Every so often a remarkable piece of work
tural phenomenon for its historical relevance, contemporary status, and future
trajectory. This book does precisely that for online education in a clear and unam-
biguous fashion. *Online Education Policy and Practice* is a must-read for those who
wish to understand instructional technology's impact on our contemporary learning environment. Commendably free from hindsight bias this book never waivers
from its focus on quality education in the 21st century.

—**Charles Dziuban**, *Director of the Research Initiative for
Teaching Effectiveness at the University of Central Florida, USA*

Dr. Picciano is a leading researcher and author in the field of online learning and
his expertise has been recognized by the online higher education community for
more than two decades. He accurately captures the history of online learning and
provides fundamental context by situating online learning in the overall higher
education landscape. Through thoughtful reflection, he shares vital insight on the
evolution of online learning as well as well-informed projections for the future.
This book is a must-read and a trusted resource for any higher education leader
or faculty member.

—**Eric Fredericksen**, *Associate Vice President for Online Learning &
Associate Professor in Educational Leadership, University of Rochester, USA*

Dr. Picciano has been a leader in educational technology and online learning for
over a quarter of a century. He brings his deep experience to bear as he explores
how new technologies will affect the future of higher education by examining
how they have evolved and changed higher education today. The result is a com-
pelling and thought-provoking read.

—**Karen Swan**, *Stukel Distinguished Professor of Educational Leadership,
University of Illinois Springfield, USA*

As important as the history of online learning may be, an understanding of its
future direction and potential is critical to the higher education enterprise. Online
education in all of its forms may, in fact, be the only means available to address
the tripartite challenges of the iron triangle: access, quality, and cost. This book is,
therefore, an important addition to the reading list of anyone concerned about the
future of higher education.

—**Joel Hartman**, *Vice President for Information Technologies & Resources
and CIO, University of Central Florida, USA*

ONLINE EDUCATION POLICY AND PRACTICE

In *Online Education Policy and Practice: The Past, Present, and Future of the Digital University*, Anthony Picciano provides an in-depth look at the formation and development of online education in American higher education. He establishes online education as part of the evolution of instructional technology in which college faculty and researchers played an integral role. He traces in great detail the beginnings of online education in the 1990s, just before the dawn of the ubiquitous Internet. He clearly examines the waves or phases of online education over the past twenty years, including the major developments of fully online courses and programs, blended learning, and the rise and fall of the MOOC phenomenon. He also speculates on the future, dividing this timeframe into a near future and a more distant future. He is both optimistic and cautious in his speculations about the digital university. Policymakers, administrators, educators, and government and private funders interested in higher education will not find a more complete treatment of the past, present, and future of online education as the one in this book. Dr. Picciano reserves a particular place for the faculty who more than any other segment of higher education will be most affected by online education in the coming years.

Anthony G. Picciano is Professor and Executive Officer of the PhD Program in Urban Education at the City University of New York Graduate Center and Professor of Education Leadership at Hunter College.

ONLINE EDUCATION POLICY AND PRACTICE

The Past, Present, and Future of the Digital University

Anthony G. Picciano

Routledge
Taylor & Francis Group

NEW YORK AND LONDON

First published 2017
by Routledge
711 Third Avenue, New York, NY 10017

and by Routledge
2 Park Square, Milton Park, Abingdon, Oxon OX14 4RN

Routledge is an imprint of the Taylor & Francis Group, an informa business

Library of Congress Cataloging-in-Publication Data
Names: Picciano, Anthony G., author.
Title: Online education policy and practice : the past, present, and future
    of the digital university / Anthony G. Picciano.
Description: New York, NY : Routledge, 2016. | Includes bibliographical
    references and index.
Identifiers: LCCN 2016019062 | ISBN 9781138943629 (hardback) |
    ISBN 9781138943636 (pbk.) | ISBN 9781315672328 (ebook)
Subjects: LCSH: Education, Higher—Effect of technological innovations on. |
    Internet in higher education. | Web-based instruction. | MOOCs
    (Web-based instruction)
Classification: LCC LB2395.7 .P55 2016 | DDC 371.33/44678—dc23
LC record available at https://lccn.loc.gov/2016019062

ISBN: 978-1-138-94362-9 (hbk)
ISBN: 978-1-138-94363-6 (pbk)
ISBN: 978-1-135-67232-8 (ebk)

Typeset in Bembo
by Apex CoVantage, LLC

Printed and bound in the United States of America by Publishers Graphics,
LLC on sustainably sourced paper.

To the past, present, and future pioneers of instructional technology who have, are, and will continue to make American higher education the best it can be.

CONTENTS

ILLUSTRATIONS

Figures

Tables

PREFACE

In 1993, I published *Computers in the Schools: A Guide to Planning and Administration,* with Merrill Publishing Company. At that time, all aspects of the publishing process were handled through paper transmission. Contracts, outside reviewer comments, manuscript submission, editing, and the final copy work were done by sending paper back and forth between the author and the respective parties. I maintained an entire shelf in my library bookcase containing all of the correspondence and drafts that were exchanged. Correspondence with the publishing agents and editors, all of whom operated in Columbus, Ohio, relied on the regular mail. The sum total of postage costs ran into thousands of dollars.

In 2015, I began this project with a proposal sent electronically to my editor, Alex Masulis, at Routledge/Taylor & Francis, in New York. I received reviews, comments, and eventually a contract from Alex via email. Every word of this book was keyed into Microsoft Word. I submitted my first draft electronically in March 2016 launching a six-month process of reviews and copy editing, all of which were handled via email. Furthermore, this aspect of the production was handled by individuals from around the world. The final drafts were all reviewed in Adobe pdf format. I am quite pleased, however, that this publication will be available in both traditional book form as well as in an electronic edition. It amazes me that in the space of twenty years, the creation and development of such a fundamental aspect of our culture and knowledge industry, the book, have undergone such a dramatic change. This book, in turn, examines a similar phenomenon as the higher education enterprise evolves within a digital environment. Many of the administrative and student service aspects of a college such as admissions, registration, counseling, and library services are well on their way to all-digital environments. Teaching and learning are evolving in a similar fashion albeit, a bit more slowly. This book examines this evolution—where it has been, where it is, and where it is going.

An argument might be made that the comparing education to publishing a book focuses only on the technical aspects of these enterprises and not on the deeper substantive production of ideas and knowledge. There is some basis for this argument, but the fundamental development of knowledge is being greatly enhanced by technology as well. The ability and ease with which a writer edits and re-edits material can surely lead to a refinement of one's thinking and idea generation. The ability to access information rapidly using search engines and other Internet facilities saves significant time and widens the writer's perspectives on issues further refining ideas. Lastly, the ease of maintaining contact and communication with colleagues who directly or indirectly help a writer think through ideas and positions is greatly enhanced through technology in ways that were undreamed of a few decades ago. And so it is with the educational enterprise as well.

I hope that you will find this work helpful as you consider the issues involving online education in American higher education. Quality instruction must be at the top of our priorities in the online environment as well as in the face-to-face classroom, and the quality of student learning must be maintained as the foremost goal for instruction regardless of the modality. I have enjoyed working on this book because one learns so much when trying to share knowledge with others using the written word. I sincerely hope that this book lives up to your expectations when making its purchase and wish you much success in your endeavors.

ACKNOWLEDGMENTS

This is the fourth book that I have published with Routledge/Taylor & Francis. I am very pleased with my association with this fine company. The editors and support staff there have become colleagues with whom it is a pleasure to work. First and foremost, I thank my editor, Alex Masulis, who has supported this project from the very beginning. Secondly, the support staff at Routlege/Taylor & Francis, including Daniel Schwartz, Eleanor Reading, and Jennifer Bonnar, are a talented and able group of individuals whose contributions made this book better as it came to fruition. Third, I have been blessed to be a part of the Online Learning Consortium, formerly the Sloan Consortium, where the seeds of online learning in this country were planted in the 1990s. I have had the pleasure of working with a number of amazing colleagues through this Consortium including Chuck Dziuban, Patsy Moskal, Charles Graham, Karen Swan, Peter Shea, Eric Fredericksen, Frank Mayadas, Joel Hartman, Mary Niemiec, Tanya Joostens, Meg Benke, Burks Oakley, Gary Miller, Steven Laster, Bob Ubell, Jacquie Moloney, Kathleen Ives, and others. Their friendships and collaborations have helped form many of my ideas about online education. I especially thank Chuck Dziuban and Eric Fredericksen who read early drafts and provided me with invaluable feedback and suggestions. Fourth, I have had the good fortune to spend much of my adult life at the City University of New York as a student, an administrator, and a faculty member. I have enjoyed this journey immensely because of the people who work, study, and teach at CUNY. My faculty colleagues, especially at Hunter College and the Graduate Center, have helped me become a productive scholar and researcher. My students over the years have been an inspiration to me and have helped me to become a better teacher and adviser. They combine study, work, and family responsibilities into incredibly busy days. Lastly, God has blessed me with a loving family. My grandmother, parents, brothers, children, and grandchildren were and are the air that I breathe. My wife, Elaine, has been the thirty-year partner with whom I share everything. She has been my Muse, my editor, my companion, and the best friend anyone could have.

My humble thanks to all of you!

Tony

SECTION I
The Higher Education Landscape

1

INTRODUCTION

The Ideology and Technology That Drives Higher Education Policy and Practice

In November, 2014, I gave a keynote address in New York City titled, "The Online Learning Landscape." My purpose in this talk was to provide an overview of the current state of online learning in higher education and to offer possible scenarios regarding the not too distant (three to four years) future. After the address, an associate professor from Borough of Manhattan Community College came up to me and asked if I thought that she would be out of a job in ten years. I told her that I didn't think she would be out of job, but it was very likely that the way she teaches and the way her students learn would be different, with a greater emphasis and integration of online technology. It was this conversation that started me thinking further into the future and about the potential impact of online learning on higher education and particularly on the university professoriate. A few months later, in January 2015, I was putting the finishing touches on a book about education research in online education that I was writing with colleagues from the University of Central Florida and Brigham Young University. In the concluding chapter we speculated on the future of online and blended learning research. Again, I thought about the exchange with the associate professor from Borough of Manhattan Community College. It was clear that online learning had progressed significantly since its introduction in the early 1990s, evolving as a series of stages or waves that seem to occur every seven or eight years. Before I knew it I was thinking about 2030 and beyond and the effects online learning has had and will have on higher education. This was the inspiration for this book, the purpose of which is to consider how online education in all its manifestations has influenced and will continue to influence the evolution of higher education, especially the professoriate. It has always been my position that you cannot understand where you are going unless you know where you have been. The book's title, *Online Education Policy and Practice: The Past, Present, and Future of the Digital University*, reflects this position and forms the basis for its introduction.

Changes are occurring in higher education especially in the delivery of instruction. On one level, technology is driving many of these changes. The professional and popular literature is inundated by discussions of online learning, blended learning, flipped classrooms, and massive open online courses (MOOCs). On a meta-level, technology is being used as a vehicle or maybe a wedge, to realize a neoliberal agenda that promotes market-driven approaches for many public services including higher education. Critical to this discussion is the role of faculty in shaping curriculum and pedagogy. This chapter provides an overview of the sometimes conflicting forces seeking to fundamentally change American higher education especially the what, why, and how of teaching and learning. A systems model is provided that describes the various components within a college or university needed to develop online education programs.

Defining Online Education

This book is about online education on the Internet and World Wide Web starting in the early 1990s. Although online education applications using local and wide area networks existed before the Internet, the primary model that evolved over the past twenty years relies on ubiquitous data communications that are owned and operated routinely by all segments of the population. Today, large percentages of people living in countries all over the world are using laptops, cell phones, and other mobile devices to stay connected with family, friends, and their studies. The term *online education* is used to encompass all forms of teaching and learning using the Internet. It refers to the plethora of names and acronyms that have evolved over the past two decades including: online learning, e-learning, blended learning, web-enhanced learning, hybrid learning, flipped classrooms, MOOCs (massive open online courses), and adaptive learning. Notice that the term *distance education* or *distance learning* are not included in this sentence. Distance education has an incredibly rich history around the world, and many fine scholars such as Terry Anderson (2011) and Michael Moore (2012) have contributed significant scholarship to this area. It might be argued that online education is the latest evolution of distance education. It is the position of this author that online education is not just an evolution of distance education, it is an evolution of all education. Online technology is being used in many applications that are integrated with traditional face-to-face instruction. Blended models, which might actually be the most popular use of online learning technology now and for the intermediate future, have blossomed and represent instructional applications across the wide spectrum of education.

Internet-based online education, while a natural evolution of the instructional technology that has been a part of higher education since the middle of the 20th century, is a major leap forward in faculty teaching and students learning. Online education is not simply an adjunct to the traditional classroom, it has replaced the classroom in many schools and programs. There are a number of very successful academic programs and colleges such as the University of Maryland–University

College, Western Governors University, and Rio Salado Community College that now operate almost entirely on the Internet without any bricks and mortar other than for administrative functions. Approximately 25 to 30 percent of the college population or 5.5 to 7 million students are now enrolled in at least one fully online, for-credit course in any given year (Allen & Seaman, 2016; Allen & Seaman, 2015). The differences in these estimates are based on questions of definition. An online course, as defined in the Allen & Seaman (2016) study, is one where eighty percent of the seat time is replaced by online activity. Millions of additional students are enrolled in blended or hybrid courses although accurate data on this population does not exist. For the purposes of this book, the word *blended* will be used to designate courses where some percentage of seat time is conducted online. Web-enhanced courses that do not necessarily replace seat time but have substantial Internet-based activity are also becoming commonplace at all colleges and universities. The point is about to be reached in American higher education where the majority of college courses will have some Internet components ranging from the fully online to Web-enhancements. In a mere twenty years, online education has become integral to the delivery of instruction in colleges and universities. No longer a novelty, it is becoming fully integrated into all teaching and learning. As Larry Ellison, the founder and CEO of Oracle Corp., has often been quoted as saying, "The Internet changes everything, I really mean everything" (Schlender, 1999).

Technological Change

The word *technology* derives from the ancient Greek *techne*, which translates to "art" or "craft-knowledge." It specifically refers to the knowledge and practice of making things. Technological change has been a fundamental aspect of human existence since Homo sapiens started to walk on two legs and maybe before. The use of stone tools, metals, and the wheel have each had a profound impact on how the members of our species have interacted with the environment and with each other. Aristotle wrote about and examined the dichotomy between things that occurred naturally and those that were made by humans. Francis Bacon likewise, in *New Atlantis*, written in 1623, presented a vision of society in which natural philosophy and technology coexisted in the centrality of human endeavor. Hegel's dialectics—thesis, antithesis, and synthesis—served as a foundation for Marx and Engels in terms of the effect of technology on societies and the interplay of capital and workers. In the modern era, Neil Postman (1993) refers to the dialectic of technological change and warns of its light and dark sides. Clayton Christensen (1997) sounded an alarm throughout corporate America to be aware of "disruptive technology" that can cause great firms to fail. Christensen and Eyring (2011) have since sounded a similar alarm to public service organizations including colleges. A major focus of this book will be to examine technology's influence on higher education and specifically how online technology is changing the fundamental way instruction is delivered. However, this influence cannot be separated from the larger societal influence that technology has had and will continue to have on all aspects of human endeavor.

Since the industrial revolution of the late 19th century to the present, American society and culture have embraced new technology. Automobiles, air travel, television, and mobile devices have found producers and consumers interested and willing to invest their resources. Over the past fifty years, this has been particularly true of digital technology. The computer age of the 1960s-70s gave way to the information/knowledge age of the 1980s which, in turn, gave way to the age of the Internet in the 1990s to the present. Public and private organizations and companies have changed in most aspects of their operations, including the production and delivery of goods and services. Companies such as Apple, Google, Facebook, and Microsoft, which did not exist fifty years ago, now lead the list of stocks on the Dow Jones Industrial Averages. Amazon has re-conceptualized the book retailing business. Books can now be proposed, written, edited, published, and sold without a single printed page. In education, the Florida Virtual High School, which conducts all of its teaching online, enrolls more than 100,000 students each year. The University of Phoenix enrolled more than 400,000 online students at its peak. This book will examine the impact of the Internet on the broad spectrum of higher education as well as the implications of significant developments yet to come.

Neoliberalism

The latter half of the 20th century has seen a number of nontechnological forces and movements shape American higher education as well. This country's social order is built on a combination of beliefs that permeate most of our institutions. Nationalism, belief in free market capitalism, democracy, and liberal humanistic values such as social justice are in evidence in all of our institutions including our colleges and universities. These beliefs interact in various ways and result in movements that permeate society for certain periods of time. Some are specific to political parties, others cross party lines.

One such development has been neoliberalism that has found a good deal of acceptance among government leaders from both the left and the right, liberal and conservative, Democrat and Republican. Over the past fifty years, presidents, legislators, governors, and mayors have come to embrace a neoliberal philosophy as the basis for moving government services including education to a free market system. Championed by a number of economists and government leaders, neoliberalism is a theory of political economic practices that proposes that human well-being can best be advanced by liberating individual entrepreneurial freedoms and skills. It operates within an institutional framework focused on strong private property rights, free markets, and free trade and has been characterized by policies associated with privatization, deregulation, globalization, decreased government spending and tax reduction (Harvey, 2005). Ronald Reagan and Margaret Thatcher were among the most prominent elected officials to promote the neoliberal agenda.

Among neoliberals, the very purpose of a higher education has come under greater scrutiny. For example, the term *commoditization* has evolved to refer to the deliberate transformation of the educational process into commodity form, that is, something created, grown, produced, or manufactured for the purpose of commercial transaction or exchange. Neoliberal proponents see this transformation as desirable and as a result, support developments such as student demand for employment skills, private investment (corporations and corporate-affiliated foundations) in higher education, federal government policies such as STEM, and a reprioritizing of state funding for public higher education. The commoditization of education has seen public universities and community colleges which educate the majority of students in the United States, become vulnerable to significant funding reductions by state and local governing bodies, thereby subjecting them to free market forces. This has resulted in steady increases in tuition rates, forcing students to take on more debt. While the trend of decreased public funding has existed over the past twenty years, a major acceleration occurred as a result of the great recession of 2008 when state and local revenues plummeted. This decrease in funding has been accompanied by strong and steady enrollment increases as more high school graduates enroll in college and as more adults seek advanced degrees and lifelong learning experiences. Commoditization has also weakened the position of the liberal arts and sciences that for a century or more formed the foundation of college curricula and academic programs. People on and off campus have begun to question the need to study philosophy, history, literature, and the fine arts in an era when many jobs require well-honed technical skills. The emergence of the "digital humanities" focusing on integrating technology into the liberal arts is seen as a possible savior for a number of academic programs. On the other hand, professional programs in business are seeing enormous demand by students. Even those students who major in humanities or social sciences are enrolling in business courses and in some cases taking second majors in a professional area.

Technology as a means of efficiency in government-funded activities is a major vehicle for neoliberalists and can be seen in all aspects of the privatization movement. In higher education, online education specifically is perceived as a major mechanism for technology efficiency. For-profit colleges and universities have flourished under this approach and are offered as models of a low-cost education. Policymakers point to for-profit higher education and their dependence on online education as viable alternatives to campus-based colleges requiring large spaces, buildings, physical libraries, and full-time faculty. Furthermore, the implementation of online education goes beyond the goals of distance education and is being promoted for mainstream colleges and academic programs.

The University Professoriate

In 2013, Anant Agarwal, president of edX, the MOOC venture of Harvard and MIT, during an address on online learning, commented that college teaching had not changed "in centuries": professors lecture and "students sit in neat little rows"; the typical professor from a hundred years ago and the professor today approach a group of students in a room and deliver a lecture for an hour or so. The professors in both eras would require the students to do readings, do written assignments, and take tests at one or more points during the semester. Agarwal then argued for the need to change fundamentally the way faculty teach by making greater use of online technology and new pedagogical techniques. This rhetoric has been heard many times particularly in the last twenty years, characterizing faculty as old-fashioned, coupled to their well-worn notes and methods of teaching, and afraid of the new technologies. It is overblown, trite, and unwarranted. Faculty have been at the forefront of much of the instructional technology and online learning development in this country. At the same time, the faculty have also been among the most severe critics of the new technologies. This dialectic between and among faculty is a part of higher education's culture that comes to bear on any number of issues, including how to teach. However, as coverage in the mass media increases, the prerogatives and methods of the professorate are coming under more scrutiny.

The role and responsibility of a university professor changes significantly from one institution to another. Research universities expect their faculty to secure grants and to be active scholars. Small liberal arts colleges instill in their faculty the importance of interweaving pedagogical practice, with community and social relationships. Community colleges prefer their faculty to be first and foremost excellent teachers in order to meet the needs of a diverse student body. Particular academic programs such as business, medicine, health science, social work, and education, expect faculty to be active and develop working and collaborative relationships within their professions.

Despite these differences, a good teacher must have a deep knowledge of her or his subject matter and possess effective ways of sharing it with students. A great teacher inspires students to develop their own knowledge. College faculty today are far more knowledgeable about their subject matter than their peers of a hundred years or even of fifty years ago. The average faculty member has relatively easy access to current knowledge thanks to the convenience of digital technology. The world's catalogue of books, journals, and articles are a mouse click away. Most faculty spend a good deal of their time keeping up with this large, growing, and easily accessible professional literature. Large datasets containing quantitative and/or qualitative data can be easily analyzed in ways that were impossible a few decades ago. Today's laptop, PC or iMac is ten times more powerful than the large mainframe computers of the 1960s and 1970s and gracefully allows colleagues from around the world to share their knowledge and scholarship. Anyone who has taught at any level understands that while it is important to know how to teach, it is equally important to know what to teach.

Agarwal's comment earlier in this section focused specifically on the teaching aspect of a professor. While his comment has some truth, he ignores the fact that by 2013, millions of college students were learning in fully online courses or in blended courses, developed with a significant amount of faculty design and direction. An argument can be made that faculty were heavily engaged in online learning by 2013. Not all faculty have embraced teaching online, which is their prerogative as long as they teach "well." The decision to teach with technology or not might be similar to the decision as to read a physical book or to read it on an Amazon Kindle or an Apple iPad. Some people prefer the book and some prefer the electronic reader. Should we criticize those who prefer a printed book as old-fashioned and out of touch? Most people would say not. Similarly, some faculty choose to teach online; others choose to teach in traditional face-to-face mode. Many faculty are able to teach in either mode and decide depending upon the subject matter and level of student ability. Much of the research points to the fact that some students do not do well in online environments. Daphne Koller, the president of Coursera, another MOOC venture, has commented that students who have remediation and other learning needs, and who lack the basic skills of reading, writing, and arithmetic, would probably better be served by face-to-face instruction (Koller, 2013). Even so, today's classroom faculty make much greater use of multimedia, smartboards, simulation software in laboratory sciences, gaming, etc. than ever before. The traditional "class" model of a faculty member as the center of instruction is evolving into a social construct that combines student, course content, and teacher into a seamless digital environment of instructional interactions. In sum, the characterization of faculty stuck in the ways of their predecessors one hundred years ago does not hold up.

A Systems Model for Online Education

In studying online education, in addition to understanding the role of the faculty member as teacher and the instructional support staff as assisting in design, one must also acknowledge that a range of institutional-wide decisions, plans, and activities need to be considered. While individual faculty members may develop online courses, scaling projects up to include entire academic programs requires a more system-wide organizational commitment involving multiple actors, resources, and policy considerations. There are a number of models for presenting and studying technology planning and development, but to lay the groundwork for the remainder of this book, a systems approach is provided. In fact, a carefully planned systems model is preferred to a disruptive sudden leap forward approach. Rick Levin, former president of Yale University, and CEO of the MOOC company, Coursera, cautioned:

We are still at the stage where it [online learning] is expanding the [higher education] market rather than substituting for educational offerings. The biggest effect is in bringing new learners in. Three-quarters of our learners are over the age of 22. They are beyond secondary and college years. Most of them are working and they are using it primarily for career advancement or personal enrichment in equal proportions. That is not a hugely disruptive thing at this point. That is additive, an enhancement to what we provide.

The evidence is beginning to be very clear that if properly managed and done strategically, online learning can be a net revenue enhancement. . . . Over time, there will be a tendency for institutions of higher education to want to use some high quality MOOCs in their own instructional programs. But it will take time and there will be institutional inertia that will make it slow. If we look over decades, sure disruption will happen.

(Byrne, 2015)

Figure 1.1 provides a systems model for planning instructional technology that is appropriate for the development of online education in a college or university. It takes into consideration external influences (the environment) as well as institutional-specific needs to determine goals and objectives. It also recognizes the relationships of several organizational components (governing board, college administration, faculty, and operational units) that engage in and are required for major technological initiatives.

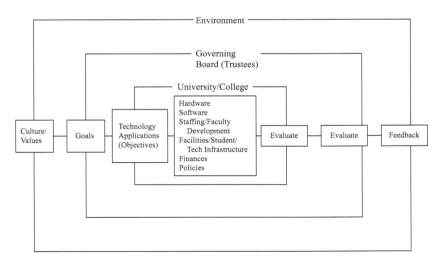

FIGURE 1.1 Systems Model for Planning Instructional Technology

Goals and Objectives

Colleges and universities have different missions and goals, serve different constituents, and will approach online education in different ways. The Carnegie Classification of Institutions of Higher Education starts with six basic categories:

- Associate degree colleges
- Baccalaureate colleges
- Masters colleges and universities
- Doctoral-granting universities
- Special focus institutions
- Tribal colleges

The classification expands considerably depending upon the nature of the academic programs, size of the student body, locale, nonprofit or for-profit status, and level of research. Community colleges, for example, provide access to higher education as their primary goal. They generally serve local commuter student populations by offering a range of academic programs designed to enhance employment opportunities or to enable students to transfer to a four-year institution. Private four-year liberal arts colleges focus on providing a high-quality undergraduate experience for their largely residential students. Social life and campus experiences at a private liberal arts college are as important as the academic programs. Research institutions offer a variety of four-year and graduate programs and in addition are active in securing grants, corporate contracts, and other external funding. Faculty at these institutions see research, scholarship, and grantsmanship as primary responsibilities. How these institutions approach online education will differ. A community college might seek to use fully online courses and programs as vehicles to broaden student access or to help enrolled students remain in their programs when family, financial, and other responsibilities pressure them to withdraw. The four-year liberal arts college might prefer to take advantage of the pedagogical benefits of blended learning applications that can be integrated into traditional classrooms. Research institutions might use online education to extend graduate expertise or to brand their programs nationally or globally.

Online education applications (objectives) are growing substantially every year. Converting what have been traditional, face-to-face courses into fully online courses has become commonplace, and the development of completely online programs is being done on a more regular basis. Once a college or university has successfully developed a fully online course or program, the tendency is to develop more courses and programs until they have reached a saturation point. There has also been substantial acceptance of blended learning, particularly in traditional or mainstream higher education. The blended learning modality is perceived as the best of both learning modalities—face-to-face and online.

The major components of an online education application are:

- Hardware
- Software
- Staffing/faculty development
- Facilities/student/tech support infrastructure
- Finances
- Policies

These components are fundamental to every technology initiative and need to be considered for an online education application as well. In the following paragraphs, several current and important issues with respect to each component will be presented.

Hardware

The fundamental hardware required for online education applications is not particularly complex but should be consistent with an overall institutional technology plan. Essentially hardware for online education consists of servers that can support a network size appropriate for the institution. The network must also integrate with the hardware used for the institution's database management system as well as some type of course or learning management system. The vast majority of colleges and universities have established such a hardware facility in house or have contracted out with a service or cloud provider.

The hardware that the faculty and others involved with the online education application will have available to them also needs to be considered. Desktop computers are common but increasingly, the world has moved to mobile technology (i.e., laptops, iPads, Androids). When launching an online education application in the present time, colleges and universities increasingly are investing in laptop and mobile technology for their faculty.

Software

The critical software for an online education application is a course management system (CMS) also referred to as a learning management system (LMS). Many colleges acquire a CMS or contract with a vendor to host their applications. This was not the case in the early days of online education when institutions had to develop their own CMS platforms. Blackboard, Canvas, and Desire2Learn are three dominant providers of this type of software. Moodle, a free, open source software, is also used by a number of colleges as their CMS.

An alternative to acquiring a CMS and developing online courses in-house is outsourcing course development to a third party vendor. Companies such as Pearson's Embanet—Compass Knowledge Group, Bisk Education, and Colloquy provide a variety of support services including online course and program development. Several MOOC providers are also providing these services. While this might be an administratively easy way for a college or university to get started in online education, the costs can be significant. Before taking this approach, colleges generally should undertake a careful cost-benefit analysis.

In addition to a basic CMS, specialized software for assessment, adaptive learning, learning analytics, and gaming might also be considered.

Staff/Faculty Development

A significant issue in developing or expanding online education is the readiness and commitment of staff and faculty. Faculty "buy in" is particularly critical. In many colleges and universities, adjunct faculty teach the online courses because full-time faculty are unwilling or unable to do so. This is not a desirable situation. Allen & Seaman (2012) in a national study of faculty attitudes observed:

> Faculty report being more pessimistic than optimistic about online learning. Professors, over all, cast a skeptical eye on the learning outcomes for online education. Nearly two-thirds say they believe that the learning outcomes for an online course are inferior or somewhat inferior to those for a comparable face-to-face course.
>
> *(Allen & Seaman, 2012, p. 2)*

There is no silver bullet that will automatically change faculty attitudes; however, administrators need to engage and involve faculty in any plans and decisions that are important to the institution and provide ongoing professional development as needed. Characteristics of effective professional development include:

- **Pedagogical principles**—start with the assumption that good pedagogy (i.e., social construction of knowledge, student interaction, instructor responsiveness) drive online learning technology.
- **Hands-on activities**—participants need to use equipment and be allowed to experiment and make mistakes.
- **One-on-one coaching**—group work is a good start but at some point faculty will need one-on-one assistance as they try different features.
- **Train the trainers**—identify faculty in departments who have an interest in helping other faculty and provide them with assistance and released time so that they can be available to help other faculty.
- **Make sure that faculty have proper equipment**—online education will require faculty to be available for student inquiries. While desktop computers are fine, laptops are far more convenient for teaching online.
- **Provide incentives**—faculty new to online teaching deserve rewards for taking the time and effort to do so. Without a doubt, teaching online takes more time in preparation and teaching, especially for beginners.

> **Start with smaller modules**—developing a fully online course may be daunting for someone who has never done so. It might be better to start with smaller course modules rather than the entire course.

A good instructional design team is also critical for professional development and needs to be at the forefront of any faculty development effort. Investing in instructional design support services becomes a requirement for successful online and blended learning courses and programs.

Facilities/Student/Tech Infrastructure

In the early days of computing, facilities and infrastructure generally referred to a single, centralized physical facility and the technical staff assigned to maintain it. This concept has changed considerably with the ubiquity of Internet technology. Faculty and students expect Wi-Fi service throughout a campus; staff provide "help desk" support and are available online. When developing online education applications, the concept of the help desk extends to all engaged faculty and students regardless of where they are. For online and blended learning courses, providing support means assisting faculty in the development of online materials and assisting faculty and students using a CMS.

For fully online programs, the level of required support increases considerably. If a college expects to attract a wide audience or student base for fully online programs, then it must invest in a full gamut of academic, library, and support services. Academic advisement, admissions, financial processing, registration, library databases, and student counseling must be provided from afar via online and telephone help facilities. This can be a daunting proposition for colleges and universities launching their first fully online programs. In fact, providing these services may be a more difficult undertaking than the development of the academic program. There are many cases where colleges have invested significantly into online program development only to find that the necessary support services were not fully considered resulting in significant delays in implementation. If students are recruited across time zones, many of these services need to be provided on a twenty-four-hour, seven-days-a-week schedule. While many colleges provide these services themselves, others are contracting with private companies for some or all of them. Successful fully online programs need good and reliable academic and student support services.

Finances

The enthusiastic and creative discussions that take place in many planning processes center on the consideration of goals, objectives, and applications. However, the hard reality of finance can sometimes temper much of this enthusiasm. Online education initiatives require funding, and for institutions just embarking on them, the investment in software and support services are significant. With the exception of colleges and universities with substantial endowments, much of higher education finds itself under serious financial constraints. Private colleges that are tuition-driven, struggle to control costs and to maintain an affordable tuition rate. Publicly funded institutions also increasingly are relying on student contributions via tuition and fees as many states have significantly reduced if not abandoned their commitment to higher education. The U.S. General Accounting Office (2014) issued a report stating that an important milestone had been reached in 2012 when, for first time in the history of our country, student tuition surpassed state appropriations for the financing of public higher education.

Policies

The last component of the planning model is the consideration of any policy issues that may arise as a result of a new or substantial expansion of online educa-tion. Changes in existing bylaws, governance documents, and collective bargaining contracts may need to be considered to ensure that institutional policies are not being bypassed or infringed upon. If a college has already developed a substantial online program, many of these policy issues may have already been addressed. Those colleges mounting new initiatives would be wise to consult their legal, faculty governance, and personnel offices for a review of policies that might relate to online education.

Evaluation

Evaluation and feedback are critical for continuing planning activities from year to year and from planning cycle to planning cycle. All constituents from govern-ing board to college administrators to faculty and support staff need to know if and how well the online education applications are achieving objectives.

About the Book

This book will speculate on the future of higher education as it becomes more dependent upon online technology for the delivery of instruction. More than just an engaging ploy, the title of the book represents a calculated risk on the part of the author to make measured predictions about the evolution of higher education over the next decade. Several scenarios for the future will be considered. First, it is likely that faculty will develop great facility with instructional technology and will integrate it seamlessly into their academic programs. Second, there will be fewer full-time, tenure-track faculty as a percentage of the total faculty and contract, adjunct faculty, and tutors will supervise a good deal of the coursework. Third, in professional programs such as business, education, health sciences, and social work, there will be an increased emphasis on work study and clinical practice. Fourth, alternate credentialing related to demonstrated competencies and life experience will grow significantly. Fifth, it is likely that in the not-too-distant future, a major new technology breakthrough will emerge that will promote even greater use of instructional technology.

This last scenario is perhaps most important because history tells us that technology developed for one purpose or activity may have significant unforeseen effects on other activities. Best-selling author Steven Johnson in *How We Got to Now: Six Innovations that Made the Modern World,* observes that technological innovations "have set in motion a much wider array of changes in society than you might reasonably expect" (Johnson, 2014, p. 2). He goes on to describe innovations to prove his point. For instance, Johannes Gutenberg's printing press created a surge in demand for eyeglasses because the "new" or expanded practice of reading made many Europeans realize that they were far-sighted. Or more recently when Google launched its search software in 1999, it was a breakthrough improvement over any previous search mechanisms for exploring the World Wide Web's trove of information. The entire World Wide Web became more useful and functional. However, several years later when Google started selling advertisements tied to search requests, the nature of advertising changed dramatically. Advertisement agencies and their company clients flocked to Google and other Web-based services to promote products. Johnson goes on to comment that a case can be made that Google's evolution in advertising "hollowed out the advertising base of local newspapers" thereby having serious consequences for newspaper journalism in general as previous lucrative advertising contracts declined (Johnson, 2014, p. 7). The same is likely true for instruction; a major new technology will evolve that will have significant repercussions on many human endeavors including education.

Organization of the Book

The book is divided into two sections. Section I examines the higher education landscape, including issues, challenges, technology development, and the role of the faculty in colleges and universities. Section II focuses on the evolution of online education. It looks back to the 1990s and speculates on the post-2030 future.

The Chapters

This chapter as well as Chapter Two are meant to lay the groundwork for the reader by examining the major ideological, societal, and technological developments that are shaping American higher education. Chapter Three focuses entirely on college faculty. Chapter Four explores the close relationship of higher education and technological development. Chapters Five through Eight chronologically present the waves of online education beginning in 1990s to the present. Chapters Nine and Ten speculate on future technological developments that will likely have major influences on higher education as well as society in general. An epilogue concludes the book. Brief summaries of the remaining chapters follow.

Chapter 2—American Higher Education at the Crossroads

This chapter focuses on the larger socio-economic forces shaping American higher education. Issues such as mission and purpose, public funding, student debt, and commoditization are presented as they relate to a common neoliberal philosophy that promotes market-driven approaches, privatization, and corporate solutions to public services including higher education. Each sector of American higher education including the public universities, community colleges, research universities, nonprofit private colleges, and for-profit colleges is discussed individually. The chapter also examines technology as a major vehicle for supporting the neoliberal agenda, especially as related to academic programs, curriculum, and pedagogy.

Chapter 3—Are the Faculty the University?

This chapter explores the role and position of the university professoriate. Basic data are provided for key faculty characteristics such as gender, race, salary, and full-time/part-time status. The chapter also traces the rise of contingent and adjunct faculty over the past several decades. It concludes with a discussion of faculty governance.

Chapter 4—Higher Education, Digital Technology, and Instruction

Higher education has maintained a close relationship with digital technology for the past seventy to eighty years. College faculty and researchers were involved with many of the important breakthroughs in the design and development of computing equipment going back to World War II. American higher education played a critical role in developing and designing pivotal elements within the digital technology evolution that commenced in the 20th century and continues today. The stories of visionaries who foresaw and modeled computer hardware and software that would usher in technologies for all aspects of our societal endeavors are presented. This chapter also focuses on education leaders who envisioned technology as a tool in teaching and learning. Computer-based education owes a lot to these individuals even though early applications proved to be limited. The chapter closes with the stories of three developments, outside of computer-based education, that nonetheless resulted in major contributions on the part of American higher education.

Chapter 5—The First Wave: Beginnings (1993–1999)

Online learning technology can be seen as developing in five waves starting in 1993 and continuing through the 2020s. The first wave of online and blended learning commenced with the establishment of the Internet in the early 1990s. The most common technology of the first wave was based on slow-speed, dial-up modem lines. As a result, many of the earliest online learning courses were text-based and relied heavily on asynchronous learning. Digital multimedia was difficult and time-consuming to develop and was incredibly slow in downloading to student computers. The main pedagogical model was an interactive, asynchronous learning network made popular by the Alfred P. Sloan Foundation's grant program titled, *Anytime/Anyplace Learning*. Software such as learning/course management systems was rudimentary and a number of schools had to develop their own course-delivery platforms.

The colleges and universities most interested in online learning development during this decade were those that had established distance education programs using other modalities such as television, radio, and course packs. Public institutions such as Athabasca University, the Penn State World Campus, and the University of Maryland–University College, were early leaders in the development of online learning programs. For-profit colleges such as the University of Phoenix, a subsidiary of the Apollo Education Group, invested heavily in developing fully online learning programs.

Chapter 6—The Second Wave: Blending Into the Mainstream (Early 2000s)

By the early 2000s, Internet technology had advanced to the point where many people were able to afford high-speed cable modems and digital subscriber lines (DSL). This enhanced connectivity opened up the possibility of incorporating multimedia (pictures, sound, video) into online learning development. Social media such as blogs, wikis, and YouTube also came on the scene, allowing for greater interaction. Faculty from around the world began sharing learning tools and objects in digital depositories such as Merlot. Perhaps the most important development of this second wave was that Internet technology was no longer seen solely as a vehicle for distance education but could be used in mainstream education in almost any class and for teaching any subject matter. The predominant pedagogical model of this wave was blended learning, as faculty began to use online facilities to enhance their courses and to replace some seat time in regular face-to-face courses. Courses were designed to take pedagogical advantage of the best of both worlds of fully online and face-to-face modalities.

During this second wave, many colleges and universities scaled up their online and blended learning activities. Learning/course management systems such as

Blackboard, Desire2Learn, and Moodle were acquired. Online, for-profit colleges expanded their programs significantly as venture capital flooded into the sector. While mainstream higher education embraced the blended model, the fully online model continued to be the mainstay of the for-profit colleges mainly because it was cost effective for institutions that did not have brick and mortar campuses.

Chapter 7—The Third Wave: The MOOC Phenomenon (2008–2013)

The term *MOOC* (Massive, Open, Online Course) was coined in 2008 by Dave Cormier and Bryan Alexander to describe an online course led by George Siemens and Stephen Downes. The course enrolled more than 2,000 students. With this course, the third wave of online learning development began. In 2011 Stanford University offered several MOOCs one of which, led by Sebastian Thrun and Peter Norvig, enrolled more than 160,000 students. Thrun shortly thereafter started Udacity, a company designed to provide MOOC materials to colleges and universities. A few months later, Andrew Ng and Daphne Koller, both from Stanford University, launched Coursera, another MOOC provider. Both Udacity and Coursera received extensive start-up funding from Silicon Valley investors. The MOOC model was grounded in improving student access to a higher education and cost effectiveness. The emphasis was surely on "massive" enrollments and courses that were enrolling hundreds of thousands of students attracted deserved attention. Education policymakers saw MOOCs as a way to cut costs for higher education. The general media engaged in a frenzy, and The *New York Times* declared 2012 as "The Year of the MOOC."

By the end of 2013, the media's infatuation with MOOCs receded. A major development that spurred a backlash took place at California's San Jose State University where a well-publicized experiment was conducted in which several blended learning courses in mathematics and statistics were developed by Udacity. In comparing completion rates and grades, students taking the MOOC courses did not fare as well as students in previous years' face-to-face courses. Subsequently, in December 2013, Sebastian Thrun, the founder of Udacity, opened himself and his company up to criticism in an interview with *Fast Company*, where he was quoted as saying that he was throwing in the towel and that "we [Udacity] have a lousy product."

Chapter 8—The Fourth Wave: The Reconciliation of Blended and MOOC Technologies (2014–2020)

The fourth wave arrived in 2014 wherein blended learning technologies that allowed for more extensive and personal faculty interaction were reconciled with well-financed course content as developed by MOOC providers and others. The fourth wave model extends and combines the developments of the second wave (blended learning) and the third wave (well-designed MOOC content) and incorporates a variety of pedagogical approaches using multiple formats and instructional tools. Social- and multimedia use has expanded, as students rely more heavily on portable devices (laptops, tablets, PDAs) for accessing and participating in course activities. In addition, a number of new facilities and approaches that were in their nascent stages in previous waves have expanded. These include:

1. Big data/learning analytics
2. Adaptive or differentiated learning
3. Expansion of competency-based instruction
4. Open educational resources (OER)
5. Interactive media (games, simulations, and multiuser virtual environments)
6. Mobile technology

All of these, as well as traditional lectures, class discussions, laboratory work, and internships, that are typical in face-to-face classes, are at the disposal of faculty. Private investors are also making significant commitments of finance to companies such as Pearson that are providing a host of services for online education. In sum, the fourth wave is categorized primarily as one where pedagogy is driving technology in a comprehensive and sophisticated blended learning environment relying on a variety of digital resources developed by individual faculty, by well-financed MOOC companies, and by corporate education service providers

Chapter 9—The Fifth Wave: Maturation (2021–2029)

During the fifth wave, online learning will have matured and Internet technology will be integrated into the vast majority of college instruction. A wide variety of delivery designs, some fully online and some blended will be the rule throughout higher education. Students will come to expect that every course will have online components. Fully online programs will be as common as face-to-face programs. During this period, policymakers will question the need for faculty as teachers. Faculty will be seen more as designers and supervisors of courses. Tutors will be used to monitor instruction and assist students but will not necessarily be expected to teach course content. During this wave, there will be major conflicts among policymakers, administrators, and faculty over what is taught, why it is taught, and how it is taught. There will be a broad movement to digital instruction.

Chapter 10—2030 and Beyond

This chapter examines possible new digital technologies that will have major impact on most human endeavors including higher education in the year 2030 and beyond. Predicting what will happen in the future is difficult; timing in particular is very speculative. The work of futurist Ray Kurzweil is featured with regard to the singularity, when man-machine technology will begin to outperform human brain functions and will begin to repair and replicate itself. While there are skeptics, it is likely that technologies augmenting the human brain will evolve. Neural implants, intelligent self-generating nanobots, and brainnets are likely to become realities in the post 2030 timeframe. Many of these technologies will rely on supercloud computer networks far more advanced than the cloud computing of the present day. Artificial intelligence will dominate much of the man-machine interface technologies and concerns will arise about the loss of control over humanity's future.

Epilogue

The book ends with a brief epilogue calling for higher education to change and adapt, to use technologies that are beneficial, and to question those that are not. But most important, do not ignore them.

References

Agarwal, Anant (2013, November). *Reinventing education.* Keynote presentation at the 19th Annual Sloan Consortium Conference on Online Learning. Orlando, FL. Retrieved from: from: http://olc.onlinelearningconsortium.org/conference/2013/aln/reinventing-education

Allen, E. & Seaman, J. (2012). *Conflicted: Faculty and online education,* 2012. Needham, MA: Babson College Survey Research Group.

Allen, E. & Seaman, J. (2015). *Grade level: Tracking online education in the United States.* Needham, MA: Babson College Survey Research Group.

Allen, E. & Seaman, J. (2016). *Online report card: Tracking online education in the United States.* Needham, MA: Babson College Survey Research Group.

Anderson, T. (Ed.) (2011). *The theory and practice of online learning* (2nd Edition). Athabasca, Canada: AU Press.

Byrne, J.A. (May 6, 2015). Coursera CEO: Reports of mass disruption to higher ed greatly exaggerated. Interview with Rick Levin. *Poets and Quants.* Retrieved from: http://poetsandquants.com/2015/05/06/coursera-ceo-employers-recognizing-the-value-of-online-learning/ Accessed: May 6, 2015.

Christensen, C. (1997). *The innovator's dilemma: When new technologies cause great firms to fail.* Boston: Harvard Business Review Press.

Christensen, C. & Eyring, H.J. (2011). *The innovative university: Changing the DNA of higher education from the inside out.* San Francisco: Jossey-Bass, Inc.

Harvey, D. (2005). *A brief history of neoliberalism.* Oxford: Oxford University Press.

Johnson, S. (2014). *How we got to now: Six innovations that made the modern world.* New York: Riverhead Books.

Koller, D. (2013, November). *Online learning: Learning without limits.* Keynote presentation at the 19th Annual Sloan Consortium Conference on Online Learning. Orlando, FL.

Moore, M.G. (Ed.) (2012). *Handbook of distance education* (3rd Edition). New York: Routledge.

Postman, N. (1993). *Technopoly: The surrender of culture to technology.* New York: Vintage Books.

Schlender, B. (May 24, 1999). Larry Ellison Oracle at Web Speed: "The Internet changes everything," and the CEO of Oracle is living proof. *Fortune Magazine.* Retrieved from: http://archive.fortune.com/magazines/fortune/fortune_archive/1999/05/24/260276/index.htm Accessed: November 21, 2015.

U.S. General Accounting Office (2014). *Report to the Chairman, Committee on Health, Education, Labor, and Pensions, United States Senate. HIGHER EDUCATION State Funding Trends and Policies on Affordability.* Washington, D.C.: GAO-15-151.

2

AMERICAN HIGHER EDUCATION AT THE CROSSROADS

American higher education has reached an important juncture in its history. Government officials, policymakers, corporate America, and the media are calling for changes in the way higher education operates and questioning its purpose and mission. Nevertheless, a careful examination of the issues portends good news as well as concerns. On the positive side, student interest and demand for higher education opportunities continue to grow due to a number of factors, including an American culture that values education and encourages young people to stay in school and attain as much academically as well as the knowledge that lifetime earnings for college graduates substantially outpace those without a degree. According to the Pew Research Center (2014), the earnings gap between young adults with and without bachelor's degrees has stretched to its widest level in forty-eight years. Young adults with just a high-school diploma earned 62 percent of the typical salary of college graduates, down from 81 percent in 1965, the earliest year for which comparable data are available. The result is that the overall trend in enrollments in degree-granting postsecondary institutions continues to increase with projections by the U.S. Department of Education indicating an increase from approximately 19 million students in 2014 to 24 million by 2022 (Hussar & Bailey, 2013). The percentage of secondary school graduates enrolling in college is also at an all-time high. The Center for Public Education (2014) estimated that 88 percent of high school graduates will enroll in college by age 26. World rankings of colleges and universities consistently have American institutions leading all other countries. In 2014, *The (British) Times* rankings had American colleges and universities occupying 74 of the top 200 spots. It is no wonder that in a 2014 survey of college leaders, two-thirds of public institution presidents think that higher education is headed in the right direction, as do well over half of their private campus peers (Selingo, 2014).

Despite this rosy picture, there is reason for concern. First, in the world rankings cited, the 74 American colleges at the top are all research universities, while the vast majority of students in the United States attend public and private teaching colleges. Second, although more students are enrolling in college than ever before, far too many are not graduating. Many who do graduate frequently take in excess of six years to finish, thereby increasing costs for both students and schools. Third, state funding for public higher education on a per student basis is decreasing and projections indicate that it will disappear altogether in some states—this at a time when industrialized countries in Asia and Europe have begun to invest heavily in their higher education systems. Fourth, lower state funding has led to significant tuition increases that exceed inflation which, in turn, have resulted in greater student debt upon graduation. Forty million Americans collectively owe more than $1.3 trillion in student loans, surpassing all other kinds of consumer borrowing except for mortgages (U.S. Department of Education, 2014). Furthermore, the percentage of borrowers who are defaulting on their student loans is increasing substantially. Fifth, there are growing questions about the quality and purpose of a higher education. Richard Arum of New York University and Josipa Roksa of the University of Virginia caused ripples throughout the higher education community in 2010 with their book, *Academically Adrift: Limited Learning on College Campuses.* Based on a study of more than 2,300 undergraduates at 24 colleges, they concluded that 45 percent of students show no significant improvement in the key measures of critical thinking, complex reasoning. and writing by the end of their sophomore years, and after four years, 36 percent of students do not demonstrate significant improvement (Arum & Roksa, 2010). Sixth, policymakers increasingly are promoting commoditization and experiential and competency-based learning in academic programs and are urging colleges and universities to revise their role in preparing individuals for the public good and to concentrate more narrowly on job creation and skills development.

In sum, there are thousands of articles, books, essays, and opinion pieces that paint a rosy picture for American higher education and thousands more that present an enterprise in dire need of reform. The facts are that there is lot of good that can be said about American higher education, as well as issues that need to be addressed. John Hennessy, President of Stanford University, at the Annual Meeting of the American Council on Education in 2015, gave a keynote address titled *Information Technology and the Future of Teaching and Learning,* and declared:

> American higher education isn't broken. . . . It's still "the envy of the world." But it has to reckon with serious problems, including rising costs and falling degree-completion rates. . . . My goal is to provide a higher education that is affordable, accessible, adaptable, and enhances student learning.
> *(Howard, 2015)*

The Political-Economic Forces Shaping Higher Education Policy and Practice

Yuval N. Harari (2015), in his best-seller, *Sapiens,* identifies three dominant themes influencing American thinking and policy formulation: nationalism, free market-capitalism, and liberal humanism. Nationalism has been a force in America since its inception in the 1700s. Americans possess a spirit of national competitiveness and pride that affects all endeavors. The military, private corporations, professional sports, and American universities compete internationally for contracts, goods, services, prestige, research projects, and influence. Student protests against the Vietnam War in the 1960s and the general distrust that evolved during the Iraq War in the early part of the 21st century can be viewed as justifiable deviations rather than serious abandonment of nationalistic tendencies. The response to the attack on the World Trade Center in 2001 is evidence of how quickly the American people will unite against threats from outside the country's borders. And while conflicts may arise around overzealous displays, nationalism is generally accepted as a basic aspect of American life that influences people's feelings, governmental policies, and social institutions including colleges and universities. Free market capitalism and liberal humanism, on the other hand, vie for influence over the country, its people, and its institutions.

The media frequently promote the idea that political and economic battle lines are drawn between major political factions over the emphasis on free markets or humanistic social policies: conservatives versus liberals; Republicans versus Democrats. The closeness of recent national elections seems to indicate that the country is divided by these two viewpoints. However, rather than a dichotomy, a continuum may be a more appropriate characterization. There are surely moderates within both political parties. A free market conservative on one issue might be a humanistic liberal on another and vice versa. Take, for instance, the privatization of K–12 public education. Conservative Republicans, during the presidency of George W. Bush, supported the idea of market forces driving public education policy, the result of which was No Child Left Behind (NCLB) legislation in 2001. Hallmarks of NCLB included charter schools, private tutoring, and expansion of testing and assessments, all indicative of market-driven thinking. However, a number of liberal Democrats, including Ted Kennedy were very supportive at least in part of NCLB. Furthermore, many NCLB provisions have been continued by President Barack Obama in his signature Race to the Top (RTTT) education program. A case can be made that, with respect to social policies including education, common political-economic ground has evolved. Neoliberalism may be the basis for this common ground with regard to education policy. In fact, there may have been an "emphatic turn towards neoliberalism" in political-economic practices and thinking since the 1970s (Harvey, 2005).

Neoliberalism and Higher Education

Neoliberalism is associated with the work of economists Friedrich von Hayek and Milton Friedman. Friedrich von Hayek, an Austrian economist and winner of the Nobel Prize in 1974, who moved to the United States to teach at the University of Chicago from 1950 to 1962, posited that without government interference, marketplace competition would create ideal social institutions. In *The Road to Serfdom*, Hayek argued that free market competition results in the production of goods wanted by the public. And that competition is the best way of assuring the lowest consumer price (Hayek, 1962). Milton Friedman, a colleague of Hayek's at the University of Chicago and the 1976 Nobel Prize winner, advocated applying the principles of the free market to public education by allowing parents free choice of a school for their children. Friedman proposed the use of a government-financed voucher that parents could redeem "for a specified maximum sum per child per year if spent on 'approved' educational services" (Friedman, 1962, p. 89). He also argued that vouchers would overcome the class stratification embodied in the existence of rich and poor school districts. He suggested, "Under present arrangements, stratification of residential areas effectively restricts the intermingling of children from decidedly different backgrounds" (Friedman, 1962, p. 92).

In general, free market ideologists argue that competition at all levels of the education market will result in improving the quality of education available to the American public. In the 1970s, several American think tanks earnestly began promoting free market ideas. In his 1991 book, *The Idea Brokers and the Rise of the New Policy Elite*, James Smith described this development: "In the early 1970s, executives in a handful of traditionally conservative foundations redefined their programs with the aim of shaping the public policy agenda and constructing a network of conservative institutions and scholars" (Smith, 1991, p. 181).

One of the leaders and early spokesperson of this movement was William Simon, who left his job in 1976 as Secretary of the Treasury in the Nixon and Ford administrations to become head of the John Olin Foundation, whose purpose, in Simon's words, "is to support those individuals and institutions who are working to strengthen the free enterprise system" (Simon, 1978, p. 233).

In Simon's 1978 book, *A Time for Truth*, he warned that public thinking was dominated by a liberal establishment. This argument was reflected in the book's foreword, written by free market advocates Milton Friedman and Friedrich von Hayek. In the preface, Friedman sounded the alarm that intellectual life in the United States was under the control of "socialists and interventionists, who have wrongfully appropriated in this country the noble label 'liberal' and who have been the intellectual architects of our suicidal course" (Friedman, 1978). Applying the concepts of the marketplace to intellectual life, Friedman further argued that the payoff for these "liberals" was support by an entrenched government bureaucracy. In other words, the liberal elite and the government bureaucracy fed off each other. Coining a phrase that would be repeated by conservatives throughout the rest of the twentieth century, Friedman contended that "government is the problem, not the cure" (Friedman, 1978). According to Friedman, saving the country required a general understanding of the importance and acceptance of the free market. To undermine the supposed rule of a liberal intelligentsia, Simon urged the business community to support those intellectuals who advocated the importance of the free market. Simon called on business people to stop supporting colleges and universities that produced "young collectivists by the thousands" and media "which serve as megaphones for anti-capitalist opinion." In both cases, Simon insisted, business people should focus their support on university programs and media that stress pro-capitalist ideas (Simon, 1978, pp. 232–233). Simon further calculated that an important step should involve business people rushing "multimillions to the aid of liberty, in the many places where it is beleaguered." Upon receiving the largess of business, he insisted, "Foundations imbued with the philosophy of freedom . . . must take pains to funnel desperately needed funds to scholars, social scientists, writers, and journalists who understand the relationship between political and economic liberty" (Simon, 1978, p. 230).

While neoliberalism derives from a belief in the benefits of unfettered free markets, it evolved into a very influential political force in the United States and beyond. Political figures such as Ronald Reagan and Margaret Thatcher became major proponents of free market enterprise and of getting government out of the way of private industry. Their leadership as well as the groundwork of Simon and others has resulted in a powerful presence of neoliberal thought in many of our institutions. David Harvey describes neoliberalism thus:

> in the first instance it is a theory of political economic practices that proposes that human well-being can best be advanced by liberating individual entrepreneurial freedoms and skills within an institutional framework characterized by strong private property rights, free markets, and free trade.
>
> *(Harvey, 2005, p. 1)*

Harvey goes on to comment, however, that advocates of neoliberalism occupy influential positions in education, in the media, in corporate boardrooms, in foundations, in key international organizations such as the International Monetary Fund and World Bank, in federal agencies, and in state capitals. They have had a pervasive effect on "ways of thought" to the point where neoliberalism has become incorporated into the way many people interpret and understand the world (Harvey, 2005, p. 3). Together, the agents of neoliberalism create narratives to press their position even if this means the destruction of existing social institutions and their frameworks.

Henry Giroux goes further than Harvey in his critique of neoliberalism and sees the movement as class struggle and refers to it as the latest incarnation of "predatory capitalism":

As a form of public pedagogy and cultural politics, neoliberalism casts all dimensions of life in terms of market rationality. One consequence is that neoliberalism legitimates a culture of cruelty and harsh competitiveness and wages a war against public values and those public spheres that contest the rule and ideology of capital. It saps the democratic foundation of solidarity, degrades collaboration, and tears up all forms of social obligation. . . . In the end, it abolishes institutions meant to eliminate human suffering, protect the environment, ensure the right of unions, and provide social provisions. It has no vision of the good society or the public good and it has no mechanisms for addressing society's major economic, political, and social problems.

(Giroux, 2013)

In terms of higher education, Giroux sees neoliberalism as promulgating a narrative in which a college becomes "a space for producing profits, educating a docile labor force, and a powerful institution for indoctrinating students into accepting the obedience demanded by the corporate order" (Giroux, 2013). In terms of the university professoriate, Giroux has great misgivings in that neoliberalism promotes the squelching of academic freedom, a rise in the number of adjunct faculty, and the view that students are basically consumers and faculty are providers of a saleable commodity. He cautions:

Too many faculty have become comfortable with the corporatization of the university and the new regimes of neoliberal governance . . . many academics have disappeared into a disciplinary apparatus that views the university not as a place to think but as a place to prepare students to be competitive in the global marketplace.

(Giroux, 2014, p. 17)

Another important aspect of neoliberalism's influence is its total faith in new technology. Harvey (2005) comments that neoliberals have an intense interest in and pursuit of information technologies and a

fetish belief that there is a technological fix for every problem. . . . Talented interlopers can mobilize technological innovations; . . . reshape common sense to their own pecuniary advantage, [develop] an inner connection between technological dynamism, instability, and dissolution of social boundaries.

(Harvey, 2005, p. 68)

In terms of present-day higher education, neoliberalism's "fetish" focuses largely on instructional technologies such as online education, big data, learning analytics, and adaptive learning, all of which will be discussed further later on in this book.

For now, let us look at the major issues facing higher education, some of which have been promulgated by neoliberal narratives.

The Expansion of Higher Education—Sectors, Enrollments, and Graduation Rates

Higher education is a growth enterprise. Every indicator and trend points to increasing demand for more higher education. For example, the number of post-secondary institutions (degree granting and nondegree-granting) increased almost 10 percent between 1999 and 2010. However, the rate of increase was different depending upon the sector (public, private, not-for-profit, for-profit). The sector designation is an important characteristic of higher education that should not be ignored. Public community colleges are different from private nonprofit four-year colleges, which are different from large, four-year public university systems. In examining the data in Table 2.1, it is obvious that most of the sectors, with the exception of the for-profit private institutions, were relatively stable during the period. In fact, much of the increase in the number of institutions between 1999 and 2010 can be attributed to the private, for-profit sector.

Student enrollments in degree-granting institutions have been on the rise for several decades. Figure 2.1 shows past enrollments and projections to 2022. The U.S. Department of Education is projecting that student enrollments in degree-granting institutions will increase almost 20 percent between 2012 and 2022, to 24 million students. Females represent approximately 57 percent of the student population. Part-time students represent 38 percent of the student population. White students represent the majority of the student population, but their percentages have been declining, from 73 percent in 1997 to a projected 58 percent by 2022. A good percentage of the increase in enrollments between the mid-1990s and 2012 can be attributed to the rise of for-profit colleges, many of which offered fully online academic programs. However, between 2012 and 2014 (see Table 2.2), enrollments in for-profit institutions decreased. Much of this can be attributed to a number of high-profile federal government lawsuits and investigations in 2010 and 2011, accusing several prominent for-profit colleges such as the University of Phoenix and Kaplan University of questionable practices regarding recruitment and financial aid as well as excessive dropout rates. The University of Phoenix has been hit particularly hard since the government investigation. Enrollments have decreased 50 percent (more than 200,000 students), thousands of employees have been laid off, and the stock has plummeted from a high of $89 a share in 2009 to $20 in 2013 (Hansen, 2013).

A comparison of the data in Tables 2.1 and 2.2 might indicate a conflicted scenario, with the number of private, for-profit colleges increasing while recent overall enrollments in these institutions decreased. These data are indicative of the unstable situation that has arisen in this sector, with many new institutions opening even though several very large for-profit universities had significant enrollment

TABLE 2.1 Number of Postsecondary Institutions in the United States

Level and control of institution	1980–81	1990–91	1999–2000	2000–01	2001–02	2002–03	2003–04	2004–05	2005–06	2006–07	2007–08	2008–09	2009–10	2010–11
Postsecondary Title IV institutions	–	–	**6,407**	**6,479**	**6,458**	**6,354**	**6,412**	**6,383**	**6,463**	**6,536**	**6,551**	**6,632**	**6,742**	**7,021**
Public	–	–	2,078	2,084	2,099	2,051	2,047	2,027	2,013	2,009	2,004	1,997	1,989	2,015
Private	–	–	4,329	4,395	4,359	4,303	4,365	4,356	4,450	4,527	4,547	4,635	4,753	5,006
Nonprofit	–	–	1,936	1,950	1,941	1,921	1,913	1,875	1,866	1,848	1,815	1,809	1,809	1,812
For-profit	–	–	2,393	2,445	2,418	2,382	2,452	2,481	2,584	2,679	2,732	2,826	2,944	3,194
Title IV nondegree-granting institutions	–	–	2,323	2,297	2,261	2,186	2,176	2,167	2,187	2,222	2,199	2,223	2,247	2,422
Public	–	–	396	386	386	339	327	327	320	321	319	321	317	359
Private	–	–	1,927	1,911	1,875	1,847	1,849	1,840	1,867	1,901	1,880	1,902	1,930	2,063
Nonprofit	–	–	255	255	265	256	249	238	219	208	191	180	185	182
For-profit	–	–	1,672	1,656	1,610	1,591	1,600	1,602	1,648	1,693	1,689	1,722	1,745	1,881

Title IV degree-granting institutions	3,231	3,559	4,084	4,182	4,197	4,168	4,236	4,216	4,276	4,314	4,352	4,409	4,495	4,599
Two-year colleges	1,274	1,418	1,721	1,732	1,710	1,702	1,706	1,683	1,694	1,685	1,677	1,690	1,721	1,729
Public	945	972	1,068	1,076	1,085	1,081	1,086	1,061	1,053	1,045	1,032	1,024	1,000	978
Private	329	446	653	656	625	621	620	622	641	640	645	666	721	751
Nonprofit	182	167	150	144	135	127	118	112	113	107	92	92	85	87
For-profit	147	279	503	512	490	494	502	510	528	533	553	574	636	664
Four-year colleges	1,957	2,141	2,363	2,450	2,487	2,466	2,530	2,533	2,582	2,629	2,675	2,719	2,774	2,870
Public	552	595	614	622	628	631	634	639	640	643	653	652	672	678
Private	1,405	1,546	1,749	1,828	1,859	1,835	1,896	1,894	1,942	1,986	2,022	2,067	2,102	2,192
Nonprofit	1,387	1,482	1,531	1,551	1,541	1,538	1,546	1,525	1,534	1,533	1,532	1,537	1,539	1,543
For-profit	18	64	218	277	318	297	350	369	408	453	490	530	563	649

Source: U.S. Department of Education, National Center for Education Statistics; Higher Education General Information Survey (HEGIS), "Institutional Characteristics of Colleges and Universities" survey, 1980–81; Integrated Postsecondary Education Data System (IPEDS), "Institutional Characteristics Survey" (IPEDS-IC:90–99); and IPEDS Fall 2001 through Fall 2010, Institutional Characteristics component. (This table was prepared December 2012.)

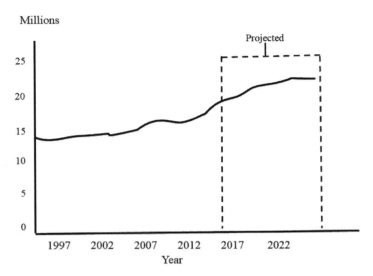

FIGURE 2.1 Enrollment Projections for Degree-Granting Postsecondary Institutions

TABLE 2.2 Actual Unduplicated Student Headcount Enrollments by Sector

Sector	FALL 2014		FALL 2013		FALL 2012	
	Enrollment	% Change from prior year	Enrollment	% Change from prior year	Enrollment	% Change from prior year
Total enrollment, all sectors	19,619,773	−1.3%	19,885,203	−1.5%	20,195,924	−1.8%
Four-year public	7,965,176	0.0%	7,964,090	0.4%	7,931,702	−0.2%
Four-year private nonprofit	3,823,465	1.6%	3,761,953	1.3%	3,714,967	0.5%
Four-year for-profit	1,315,167	−0.4%	1,321,107	−9.7%	1,463,097	−7.2%
Two-year public	6,107,337	−3.5%	6,329,631	−3.3%	6,544,820	−3.6%
Unduplicated student headcount (All Sectors)	19,258,730	−1.3%	19,511,518	−1.4%	19,791,149	−1.7%

Source: National Student Clearing House Research Center. Retrieved from: http://nscresearchcenter. org/currenttermenrollmentestimate-fall2014/#more-3770 Accessed: March 8, 2015

decreases. Regardless, the long-term trend is for enrollments to increase in all higher education. Students will likely want to go to college, and if they don't enroll in one college, they will enroll in another college. As indicated earlier in this chapter, the benefits of a college education are real. Parents, students, and adult learners understand this and see college as a necessity for career and professional goals and satisfaction. However, there is another factor to be considered in understanding enrollment trends, and that is graduation rates.

The era of most students seeking and attaining a bachelor's degree in four years is over. For decades, students have been setting their own timeframes for completing their undergraduate studies. Five, six, seven or more years are not uncommon. A pattern of students taking fewer courses, stopping out for a while, re-enrolling, and changing majors is becoming the norm, which contributes significantly to higher enrollments as more students stay in college longer. In addition, many students, especially adults and lifelong learners, attend college part-time and may never complete a degree. The same is true for students seeking associate degrees. Very few of these students will complete a degree in even three years. Tables 2.3 and 2.4 provide graduation rates for students seeking bachelor and associate/certificate degrees. For all baccalaureate students, 59 percent will graduate in six years; for associate and certificate students, 31 percent will complete within 150 percent of the "normal" time to complete a program. For the associate degree,

TABLE 2.3 Percentage of Students Seeking a Bachelor's Degree at Four-Year Degree-Granting Institutions Who Completed a Bachelor's Degree Within Six Years, by Control of Institution: Starting Cohort Year 2006

0	All institutions	Public	Private nonprofit	Private for-profit
Percent	59%	57%	66%	32%

Source: U.S. Department of Education, National Center for Education Statistics, Integrated Postsecondary Education Data System (IPEDS), Spring 2013, Graduation Rates component. See *Digest of Education Statistics 2013*, Table 326.10.

TABLE 2.4 Percentage of Students Seeking a Certificate or Degree at Two-Year Degree-Granting Institutions Who Completed a Credential Within 150 Percent of the Normal Time Required to Do So, by Control of Institution: Starting Cohort Year 2009

	All institutions	Public	Private nonprofit	Private for-profit
Percent	31%	20%	62%	63%

Source: U.S. Department of Education, National Center for Education Statistics, Integrated Postsecondary Education Data System (IPEDS), Spring 2013, Graduation Rates component. See *Digest of Education Statistics 2013*, Table 326.20.

150 percent is three years, while certificate programs can vary widely from a few months to two years. Again the data indicate that there are differences among the sectors. Baccalaureate private, nonprofit institutions have the highest graduation rates, at 66 percent, and the private for-profits have the lowest at 32 percent. For associate and certificate programs, the private, for-profit institutions have the highest graduation rates, at 63 percent, and the publics the lowest, at 20 percent. It should be mentioned that the private, for-profit institutions offer far more certificate programs, that these have much shorter completion times, in some cases several months' duration, and hence higher percentages of completion.

A critical question is why the graduation rates are so low. First, many students are taking longer to finish their academic programs by choice. Paul Attewell and David Lavin (2007), in their monumental study, *Passing the Torch*, examined the academic careers of disadvantaged women enrolled at the City University of New York over a thirty-year period and compared them to a national sample. This study was highly acclaimed and won several awards including the Grawemeyer Award in 2009 for the best book in education. Among Attewell and Lavin's conclusions was that one-third of these women took more than ten years to complete their baccalaureate degrees. The reasons vary but include a number of financial, job, and family responsibilities. This trend has evolved as American higher education has moved from a selective system to an open admissions system. While every high school graduate can now enroll in a college program, sixty years ago, this was not the case. A combination of the G.I. Bill and the move to the open admissions policies in the 1960s made higher education available to the masses. Another trend that accelerated at the time of open admissions was the percentage of students who chose to attend college part-time. Estimates vary a bit, but the so-called "traditional" residential college student who is between the ages of 18–21 and attends full-time represents less than 20 percent of total enrollments. Students, especially the large adult population, are enrolling in academic programs to fit their personal needs and lifestyles. Attending part-time and stopping out for a while is not a problem for many "nontraditional" students. They have set their own schedule for graduation.

A second reason why students do not graduate or are taking longer to graduate is the need to enroll in remedial coursework. Nationally, the number of college students who need remediation has increased significantly and can represent as much as 80 percent of an incoming class (Edelman, 2011). Many of these students will struggle in their first year and may never resolve remedial issues, at a minimum resulting in extending their time to a degree or, at worse, causing them to drop out of college altogether. There is no easy solution for this problem. Basic reading, writing, and mathematical skills are deemed necessary for engaging in and completing college studies. So either the K–12 system significantly improves the preparation of students, or remedial students are allowed to just enter regular college courses without resolving their remediation. It is not likely that this situation will change soon. The state of Florida in 2014 enacted a new law that required all of the state's public colleges and universities to presume that all students graduating from a Florida public high school after 2004 are academically prepared for college. Public colleges in Florida have the option of assessing a student's academic standing using tests, high school GPAs, and other measures—and they may advise students with limited skills to take remedial classes. In the end, though, students themselves will decide whether they want to enroll in remedial classes or enter directly into introductory courses. It is too early to predict or study the results of this policy (Ross, 2014).

Third, financial situations and the cost of higher education are also causing students to slow down their completion to a degree. Simply put, many students do not have the funds readily available to pay for tuition, or they do not want to saddle themselves with too much debt. Over a ten-year period (2002–2012), tuition increased more than 50 percent in American public colleges and universities that enroll the largest percentage of students in higher education. According to a recent U.S. Government Accountability Office Report:

> Tuition prices and out-of-pocket costs increased for students in all income [brackets] both at 4-year and 2-year public colleges, making college less affordable for students and families. Median published tuition prices for in-state students increased by 55 percent from about $3,745 in school year 2002–2003 to $5,800 in school year 2011–2012. . . . Though tuition is typically higher at 4-year colleges than at 2-year colleges, the increase over the period was similar between the two types of colleges: both increased by about 54 percent. Median published tuition also increased for out-of-state students during this period, though less dramatically than for in-state students, rising by 31 percent from the 2002–2003 school year to the 2011–2012 school year.
>
> *(U.S. GAO Report, 2014)*

While inflation counts for some of this increase, the major driver of increased tuition at public institutions has been the severe reduction in state funding. While these reductions differ from state to state, the overall trend has clearly been one of substantial decline.

Funding of Higher Education

Most sectors of higher education have experienced adverse funding issues in the 21st century, especially since the Great Recession of 2008. Colleges and universities with endowments have had to rely a little more on these endowments to support operations. Private institutions have had to raise their tuition and fees. Research universities have become more aggressive in seeking out grants and contracts even though many of these institutions have been the beneficiaries of significant annual giving by alumni and other donors. The Council for Aid to Education (CAE) reported that annual giving to American higher education had

Percentage of total revenue

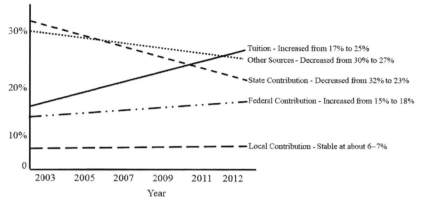

FIGURE 2.2 Revenue Sources for Public Higher Education—2003–2012

Source: U.S. GAO Analysis of Integrated Postsecondary Education Data System (IPEDS) U.S. GAO 15–151.

increased 7.6 percent in 2015 to more than $40 billion. Almost 30 percent, or $11.6 billion, went to just twenty institutions (Koenig, 2016).

The sector that has seen the most change in its funding situation has been public higher education. There are five major funding sources for public higher education in America: tuition, states, localities, federal government, and other sources (gifts, grants, contracts). Figure 2.2 provides a ten-year trend analysis. Three of the sources (localities, federal government, and other) have been relatively stable over this period. However, state funding levels, traditionally the highest sources, have decreased significantly from 32 percent to 23 percent. Most of this decrease has been made up by tuition, which has increased from 17 percent to 25 percent. And by increasing their share, localities have made up some (not all) of the state reductions for public two-year colleges. The state reductions have been most severe for four-year public university systems. It is important to note that funding reductions by the states have also occurred while enrollments have been increasing, so state systems are being squeezed on both ends. States that have instituted the largest decreases include:

- Colorado has reduced its support for higher education by nearly 69.4 percent from fiscal 1980 to fiscal 2011. At this rate of decline Colorado appropriations will reach zero in 2022. . . . Projections using more recent data find that Colorado could hit zero as soon as 2019.
- South Carolina reduced its state investment effort in higher education by 66.8 percent, from fiscal 1980 to fiscal 2011. . . . Extrapolating this trend, state funding for higher education will reach zero in 2031.

- Rhode Island reduced state higher education funding by 62.1 percent between 1980 and 2011. . . . Extrapolating this trend, state funding for higher education will reach zero in 2031.
- Arizona has reduced its annual state investment effort by 61.9 percent from fiscal year 1980 to fiscal year 2011. The trend between 1980 and 2011 will reach zero in 2032, although more recent data indicates it could be even sooner.

(Mortensen, 2012)

The implications of state funding reductions are clear. Declining state support for higher education leads directly to increased tuition charges to students. Figure 2.3 illustrates how tuition has increased in the public sector for the ten-year period between 2002–03 and 2011–12. States, in reducing if not abandoning financial support, are becoming less involved and may in fact be getting out of the higher education business. In addition:

- Many public universities are enrolling a shrinking share of students from lower-income families and competing most aggressively for the students who can afford to pay higher tuitions.
- Public institutions that can do so are aggressively recruiting nonresident students, for whom tuition charges are typically three times what state residents pay.
- Where possible, state universities are turning away from the states at the same time that the states have been turning away from their universities.

(Mortensen, 2012)

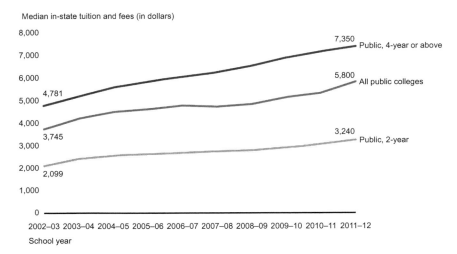

FIGURE 2.3 In-State Tuition and Fees for All Public Colleges in 2012 Constant Dollars

The policy trend in which tuition is expected to substitute for state revenue has become more dominant for several reasons, including competition for funding with other state social services. However, one of the rationales behind this policy is the idea that higher education is more of a private individual benefit than a public good. Tom Ross, president of the University of North Carolina, summarized this situation as follows:

> America is losing her way with regard to higher education. We seem to have forgotten the real value of higher education—both to our economy and to our society. We have become too focused on metrics, return on investment and job preparation. I am not suggesting these are unimportant. Rather, I would remind us that higher education offers many other—and I contend greater—benefits to our nation and its citizens and communities. . . .
>
> Today, however, America's societal commitment to investing in higher education appears to have eroded. We now spend about 2 percent more on higher education in real dollars than we spent 25 years ago, even though enrollment in our universities and colleges has grown by over 60 percent during that period. We spend about 30 percent less per student today than we did 25 years ago. As a nation, we are disinvesting in higher education, and we are beginning to pay the price. . . .
>
> We must educate policymakers about the importance of education to the fabric of our society. It is our exceptional system of higher education, both public and private, that has enabled our nation to develop the No. 1 economy in the world.
>
> *(Ross, 2015)*

One possible policy change that could significantly alter the funding patterns described is a small movement to make community colleges free. The state of Tennessee started such a program in 2015. President Barack Obama also called on the U.S. Congress to consider such a program nationally. Whether and when free community college becomes a reality is hard to say, but the idea is being considered and will likely happen eventually. The financial implication is that states and/or the federal government will make a greater funding commitment to community colleges, thereby easing the burden on students. This, in turn, may attract more students to attend community colleges and transfer to four-year colleges after receiving a two-year associate's degree. In addition to free community college, there were also calls for free four-year, public-college education from the likes of 2016 Democratic Party presidential nominees Hillary Clinton and Bernie Sanders. In a *New York Times* article titled "College for the Masses," two studies were cited that made the case that "at risk" students benefitted significantly from a four-year college education (Leonhardt, 2015). Studies by Goodman, Hurwitz, & Smith (2015) and Zimmerman (2013) show that students who typically would have difficulty being admitted into a four-year college (those who scored lower than 840 on the SAT or had less than C+ high school average) did substantially better with some college, especially if they graduated college, than those who did not. The conclusion was that a long line of research has found that education usually pays off—for individuals and societies—in today's technologically complex, globalized economy (Leonhardt, 2015).

The Purpose of Higher Education, Academic Programs, Commoditization

For the past several decades, policymakers and legislators in a number of states have been calling into question the purpose of a higher education. In recent years, governors in Florida, North Carolina, Wisconsin, New York, and Texas have called for higher education funding that focuses on job creation and growth. In January 2013, Governor Patrick McCrory (North Carolina) said he would push legislation to base funding of the state's public colleges and universities on post-graduate employment rather than enrollment.

> I'm looking at legislation right now—in fact, I just instructed my staff yesterday to go ahead and develop legislation—which would change the basic formula in how education money is given out to our universities and our community colleges. It's not based on butts in seats but on how many of those butts can get jobs.
>
> *(Binker & Sims, 2013)*

During a radio interview, McCrory also questioned the value of publicly supporting liberal arts education when the host made a joke about gender studies courses at UNC-Chapel Hill. "If you want to take gender studies that's fine, go to a private school and take it. But I don't want to subsidize that if that's not going to get someone a job" (Binker & Sims, 2013).

The term "commoditization of higher education" refers to the transformation of the educational process into commodity form, that is, something created, grown, produced, or manufactured for the purpose of commercial transaction or exchange. Neoliberalists see this transformation as desirable and support such phenomena as student demand for employment skills, private investment (corporations and corporate-affiliated foundations) in higher education, and federal government policies such as STEM. Faculty in professional academic programs such as business, teacher education, health sciences, and engineering also tend to support this trend. On the other hand, faculty in traditional arts and sciences such as history, philosophy, anthropology, and literature question it and support the importance of a liberal education that prepares students to deal with larger life and world issues.

> Liberal Education is an approach to learning that empowers individuals and prepares them to deal with complexity, diversity, and change. It provides

students with broad knowledge of the wider world (e.g. science, culture, and society) as well as in-depth study in a specific area of interest. A liberal education helps students develop a sense of social responsibility, as well as strong and transferable intellectual and practical skills such as communication, analytical and problem-solving skills, and a demonstrated ability to apply knowledge and skills in real-world settings.

(Association of Colleges and Universities, 2013)

Fareed Zakaria (2015) reminds us that the issue of a liberal education versus a more practical education is an age-old debate. In his book, *In Defense of Liberal Education*, he quotes Charles Eliot, at the time (1869) a professor at MIT, who would later become president of Harvard University, a position he would hold for forty years:

What can I do with my boy? I can afford, and am glad, to give him the best training to be had. I should be proud to have him turn out a preacher or a learned man; but I don't think he has the making of that in him. I want to give him a practical education; one that will prepare him, better than I was prepared, to follow my business or any other active calling. The classical schools and the colleges do not offer what I want.

(Eliot, 1869)

Eliot in this quote was concerned about the classical education dominated by Greco-Roman literature, history, philosophy, and language.

These two perspectives (commoditization and liberal education) are at odds with one another and have caused conflicts within the academy among administrators, faculty, and students. Several decades ago, a college graduate with almost any major could secure a decent paying position by virtue of her or his education and degree. This is no longer the case. College graduates in certain majors struggle to find employment appropriate for their level of education. There is some truth, for example, to stories of college graduates who, because they cannot find positions, take jobs driving taxicabs. In 1970, only 1 in 100 taxi drivers and chauffeurs in the U.S. had a college degree. By 2013, 15 of 100 had degrees (Orzsag, 2013). There is nothing wrong with driving a taxicab, but why would a driver invest the time and money in four or more years of college in order to do so? Would she or he have been better off bypassing college and simply going into the taxi business? Was the goal of attending college to secure a position as a taxi driver?

Within colleges and universities, concerns are growing about the place of a liberal education built on the humanities, arts, social sciences, and sciences. The liberal arts and sciences provide the curricular foundation for most academic programs at the undergraduate level and, contrary to some popular belief, are areas in which many students decide to major. In 2012, approximately one-third, or 582,750, of all baccalaureate degree graduates majored in the humanities or social sciences (U.S. Department of Education, 2013). Many of these graduates may also be taking courses, second majors, or minors in other subject areas. For instance, many liberal arts majors take education courses on the undergraduate level to become teachers. In fact, many colleges no longer offer teacher education as an undergraduate major and require students to major in other subject areas. When government officials and policy makers question the role of a liberal education that does not lead directly to a job, they exacerbate the concern of large segments of the college faculty and student populations. This in turn leads to serious discussion, if not confrontation, within the college community regarding curriculum and academic program requirements. This situation will only worsen as enrollments grow, as more students expect to secure gainful employment upon graduation, and as competition for professional positions becomes more intense. In 2014, the U.S. Department of Education was drafting guidelines requiring all colleges receiving federal financial aid to collect data on the employment records of graduates and disclose same in recruitment materials. A grand debate ensued about what it means to be an educated person and how one goes about measuring this, especially since the benefits of a liberal education may not be realized until years after graduation. To illustrate one side of this debate, here is a personal story from Frances Bronet, dean of the school of architecture at the University of Oregon, that appeared in *The Chronicle of Higher Education:*

> "There was no way I could go to school and not have an immediate return," she says. "My parents already thought that my going to school was an opportunity lost." She went to McGill University and majored in architecture and engineering—technical fields she knew would pay. Now one of her great regrets in life is not having gotten a broader liberal-arts education. "We talk about people being entrepreneurial, but it's really about being creative, thoughtful, and critical." When she taught at Rensselaer Polytechnic Institute, her department surveyed engineering alumni, asking about their education. Graduates who were a year out of college wished they had gotten more technical skills. Those who were five years out wanted more management skills. But alumni who were 10 to 20 years into their careers wanted more cultural literacy, "because they were traveling all over the world, working with cultures they never experienced before," she says.
>
> *(Carlson, 2013)*

Proponents would posit that the Frances Bonet story is not unique and that a liberal education can be the path to cultural literacy, to becoming an informed citizen, to understanding and critically analyzing complex issues, and to seeking knowledge in a variety of areas and forms.

Henry Giroux proposes:

> Pedagogy is a mode of critical intervention, one that endows teachers with a responsibility to prepare students not merely for jobs but for being in the

world in ways that allow them to influence the larger political, ideological, and economic forces that bear down on their lives.

(Giroux, 2014, p. 36)

While there are those outside the academy who continue to question its value, a liberal education will not disappear quickly from American higher education.

Adult and Lifelong Learners

Student age is related to the issue of arts and sciences programs versus professional education. Older students who are already in the job market enroll in professional programs to advance their careers. As a result, one of the major developments in American higher education over the past fifty years has been the expansion of the number of adults who attend a college or university. Table 2.5 shows the majority (55 percent) of students attending college in degree programs in 1970 were 21 years old or younger or traditional age. This is no longer the case. The projection for 2021 is that approximately 40 percent of the degree-student population will be 21 years of age or younger. During the same time period (1970–2021), students age 35 years or older will increase from 9 percent to almost 20 percent. There are a number of reasons for this, many of which relate to career needs and professional development. First, more students are seeking to advance their education beyond the baccalaureate degree. Enrollments in graduate programs, especially in high-demand areas such as business administration, keep expanding. Second, many professions, especially in health and technical areas, both in private and public employment, are requiring additional educational credentials. Third, and perhaps most important, people feel a need to expand or hone their skills and knowledge in order to compete in the employment market. This latter trend is becoming more pronounced as technology and automation accelerate the competition for jobs and employment. In 2014, *The Economist* cited a study by researchers at Oxford University predicting that:

> 47% of [all] occupations are at risk of being automated in the next few decades. As innovation wipes out some jobs and changes others, people will need to top up their human capital throughout their lives.

(The Economist, 2014, p. 11)

The Great Recession of 2008–09 may have been a harbinger of what is to come, as millions of workers in all walks of life suddenly found themselves unemployed. Many decided to switch careers and sought education credentials in other fields. While the unemployment picture in the United States has abated since the Great Recession, it has not gone away. Many people continue to be unemployed or underemployed.

In addition to degree students, there are millions of nondegree, almost entirely adult, students in colleges and universities who enroll in continuing education,

TABLE 2.5 Total Fall Enrollment in Degree-Granting Institutions, by Age: Selected Years, 1970 Through 2021

[In thousands]

Age																Projected		
	1970	1980	1990	2000	2003	2004	2005	2006	2007	2008	2009	2010	2011	2012	2013	2016	2021
1	2	3	4	5	6	7	8	9	10	11	12	13	14	15	16	17	18
All students	**8,581**	**12,097**	**13,819**	**15,312**	**16,911**	**17,272**	**17,487**	**17,759**	**18,248**	**19,103**	**20,428**	**21,016**	**20,994**	**21,253**	**21,485**	**22,194**	**23,755**
14 to 17 years old	263	257	153	131	169	166	187	184	200	195	217	202	202	207	208	219	244
18 and 19 years old	2,579	2,852	2,777	3,258	3,355	3,367	3,444	3,561	3,690	3,813	4,041	4,056	4,025	4,343	4,331	4,358	4,765
20 and 21 years old	1,885	2,395	2,593	3,005	3,391	3,516	3,563	3,573	3,570	3,649	3,945	4,101	4,174	4,386	4,368	4,361	4,603
22 to 24 years old	1,469	1,947	2,202	2,600	3,086	3,166	3,114	3,185	3,280	3,443	3,594	3,758	3,708	3,823	3,922	3,996	4,037
25 to 29 years old	1,091	1,843	2,083	2,044	2,311	2,418	2,469	2,506	2,651	2,840	3,096	3,253	3,319	3,057	3,116	3,389	3,545
30 to 34 years old	527	1,227	1,384	1,333	1,418	1,440	1,438	1,472	1,519	1,609	1,741	1,805	1,807	1,678	1,726	1,833	2,037
35 years old and over	767	1,577	2,627	2,942	3,181	3,199	3,272	3,277	3,339	3,554	3,794	3,840	3,758	3,759	3,812	4,038	4,524

Source: U.S. Department of Education, National Center for Education Statistics, Higher Education General Information Survey (HEGIS), "Fall Enrollment in Colleges and Universities" surveys, 1970 and 1980; Integrated Postsecondary Education Data System (IPEDS), "Fall Enrollment Survey" (IPEDS-EF:90–99); IPEDS Spring 2001 through Spring 2012, Enrollment component; and Projections of Education Statistics to 2021. U.S. Department of Commerce, Census Bureau, Current Population Survey (CPS), October, selected years, 1970 through 2021.

noncredit contract courses and professional development programs funded by private corporations, public agencies, trade unions, and other industry-specific organizations. It would be a mistake to consider these programs as minor or insignificant operations. The City University of New York (CUNY), for example, the third largest university in the country, enrolled 270,000 students in regular degree programs in 2013 and another 230,000 students in nondegree and continuing education courses. CUNY provides an enormous service to its constituencies by offering such an extensive array of nondegree, adult, and continuing education programs. These programs are also an important funding source for the university and are critical to a number of individual college operations. CUNY is not alone in providing these programs; many other colleges and universities, especially those in large urban centers, have made adult and continuing education an important part of their overall academic offerings.

The Role of Technology

As the forces, developments, and trends described in this chapter buffet and affect American colleges and universities, technology is seen as fundamental and integral to the health of the higher education enterprise. Whether to help reduce costs in order to serve more students, to make up for funding decreases, or to provide students with career and professional skills to compete in the job market, technology is viewed as part of the solution. Furthermore, spurred by neoliberal thinking, technology in higher education is seen by policymakers in government as well as by individuals in the private sector as critical to the country's future.

Summary

This chapter focused on the larger socio-economic forces shaping American higher education. Issues related to mission and purpose, public funding, student debt, and commoditization were presented as they relate to a common neoliberal philosophy that promotes market-driven approaches, privatization, and corporate solutions to public services including higher education. It also examined how these forces are affecting the different sectors of American higher education including the public universities, community colleges, research universities, nonprofit private colleges, and for-profit colleges. The chapter concluded by positing that technology is a major vehicle for supporting the neoliberal agenda to change basic aspects of American higher education.

References

Arum, R. & Roksa, J. (2010). *Academically adrift: Limited learning on college campuses.* Chicago: University of Chicago Press.

Association of Colleges and Universities (2013). What is a 21st century liberal education? Retrieved from: http://www.aacu.org/leap/what-is-a-liberal-education Accessed: March 14, 2015.

Attewell, P. & Lavin, D. (2007). *Passing the torch: Does higher education for the disadvantaged pay off across the generations?* New York: Russell Sage Foundation.

Binker, M. & Sims, J. (2013). *McCrory: Fund higher education based on results.* WRAL Report. Retrieved from: http://www.wral.com/mccrory-fund-higher-education-based-on-results/12037347/ Accessed: March 14, 2015.

The (British) Times (2015). Higher Education World Rankings (2014–2015). Retrieved from: http://www.timeshighereducation.co.uk/world-university-rankings/2014-15/world-ranking Accessed: March 7, 2015.

Carlson, S. (April 22, 2013). How to assess the real payoff of a college degree. *The Chronicle of Higher Education.* Retrieved from: http://chronicle.com/article/Is-ROI-the-Right-Way-to-Judge/138665/ Accessed: March 15, 2015.

Center for Public Education (September 2014). The path least taken: At a glance. Retrieved from: http://www.centerforpubliceducation.org/pathleasttaken Accessed: March 7, 2015.

The Economist (June 28, 2014). Creative destruction: A cost crisis, changing labour markets and new technology will turn an old institution on its head. Retrieved from: http://www.economist.com/news/leaders/21605906-cost-crisis-changing-labour-markets-and-new-technology-will-turn-old-institution-its Accessed: March 15, 2015.

Edelman, S. (October 23, 2011). Remedial class nightmare at CUNY. *New York Post.* Retrieved from: http://nypost.com/2011/10/23/remedial-class-nightmare-at-cuny/ Accessed: March 12, 2015.

Eliot, C. (February, 1869). The new education. *Atlantic Monthly.* Retrieved from: http://www.theatlantic.com/magazine/archive/1869/02/the-new-education/309049/ Accessed: May 2, 2015.

Friedman, M. (1962). *Capital and freedom.* Chicago: University of Chicago Press.

Friedman, M. (1978). Preface. In W. Simon (Ed.), *A time for truth* (p. xii). New York: Readers Digest Press.

Giroux, H. (March 27, 2013). The violence of neoliberalism and the attack on higher education. *Truthdig.com.* Retrieved from: http://www.truthdig.com/report/item/the_violence_of_neoliberalism_and_the_attack_on_higher_education_20130327 Accessed: March 8, 2015.

Giroux, H. (2014). *Neoliberalism's war on higher education.* Chicago: Haymarket Books.

Goodman, J., Hurwitz, M., & Smith, J. (2015). College access, initial college choice and degree completion. Working Paper 20996. Cambridge, MA: National Bureau of Economic Research. Retrieved from: http://scholar.harvard.edu/files/joshuagoodman/files/collegetypequality.pdf Accessed: April 26, 2015.

Hansen, R. J. (October 22, 2013). University of Phoenix parent to lay off 500 workers on declining enrollment. *The Arizona Republic.* Retrieved from: http://archive.azcentral.com/business/news/articles/20131022university-of-phoenix-expected-to-announce-layoffs.html Accessed: March 11, 2015.

Harari, Y. N. (2015). *Sapiens: A brief history of humankind.* New York: HarperCollins Publishers.

Harvey, D. (2005). *A brief history of neoliberalism.* New York: Oxford University Press.

Hayek, F. (1962). *The road to serfdom.* Chicago: University of Chicago Press.

Howard, J. (2015). Stanford chief wants higher ed to be 'affordable, accessible, adaptable'. *The Chronicle of Higher Education.* Retrieved from: http://chronicle.com/article/Stanford-Chief-Wants-Higher-Ed/228505/?cid=at&utm_source=at&utm_medium=en Accessed: March 16, 2015.

Hussar, W. J. & Bailey, T.M. (2013). *Projections of Education Statistics to 2022 (NCES 2014–051).* U.S. Department of Education, National Center for Education Statistics. Washington, DC: U.S. Government Printing Office.

Koenig, R. (January 27, 2016). U.S. colleges raise $40 billion; Stanford tops list at $1.6 billion. *The Chronicle of Philanthropy.* Retrieved from: https://philanthropy.com/article/US-Colleges-Raise40/235059/?cid=at&utm_source=at&utm_medium=en&elq=64c c998de79f4ae59625c94297f22e3f&elqCampaignId=2306&elqaid=7662&elqat=1&elq TrackId=5e47ae0358944d6289c952e4e90dda26 Accessed: January 27, 2016.

Leonhardt, D. (April 26, 2015). College for the masses. *New York Times.* Retrieved from: http://www.nytimes.com/2015/04/26/upshot/college-for-the-masses.html?emc= edit_th_20150426&nl=todaysheadlines&nlid=1596194&abt=0002&abg=0 Accessed: April 26, 2015.

Mortensen, T.G. (Winter 2012). *State funding: A race to the bottom.* Washington, DC: American Council on Education. Retrieved from: http://www.acenet.edu/the-presidency/columns-and-features/Pages/state-funding-a-race-to-the-bottom.aspx Accessed: March 13, 2015.

Orszag, P.R. (June 25, 2013). Why are so many college graduates driving taxis? *Bloomberg Business.* Retrieved from: http://www.bloomberg.com/news/articles/2013–06–25/why-are-so-many-college-graduates-driving-taxis- Accessed: March 14, 2015.

Pew Research Center (February 11, 2014). The rising cost of not going to college. Retrieved from: http://www.pewsocialtrends.org/2014/02/11/the-rising-cost-of-not-going-to-college/ Accessed: March 7, 2015.

Ross, J. (2014). Why is Florida ending remedial education for college students? *National Journal.* Retrieved from: http://www.nationaljournal.com/next-america/education/why-is-florida-ending-remedial-education-for-college-students-20140825 Accessed: March 12, 2015.

Ross, T. (March 15, 2015). The real value of education. *The News Observer.* Retrieved from: http://www.newsobserver.com/opinion/op-ed/article14056646.html Accessed: March 21, 2015.

Selingo, J.J. (Ed.) (2014). The innovative university: What college presidents think about change in American higher education. *The Chronicle of Higher Education.* Retrieved from: http://app.results.chronicle.com/e/es.aspx?s=2423&e=89593&elq=cd9973526e5048 45837bbada16e5b345 Accessed: March 7, 2015.

Simon, W. (1978). *A time for truth.* New York: Readers Digest Press.

Smith, J. (1991). *The idea brokers and the rise of the new policy elite.* New York: The Free Press.

U.S. Department of Education (2013). National Center for Education Statistics, Higher Education General Information Survey (HEGIS), "Degrees and other formal awards conferred", 1970–71 through 1985–86; Integrated Postsecondary Education Data System (IPEDS), "Completions survey" (IPEDS-C:91–96); and IPEDS Fall 2001 through Fall 2012. Retrieved from: http://nces.ed.gov/programs/digest/d13/tables/dt13_318.20.asp Accessed: March 14, 2017.

U.S. Department of Education (2014). Federal student loan portfolio. Retrieved from: https://studentaid.ed.gov/about/data-center/student/portfolio Accessed: March 7, 2015.

U.S. General Accountability Office Report (2014). *Highlights of higher education state funding trends and policies on affordability.* GAO Report 15–151. Retrieved from: http://www.gao.gov/assets/670/667557.pdf Accessed: March 13, 2015.

Zakaria, F. (2015). *In defense of a liberal education.* New York: W. W. Norton and Company.

Zimmerman, S. (2013). The returns to college admission for academically marginal students. Unpublished article. Retrieved from: http://pantheon.yale.edu/~sdz3/Zimmerman_JoLE_5_2013.pdf Accessed: April 26, 2015.

3

ARE THE FACULTY THE UNIVERSITY?

Isador Isaac (I.I.) Rabi was a professor of physics at Columbia University who won the Nobel Prize in 1944 for his resonance method of recording the magnetic properties of atomic nuclei. He was widely regarded as one of the top physicists of his time and was a colleague of Niels Bohr, Wolfgang Pauli, Robert Oppenheimer, and Werner Heisenberg. He refused the associate directorship of the Manhattan Project in Los Alamos in 1942, stating "he did not wish to make the culmination of three hundred years of physics into a weapon of mass destruction" (Bird & Sherwin, 2006). Rabi was instrumental in establishing Brookhaven National Laboratory and Nevis Labs (Columbia University). He was also generally credited with giving European physicists the idea for establishing CERN (Conseil Européen pour la Recherche Nucléaire) Laboratory in Geneva. Rabi, however, is particularly remembered for his interesting encounter with Dwight D. Eisenhower, the then-president of Columbia University. In 1948, at their first meeting, Eisenhower was congratulating Rabi on his Nobel Prize for Physics, adding that he was always happy to see "one of Columbia's employees honored." The remark, it is recorded, drew from Rabi a careful response: "Mr. President, the faculty are not *employees* of the University—they *are* the University." This was the beginning of a twenty-year friendship between the two (Devons, 2001).

Professors today would like to think that Rabi's position on the importance of the faculty still holds true, and in fact in many, not all, universities, there is some truth to it. Faculty-governing documents, collective-bargaining agreements, and institutional bylaws that give professors extensive responsibilities and powers to hire new colleagues, to grant tenure, to establish curricula, and to evaluate teaching and learning are well-established in many of the universities in the country. However, this is not the case in all institutions. A number of mostly private nonprofit and for-profit colleges have essentially bypassed faculty prerogatives in terms of governance and have established administrative control over all aspects of policies, procedures, and operations. A number of institutions such as the University of Phoenix employ a minimal number of full-time teaching faculty and instead appoint instructors on term by term or semester contracts. Just about all personnel, curriculum, and teaching standards are controlled by the administration.

The role of college faculty and the nature of their work has long been the subject of scrutiny. Still quoted today is the George Bernard Shaw line from his 1905 play *Man and Superman*: "He who can, does: He who cannot, teaches." Shaw is also famous for: "A fool's brain digests philosophy into folly, science into superstition, and art into pedantry. Hence university education." Shaw was a great wit, satirist, and, among other things, the cofounder of the London School of Economics, one of the major public research universities in the world.

Readers familiar with organization theory might recall discussions about formal and functional authority in decision making. Formal authority is rooted in the official organizational structure and positions of authority as defined by bylaws and governing boards. Major decisions are made in a vertical hierarchy or through an established chain of command as is done in most for-profit entities such as private corporations. However, it is also recognized that functional authority might influence or reside horizontally in an organization because of professional knowledge and expertise. Amitai Etzioni in his seminal work, *Modern Organizations*, notes:

> Administration assumes a power hierarchy. Without a clear ordering of higher and lower in rank, in which the higher in rank have more power than the lower ones and hence can control and coordinate the latter's activities, the 'basic principle of administration is violated; the organization ceases to be a coordinated tool. However, knowledge is largely an individual property; unlike other organization means, it cannot be transferred from one person to another by decree. . . . It is this highly individualized principle which is diametrically opposed to the very essence of the organizational principle of control and coordination by superiors—i.e. the principle of administrative authority. In other words, the ultimate justification for a professional act is that it is, to the best of the professional's knowledge, the right act.
>
> *(Etzioni, 1964, pp. 75–76)*

Mintzberg takes this a step further and presents the concept of a professional bureaucracy, which emphasizes reliance on the

> coordination on the standardization of skills and its associated design parameters, training and indoctrination. It hires duly trained and indoctrinated specialists—professionals—for the operating core, and then gives them considerable control over their own work. In effect, the work is highly specialized in the horizontal dimension, but enlarged in the vertical one. Control

over his own work means that the professional works relatively independently of his colleagues, but closely with the clients he serves . . . and there is less power of the office and much more power of expertise.

(Mintzberg, 1979, pp. 50–52)

Mintzberg applies his concept to faculty in colleges and universities:

They [the faculty] also seek collective control of the administrative decisions that affect them, decisions, for example, to hire colleagues, to promote them, and to distribute resources. . . . Every university professor, for example, carries out some administrative duties and serves on committees of one kind or another to ensure that he retains some control over the decisions that affect his work. Moreover, full-time administrators who wish to have any power at all in these structures must be certified members of the profession, and preferably be elected by the professional operators or at least appointed with their blessing.

(Mintzberg, 1979, p. 56)

In sum, faculty possess professional expertise and knowledge that has allowed them significant leeway and functional authority to influence decisions in colleges and universities. This has evolved over time and, while challenged in some institutions, still permeates a good deal of what occurs in American higher education and particularly the nonprofit and public sectors. Examples of faculty structures and functional authority will be discussed later on in this chapter.

Critical to understanding the role of the faculty is defining what it is that they are expected to do. This depends upon the nature of the institutions, level of study, and academic programs. Large universities with well-established graduate programs expect faculty to secure grants and contracts to fund research projects. Community colleges expect faculty to be excellent teachers who are attuned to the needs of students, many of whom struggled academically in high school. Faculty in programs such as business, medicine, health science, and education are expected to do service in their professions as well as develop relationships with businesses, hospitals, and public schools. Scott Walker, governor of Wisconsin, sparked interest in the question during budget negotiations in 2015 that included his proposal to cut state appropriations for the University of Wisconsin system by $300 million when he remarked that the universities "might be able to make up savings just by asking faculty and staff to consider teaching one more class a semester." As reported in the *Milwaukee-Wisconsin Journal Sentinel*:

The governor's comment . . . bares "one of the most enduring sources of friction" in American higher education: What is the primary function of the faculty? On one side of the question are critics of universities who see it as working with students in the classroom. On the other are defenders

of advancing knowledge through research, and sharing it in ways that go
beyond the classroom.

(Herzog & Marley, 2015)

The question is part of a debate that goes back decades about the role of faculty
as teachers and scholars. In 1967, then-Governor Ronald Reagan of California
asserted that taxpayers should not be "subsidizing intellectual curiosity. . . . Learning for learning's sake might be nice, but the rest of us shouldn't have to pay for it.
A higher education should prepare students for jobs" (Berrett, 2015). The message
was clear—faculty should teach and prepare students to contribute to the economy. The *Los Angeles Times* editorial page the following day warned that Governor
Reagan's budget cuts and "tampering" with higher education threatened to create
second-rate institutions. "If a university is not a place where intellectual curiosity
is to be encouraged, and subsidized," the editors wrote, "then it is nothing." The
two views of the faculty role had long existed in uneasy equilibrium. On that day
in 1967, "the balance started to tip toward utility in ways not even Reagan may
have anticipated" (Berrett, 2015).

Who Are the Faculty?

According to the National Center for Education Statistics, there are approximately
1.5 million full- and part-time faculty working in American colleges and universities (see Figure 3.1). Faculty include professors, associate professors, assistant
professors, instructors, lecturers, assisting professors, and adjunct professors. From fall
1991 to fall 2011, the number of full-time instructional faculty in degree-granting

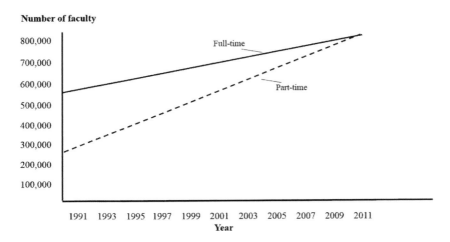

FIGURE 3.1 Number of Instructional Faculty in Degree-Granting Postsecondary Institutions, by Employment Status: Selected Years, Fall 1991 Through Fall 2011

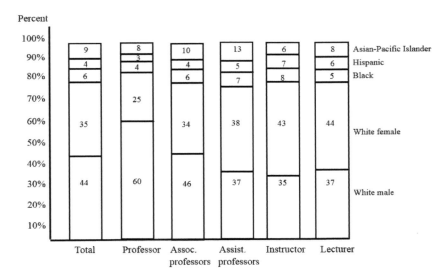

FIGURE 3.2 Percentage of Full-time Instructional Faculty Whose Race/Ethnicity Was Known, in Degree-Granting Postsecondary Institutions, by Academic Rank, Selected Race/Ethnicity, and Sex: Fall 2011

postsecondary institutions increased by 42 percent (from 536,000 to 762,000), while the number of part-time faculty increased by 162 percent (from 291,000 to 762,000). As a result of the faster increase in the number of part-time faculty, the percentage of faculty who were part-time increased from 35 to 50 percent during this period. The year 2011 is considered pivotal because it was the first time since data have been collected that the number of part-time faculty equaled the full-time faculty. The increase in the number of part-time faculty was most pronounced in private for-profit colleges. The overall twenty-year trend is quite clear.

Figure 3.2 provides a demographic profile of full-time faculty. Seventy-nine percent of the full-time faculty are white, and 55 percent are male. These percentages vary depending upon the professorial rank. For example, 60 percent of full professors are white males.

Most four-year degree programs require full-time faculty to have a PhD. And while two-year programs have high percentages of full-time faculty with master's degrees, the trend increasingly is to hire PhDs. As a result, college faculty comprise the most educated group of people in the country. According to the Council of Graduate Schools (2010), the median time to a PhD is approximately eight years. In some disciplines, the median is more than ten years. The calculation of this median becomes complicated due to a high degree of stopping in and out on the way to graduation. The average age of someone who receives a PhD is 33 years, demonstrating that most full-time college faculty have spent a good part of their 20s and 30s studying rather than working and

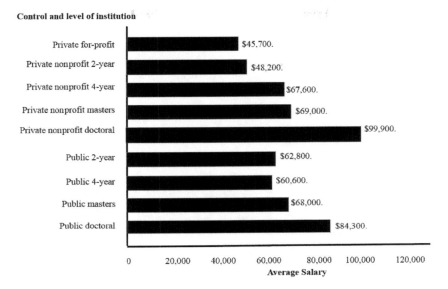

FIGURE 3.3 Average Salary of Full-time Instructional Faculty on Nine-Month Contracts in Degree-Granting Postsecondary Institutions, by Control and Level of Institution: 2012–13

earning a decent salary. The average salary for a newly minted PhD hired as a full-time assistant professor is in the $60,000-plus range, varying from institution to institution. Figure 3.3 provides data on the average salaries of full-time faculty. Faculty in doctoral institutions are the most highly paid, at approximately $100,000 per nine-month appointment. Faculty at private, for-profit institutions earn $45,700 on average. The progression of promotion from assistant to associate and then to full professor normally takes fifteen to twenty years, assuming that appropriate criteria, which normally includes a comprehensive scholarship record, are met. There are benefits unique to the professoriate such as an annual salary that is figured on a nine-month basis so that summer can be used for scholarship or to supplement one's income by additional teaching or contract work. In general, beginning assistant professors struggle a bit financially, but as their careers advance, the majority of full-time faculty lead comfortable but not necessarily rich lives in their mid-40s and beyond.

As an aside, it is well known that at many universities, especially those that are involved in Division 1 sports programs, the most highly paid personnel are sports coaches and managers. For example, at Duke University, basketball coach Mike Krzyzewski's total compensation was $9.6 million in 2015, while President Richard Brodhead earned $1.1 million. At the University of Louisville, Coach Rick Patino earned $5.7 million. At the University of Michigan, football coach Jim Harbaugh earned $5.7 million (Snyder, 2015). These salaries frequently are irksome to faculty who believe they are the university. One might ask: Why do these coaches make such high salaries? The answer is because collegiate sports generate profits. In addition, they build school spirit among students and alumni, who are yet another important source of income. The Duke University basketball program in 2014 generated revenue of $27 million and netted a profit of almost $13 million (Sherman, 2015).

Contingent Faculty

The term "contingent" refers to faculty who serve in nontenure-bearing lines and who work with minimal protection of job security, or at least not the same protection that tenured faculty members enjoy. The number of contingent faculty has grown considerably and, according to the American Association of University Professors, accounts for three-quarters of all college teaching positions (AAUP, 2014). Contingent faculty include adjunct positions, post-doctorates, teaching assistants, nontenure-track full-time faculty, clinical faculty, and contractual faculty. Part-timers or adjuncts make up the largest percentage of the contingent population.

The plight of part-time faculty has been likened to that of migrant farm workers in the 1960s. A group from the University of Wisconsin even produced a video titled *Degrees of Shame—Part-time Faculty: Migrant Workers of the Information Economy* (Wolf, 1997). The comparison to migrant workers is a bit of an exaggeration; however, the video does make the point that many part-time faculty move from position to position to eke out a living. In 2014, PBS aired a program documenting the life of Mary-Faith Cerasoli, an adjunct professor of Spanish and Italian who taught at the Bronx and Manhattan campuses of Mercy College and Nassau Community College in New York. She was also homeless. Ms. Cerasoli has a master's degree from Middlebury College. Her annual salary was $22,000, but because she put together a full course load, she was ineligible for public assistance. Since she couldn't afford a place to live, she lived off the generosity of others, staying with friends and sometimes sleeping in her car (Pathe, 2014).

The Coalition on the Academic Workforce (2012) conducted a national survey of part-time faculty and concluded that colleges and universities were not adequately supporting this population. Key findings included:

- The median pay per course, standardized to a three-credit course, was $2,700 in fall 2010 and ranged in the aggregate from a low of $2,235 at two-year colleges to a high of $3,400 at four-year doctoral or research universities. While compensation levels varied most consistently by type of institution, part-time faculty respondents report low compensation rates per course across all institutional categories.
- Part-time faculty respondents saw little, if any, wage premium based on their credentials. Their compensation lagged behind professionals in other fields with similar credentials, and they experienced little in the way of a career ladder (higher wages after several years of work).

- Professional support for part-time faculty members' work outside the classroom and inclusion in academic decision making was minimal.
- Part-time teaching is not necessarily temporary employment, and those teaching part-time do not necessarily prefer a part-time to a full-time position. Over 80 percent of respondents reported teaching part-time for more than three years, and over half for more than six years. Furthermore, over three-quarters of respondents said they have sought, are now seeking, or will be seeking a full-time tenure-track position, and nearly three-quarters said they would definitely or probably accept a full-time tenure-track position at the institution at which they were currently teaching if such a position were offered.
- Course loads varied significantly among respondents. Slightly more than half taught one course or two courses during the fall 2010 term, while slightly fewer than half taught three or more courses"

(Coalition of Academic Workforce, 2012)

The study found that 94 percent of part-time faculty respondents held graduate degrees: 40.2 percent reported a master's degree as their highest level of educational attainment, 30.4 percent a doctorate, 16.7 percent a professional degree or other terminal degree, and 7 percent completed all work but the dissertation toward a doctoral degree. There is something wrong when a higher education system that produces so many individuals with advanced credentials does not or cannot provide decent working conditions for them. Administrators have argued for decades that their colleges cannot afford to improve adjuncts' salaries without passing the cost onto students in the form of higher tuition.

There are some indications that the situation is changing, thanks largely to organized labor. Part-time instructors at some colleges have managed to win major improvements in their pay, benefits, job security, and overall working conditions. At Tufts University, for instance:

> Even before part-time instructors at Tufts University voted to form a union in September 2013, they earned more per course than their peers at most other Boston-area colleges. Tufts's administration did little to oppose their unionization, and their first contract provides them with pay increases, professional-development funds, guaranteed interviews for open full-time positions, and opportunities to earn two- or three-year contracts after several years with good performance reviews. James M. Glaser, dean of Tufts's School of Arts and Sciences, says Tufts respects the adjuncts' contributions and wants them to "feel like they have been treated well by the administration."
>
> *(Schmidt, 2015)*

The situation of adjunct faculty is causing some institutions to rethink their full-time workforce policies by hiring more faculty on nontenure-bearing, contract positions. This allows them to provide full-time status to faculty and, in many cases, to former adjuncts, without the commitment of lifetime employment that tenure would provide. Typically, such contracts last from two to five years and are renewable. At New York University, for example, contractual faculty are given five-year appointments. Their salaries are comparable to faculty in tenure-bearing positions. They have heavier teaching loads but are not required to engage in extensive research or scholarship to maintain their positions. As budgets tighten, this model is being adopted by more and more colleges in order to avoid the risk and disruption of retrenching tenured faculty.

Tenure and Academic Freedom

The policy of tenure (from the Latin *tenere*, meaning "to hold or keep") carries with it the guarantee of lifetime employment. Tenure is rarely revoked except in dire institutional financial exigency or for the most egregious behavior on the part of a faculty member. It is common practice in all levels of education and has its roots in in the concept of academic freedom. There is a long history of tenure that goes as far back as the middle ages. Scholars were assured safety in their academic pursuits as early as 1158, when the Holy Roman Emperor Frederick Barbarossa issued an edict protecting scholars (Metzger, 1973). In the 19th century, professors at colleges and universities worked at the pleasure of governing boards of trustees. There were instances where board members and major donors mandated the ouster of faculty members who did not perform to their liking. This system began to change in the early part of the 20th century. Harvard University, Columbia University, and the University of Chicago implemented policies prohibiting donors from advocating for the termination of faculty members (Cameron, 2010). New Jersey became the first state to pass tenure legislation when, in 1910, it granted fair-dismissal rights to college professors. With the emergence of unionization in higher education in the 20th century, tenure became an important element of collective bargaining and faculty contracts. Tenure at the college level is generally granted after seven years of employment and upon documentation of scholarly publications and research in the faculty member's area of expertise. While teaching and service to the institution and community are generally part of the tenure application packet, it is well understood in many institutions that scholarship is the most critical criterion for tenure. This is a very different from the tenure process at the K–12 level, which is generally based on three years of service and the candidate's record of teaching.

Tenure has its supporters and its detractors. Faculty generally support tenure and see it as protection of their academic freedom. It also tends to commit faculty to their institutions for the long term. There have been several studies examining the effects of faculty status (full-time, tenured versus part-time, nontenured) on graduation rates. Using institutional data from The College Board, Ehrenberg and

Zhang (2004) concluded that the use of part-time and full-time nontenure-track faculty adversely effects undergraduate students enrolled at four-year colleges and universities by reducing their five- and six-year graduation rates, and furthermore:

> For any given size increase in the shares of either part-time or full-time non tenure-track faculty, the magnitudes of these negative effects appear to be larger at public institutions than they are at private institutions and they appear to be largest at the public masters' level (comprehensive institutions). Other factors held constant, a 10 percentage point increase in the percentage of part-time faculty at a public masters' level institution is associated with about a 3 percentage point reduction in the graduation rate at the institution and a 10 percentage point increase in the percentage of full-time faculty that are not on tenure-track lines is associated with about a 4.4 percentage point reduction in the graduation rate at the institution.
>
> *(Ehrenberg & Zhang, 2004, p. 11)*

Another study by Sav (2012) had mixed results when examining the effects of faculty status on graduation rates. Using stochastic modeling on a panel of 318 public doctoral and master's degree classified U.S. universities, results indicate that:

> Across all model specifications, increases in the proportion of tenured faculty was found to produce efficiency gains in producing student academic success as measured by graduation rates. In pooling observations, the findings suggest that tenure track faculty presumably immersed in tenure producing research requirements are inefficient in increasing student graduations. However, tenure track faculty and their research output appears to be valuable and efficiency producing among research intensive, doctoral level universities. In contrast, the inefficiency effect of tenure track faculty emerges as insignificant in the less research intensive master level sector.
>
> *(Sav, 2012)*

Of course, there are individuals who take unfair advantage of the benefits that a system like tenure provides. Examples exist in most colleges and universities of faculty who use tenure in ways that are not particularly beneficial to students, to colleagues, or to their institutions. Instances of faculty becoming "lazy or complacent" do occur and are difficult to deal with (Cameron, 2010, p. 8). Bryan Caplan, a professor of economics at George Mason University, in a piece titled *How Lazy Is the Professoriate?*, commented:

> When I look around academia, I see lazy people everywhere. Many professors virtually retire the day they get tenure. . . . On a gut level, professors who don't publish appall me. Untenured professors who don't publish actually baffle me. How can they squander their once-in-a-lifetime opportunity?

> On reflection, though, the amazing thing about professors isn't that they accomplish so little. The amazing thing about professors is that they accomplish anything at all. They may look lazy to outside observers—and even to each other. But considering their situation, professors are amazingly industrious.
>
> *(Caplan, 2011)*

Most faculty are dedicated and work diligently beyond the receipt of tenure to advance themselves in their profession, keeping in mind that research and scholarship are as important if not more important than teaching in many colleges and universities.

Academic freedom was the basis for establishing the policy of tenure in order to protect faculty from arbitrary dismissal because of philosophical differences with governing board members and trustees. Faculty should be free to present their views and opinions in their teaching and scholarship without concern for retribution. Cary Nelson (2010), president of the American Association of University Professors in an article in *Inside Education*, stated that:

> Academic freedom means that both faculty members and students can engage in intellectual debate without fear of censorship or retaliation. . . . Academic freedom establishes a faculty member's right to remain true to his or her pedagogical philosophy and intellectual commitments. It preserves the intellectual integrity of our educational system and thus serves the public good.
>
> *(Nelson, 2010)*

Academic freedom does not mean that a faculty member can say anything she wishes. For instance, a faculty member cannot harass, threaten, intimidate, ridicule, or impose his or her views on students. However, as defined by Nelson, it is an important principle upon which higher education is founded in this country. It enables the faculty as a whole to seek truth by promoting and presenting multiple views on societal issues while protecting them from unfair retribution.

In the present day, the subject of the limits of academic freedom must extend beyond classroom discussions and into the realm of electronic and mass media. For instance, consider the following:

> A professor of American Indian studies takes to Twitter to denounce Zionism. A senior lecturer in business communication posts racist, homophobic comments on Facebook about an investigation into the shooting death of a 12-year-old. A journalism professor tweets, after a mass shooting, that the National Rifle Association has blood on its hands.
>
> Social-media eruptions like these have produced the kind of headlines that make colleges cringe. They've had seriously negative consequences for

the scholars involved and, in some cases, for institutions. They've also raised an urgent question for administrators: As more and more faculty and staff members lead active lives online, publicly sharing their work along with personal opinions, what can colleges do to protect themselves from fallout while preserving the core values of academic freedom and free speech?

(Smale, 2015)

The comments here resulted in repercussions for the three faculty members involved. Opportunities for scholars to share controversial opinions existed long before social media, but the speed and outreach of these media have added a whole new element to the meaning of academic freedom. It is one thing to say something controversial in a class of thirty students and another to create a blog posting that can be seen by millions. Colleges and universities are being forced to re-evaluate their academic freedom policies and to separate them from the right to free speech. Boundaries are being drawn between what individual faculty members say as part of their college activities and duties versus what is done outside. However, the lines are blurred and complex, as more faculty use social media for their class activities. In sum, academic freedom as a faculty protection is as important now as it has ever been. Its preservation is challenging many colleges and universities to make adjustments, given the availability of ubiquitous electronic communications.

Shared Governance (Faculty Senates, Unions, and Academic Department Prerogatives)

Vying for control of a college occurs in an arena commonly referred to as shared governance. It is here that the faculty can often exert its "we are the university" mentality. The nature of shared governance is far from consistent within American higher education. In some colleges, faculty governing bodies maintain complete control over critical processes such as academic programs, curriculum, teaching standards, and assessments. In other colleges, especially at for-profit, private institutions, shared governance is pretty much nonexistent, and control of all processes rests with the administration. There are three distinct areas where shared governance and hence faculty control dominate: in faculty senates or councils, in unions/collective bargaining, and in academic departments.

Faculty Councils

Faculty councils or senates exist in most colleges and universities within the public and nonprofit private sectors of higher education. Their responsibilities can vary significantly but generally focus on academic matters related to curriculum, programs, and assessment. They may also be involved with personnel issues related to evaluation policies and can be asked to appoint individuals to fill positions on search committees for senior administrative officers. One of their most controversial prerogatives is the vote of no confidence in a president or other senior administrator. It is infrequently invoked, but when it is, it gets a good deal of media attention. Although generally problematic for the administration, several recent votes of no confidence of President John Sexton at New York University did not result in a dismissal. A well-publicized dismissal occurred in 2005, when Harvard University's Faculty of Arts and Sciences voted no confidence in President Lawrence Summers following statements he made about women and science. Many credit this action as the reason why Summers was asked to resign by Harvard's governing board (Jaschik, 2005). On the other hand, faculty councils can be helpful in administering an institution. Academic program and curricular decisions generally receive a thorough vetting through processes established by the faculty council. This review process restricts quick or hasty changes to academic programs and maintains stability for the institution. Stability, however, can lead to stagnation if overdone.

Faculty councils, like many governing bodies, are at times vulnerable to college politics and self-serving interests. Faculty representatives may seek to maintain a college-wide curriculum that includes requirements that favor their particular academic programs and departments. For example, courses that are included in undergraduate basic distribution or general education requirements might be protected by faculty senators who represent the departments in which these courses are offered. Faculty from these programs (as do many other faculty) believe in the benefits of a broad foundational education. William Bowen, former president of Princeton University, and Eugene Tobin have a book titled *Locus of Authority: The Evolution of Faculty Roles in the Governance of Higher Education* that focuses on a number of governance issues that they believe are hindering colleges and universities from effecting changes from within. In the introduction, the authors clearly state that their "focus is on the faculty of arts and sciences at four-year colleges and universities (Bowen & Tobin, 2015, p. 7). Bowen and Tobin express concerns and question the wisdom of giving faculty governing councils broad responsibilities or veto powers over programmatic decisions that can have significant resource implications.

On the other hand, a good relationship between the administration and the faculty council can result in a great deal being accomplished to the mutual satisfaction and benefit of all. A faculty council might even be helpful to a president in dealing with boards of trustees. In 2012, a well-publicized case involved the ouster of President Teresa Sullivan of the University of Virginia (UVA), who was asked to resign by the UVA Board of Visitors due to "philosophical differences" (Johnson, Kumar, & de Vise, 2012). Sullivan was seen as an administrator who sought to bring change from the ground up through a process of building consensus and empowering individual academic units; she was popular among the faculty, students, and other constituents. When word of the board's action against Sullivan became public, the General Faculty Senate, led by Professor George Cohen, was joined by other university bodies in mounting an effective campaign to have Sullivan reinstated. This was done in June 2012. While there have been concerns expressed about faculty councils, they remain an important aspect of shared governance in American higher education.

Faculty Unions

Faculty unions maintain an important position in shared governance, although they are very different than faculty councils, focusing instead on issues related to salary, working conditions, and procedural protections for academic freedom, tenure, and promotion. They rarely are involved in curricular or academic programming issues. Faculty unions emerged in the early part of the 20th century as part of the country's overall national labor movement. Historically, unions have been more successful in public universities than private schools because of the labor laws governing state and public employees. The NEA (2015) estimates that unions represent almost 400,000 college faculty, the vast majority of whom work in the public sector. Chapters in several large states that have labor-friendly laws, such as California, New York, and Illinois, dominate the percentage of unionized faculty. Interest and membership in unionization has increased in recent years due to efforts on the part of graduate students and adjunct faculty to organize.

Unionization in the private sector was curtailed in 1980, when the U.S. Supreme Court ruled that the structure of private higher education was such that faculty members had substantial managerial authority and thus couldn't be considered employees and had no entitlement to collective bargaining. When deciding if faculty members were managerial, the question the court considered wasn't whether presidents and boards of trustees had final right of approval but whether the faculty had "effective recommendation or control." The court also ruled that public colleges and universities were subject to state and local labor laws, many of which entitled faculty and other public employees to form unions. A recent ruling by the National Labor Relations Board, however, might reopen the issue of faculty unionization in private colleges and universities. As reported in *Inside Higher Ed*:

> The National Labor Relations Board issued a ruling in December [2014] that could clear the way for much more unionization of faculty members at private colleges and universities.
>
> The ruling rejected the claims of Pacific Lutheran University that its full-time, non-tenure track faculty members are managerial employees and thus are not entitled to collective bargaining. In doing so, the NLRB offered a set of standards for evaluating whether faculty members are managerial as described by the U.S. Supreme Court in its 1980 ruling in *NLRB v. Yeshiva University,* a decision that has largely made unionization impossible for tenure-track faculty members at private colleges and universities.
>
> Last week's NLRB ruling suggested tools for evaluating whether private college faculty members have enough power to be considered managerial, and the standards set appear likely to be used by unions to say that faculty

members at many private colleges—even those on the tenure track—aren't managerial, and are thus entitled to unionize.

(Jaschik, 2015)

This ruling will likely be challenged in the courts, and its overall effect on collective bargaining in private education is yet to be determined.

Faculty unions have been active in following developments and issues in instructional technology, especially those as related to workload, differential compensation, and intellectual property. As early as the 1990s, large public faculty unions such as the Professional Staff Congress (PSC) at the City University of New York (CUNY) have actively monitored initiatives in these areas. In June 1997, the PSC declared a moratorium on all distance learning development at CUNY in response to several small-scale initiatives in online learning. CUNY had minimal experience in distance education, and the PSC wanted to establish basic policies and principles governing faculty participation. Subsequently a joint faculty-management committee was formed, and a letter of understanding was approved by the university and the union allowing online initiatives to continue. Similar scenarios have played out at many colleges and universities since.

The long-term future of faculty unions is murky at best. Organized labor has been under continuous attack in this country since President Ronald Reagan fired 11,000 air traffic controllers in 1981. In recent years, a number of states have sought to curtail public unions. Wisconsin sharply limited union rights in 2011 when the legislature enacted laws that prohibited employees from bargaining over anything but wages, outlawed strikes, and did away with the practice of binding arbitration in favor of the state agencies' right to set contract terms unilaterally. In the past decade, state legislatures have passed laws restricting public employees' collective bargaining rights in Tennessee, Oklahoma, Michigan, Maine, and Pennsylvania (Lafer, 2013). Such actions will continue in the years ahead and will inhibit the growth of new unions and restrict the power of existing ones, especially those in public higher education.

Departmental Prerogatives

Academic department chairpersons and faculty departmental committees enjoy a number of prerogatives and responsibilities that greatly influence programs, curricula, and personnel. Department chairpersons may be elected by faculty peers, appointed by senior administrators, or assume the office through some combination of the two. Members of departmental committees generally are elected by their peers. Department chairpersons and departmental committees such as personnel, curriculum, budget, and student affairs exercise broad responsibilities over matters related to academic programming, curriculum, resource allocation, and faculty. For example, chairpersons, with the approval of department personnel committees, recruit and select new faculty, establish teaching schedules, evaluate faculty performance, and make recommendations for promotion, tenure, and dismissal. No other administrators or institutional bodies have more influence over the professional growth and development of individual faculty. In the *NLRB v. Yeshiva University* U.S. Supreme Court decision mentioned earlier, this was the basis for ruling that college faculty were not simply employees but exercised substantive managerial authority. As a result of their managerial responsibilities, the court ruled that they were not entitled to collective bargaining. Bowen and Tobin (2015) also alluded to the significance of "faculty responsible for decisions about the selection, advancement, and termination of peers" (p. 210).

Within academic departments, the actions of chairpersons and members of influential committees can frequently be the objects of intense political struggles. Faculty philosophical differences as well as intense competition for resources can make politicians at the highest levels of government take notice. President Woodrow Wilson was fond of saying that "Washington was a snap after Princeton." Henry Kissinger, who negotiated the Paris Peace Treaty that ended the Vietnam War, has been quoted as saying that: "Academic politics are so vicious because the stakes are so small" (Quote Investigator, 2013).

Perhaps the greatest concern about the power of academic departments is that their focus may be entirely on their individual disciplines. This silo effect inhibits an institution from developing programs and research projects that require interdisciplinary approaches. Major scientific advances in areas such as neuroscience, big data, and human genome research have relied on interdisciplinary teams, and many colleges have been able to build successful interdisciplinary programs in areas such as women's studies, urban education, and cognitive science. This being said, the traditional academic departments might not be the best organizational structure in a world that is becoming more interdisciplinary in nature. Furthermore, without organizational structures above the academic department with comparable powers and responsibilities, the ability of the entire college or university to move forward may be hindered. Mark C. Taylor (2009), a professor of religion at Columbia University, in an op-ed piece for the *New York Times* went so far as to call for the abolition of academic departments:

> The division-of-labor model of separate departments is obsolete and must be replaced with a curriculum structured like a web or complex adaptive network. Responsible teaching and scholarship must become cross-disciplinary and cross-cultural.
>
> Just a few weeks ago, I attended a meeting of political scientists who had gathered to discuss why international relations theory had never considered the role of religion in society. Given the state of the world today, this is a significant oversight. There can be no adequate understanding of the most important issues we face when disciplines are cloistered from one another and operate on their own premises.

> It would be far more effective to bring together people working on questions of religion, politics, history, economics, anthropology, sociology, literature, art, religion and philosophy to engage in comparative analysis of common problems. As the curriculum is restructured, fields of inquiry and methods of investigation will be transformed.
>
> *(Taylor, 2009)*

On the other hand, Jerry A. Jacobs (2009), professor of sociology and education at the University of Pennsylvania and a former editor of the *American Sociological Review*, questions the need to abolish discipline-based academic departments. He posits that interdisciplinary studies depend upon the presence of strong disciplines and that departments teach techniques needed to conduct high-quality research. He cautioned:

> Interdisciplinarity is not a panacea. . . . Some interdisciplinary experiments will be stillborn; some interdisciplinary units will prove unwieldy and fracture of their own accord. Remember a cautionary tale from the past: Harvard's department of social relations proved unable to unify anthropology, psychology, and sociology and finally agreed to a divorce in 1972 after more than 20 years of marriage.
>
> *(Jacobs, 2009)*

Taylor and Jacobs each make important points; however, the solutions to this structural dilemma will vary based not on compromise but on need. Institutions that want to engage in high-end interdisciplinary research will fund and establish structures such as research centers that bring together scholars from across disciplines to conduct their work. Other institutions that focus less on research and more on teaching will be slower to move toward interdisciplinary-based structures and will continue academic departments.

Upon examining shared governance in each of its manifestations (faculty councils, unions, and academic department prerogatives), it seems unlikely that shared governance will be eliminated from American higher education in the near future. Faculty and senior administrative leaders will try to find common ground where both can function well and carry out the mission, goals, and objectives of their institutions.

Faculty Accomplishments in Research

A fitting conclusion to this chapter is a brief commentary on the accomplishments of college and university faculty. Faculty contributions to science, medicine, economic development, the arts, and every conceivable area of inquiry are far too numerous to mention. Jonathon Cole, in his seminal work, *The Great American University*, considered having an appendix that would list "the thousands of discoveries, inventions, innovations, devices, concepts, techniques, and tools that were born in American colleges and universities" (Cole, 2009). Instead he created a website (http://university-discoveries.com) where a visitor can navigate through a great collection of these accomplishments. To these ends, faculty have provided their intellectual and creative talents with the assistance in many cases of the federal government, which provided necessary financial resources. Luminaries such as Albert Einstein, Barbara McClintock, Jonas Salk, and Gertrude Elion are among the faculty at American universities who made major contributions to the betterment of humankind. Faculty such as J. Robert Oppenheimer, Enrico Fermi, and Alan Turing provided the service of their minds to help end World War II. In the present day, the vast majority of awardees of the Nobel Prize in science are faculty. For example:

- Of the last ten awardees in physiology and medicine, nine had university affiliations, five from American institutions.
- Of the last ten awardees in economics, ten had university affiliations, eight from American universities.
- Of the last ten awardees in chemistry, nine had university affiliations, six from American universities.

Despite this vast contribution on the part of the professoriate, there may be a stagnating trend (see Table 3.1) that indicates that the federal government investment

TABLE 3.1 Higher Education R&D Expenditures, by Source of Funds and R&D Field: FYs 2003–2013 (dollars in millions)

| R&D field and fiscal year | All R&D expenditures | Source of funds | | | | |
		Federal government	State and local government	Institution funds	Business	All other sources
Total, S&E and non-S&E						
2003	41,470	25,307	na	na	na	na
2004	44,839	28,304	na	na	na	na
2005	47,535	29,957	na	na	na	na
2006	49,645	30,909	na	na	na	na
2007	51,590	31,241	na	na	na	na
2008	54,114	32,101	na	na	na	na
2009	57,288	33,443	na	na	na	na
2010	61,257	37,477	3,853	11,941	3,198	4,788
2011	65,282	40,771	3,829	12,612	3,180	4,891
2012	65,744	40,151	3,695	13,635	3,272	4,991
2013	67,041	39,470	3,658	14,974	3,501	5,438

Source: National Science Foundation, National Center for Science and Engineering Statistics, Higher Education Research and Development Survey. S&E = Science & Technology Data from survey cycle FY 2013, as of 31 July 2014.

in higher education research and development began to slow in 2012. Or this may be a momentary blip. If it is a trend and reductions continue, college and universities will be forced to seek funds from other sources or reduce their research and development efforts. The latter could prove unfortunate, if not disastrous, especially since other countries such as China are making significant new investments into all aspects of their higher education systems and especially in research.

Summary

This chapter examined the university professoriate. Basic data were provided about key characteristics such as gender, race, salary, and full-time/part-time status. The chapter traced the rise of contingent faculty over the past several decades. It also examined faculty regarding the governance in faculty councils, unions, and academic departments. It concluded with a brief description of the major contributions to society that university faculty have made.

References

American Association of University Professor (2014). Background facts on contingent faculty. Retrieved from: http://www.aaup.org/issues/contingency/background-facts Accessed: March 27, 2015.

Berrett, D. (January 26, 2015). The day the purpose of college changed. *The Chronicle of Higher Education*. Retrieved from: http://chronicle.com/article/The-Day-the-Purpose-of-College/151359/?cid=at&utm_source=at&utm_medium=en Accessed: March 22, 2015.

Bird, K. & Sherwin, M.J. (2006). *American Prometheus: The triumph and tragedy of J. Robert Oppenheimer*. New York: Alfred A. Knopf.

Bowen, W. & Tobin, E.M. (2015). *Locus of authority: The evolution of faculty roles in the governance of higher education*. Princeton: Princeton University Press.

Cameron, M. (2010). Faculty tenure in academe: The evolution, benefits and implications of an important tradition. *Journal of Student Affairs at New York University*, 6. Retrieved from: http://steinhardt.nyu.edu/scmsAdmin/media/users/lh62/CameronJoSA_.pdf Accessed: March 27, 2015.

Caplan, B. (September 26, 2011). How lazy is the professoriate? Library of Economics and Liberty. *Econlog*. Retrieved from: http://econlog.econlib.org/archives/2011/09/how_lazy_is_the.html Accessed: March 28, 2015.

Coalition on the Academic Workforce (2012). A portrait of part-time faculty members. Retrieved from: http://www.academicworkforce.org/CAW_portrait_2012.pdf Accessed: March 27, 2015.

Cole, J. (2009). *The great American university*. New York: Public Affairs.

Council of Graduate Schools (2010). *Research report: Data sources: Time-to-degree for doctorate recipients*. Washington, DC: Council of Graduate Schools. Retrieved from: https://www.cgsnet.org/ckfinder/userfiles/files/DataSources_2010_03.pdf Accessed: March 23, 2015.

de Vise, D. & Kumar, A. (June 17, 2012). U-Va. board leaders wanted President Teresa Sullivan to make cuts. *The Washington Post*. Retrieved from: http://www.washingtonpost.com/local/education/u-va-board-leaders-wanted-president-teresa-sullivanto-make-cuts/2012/06/17/gJQA4ijrhV_story.html Accessed: March 29, 2015.

Devons, S. (Summer 2001). *I.I. Rabi: Physics and science at Columbia, in America, and worldwide.* Living legacies: Great moments and leading figures in the history of Columbia University. Retrieved from: http://www.columbia.edu/cu/alumni/Magazine/Summer2001/Rabi.html Accessed: March 22, 2015.

Ehrenberg, R.G. & Zhang, L. (2004). *Do tenured and tenure-track faculty matter?* Cambridge, MA: National Bureau of Economic Research. Retrieved from: http://www.nber.org/papers/w10695.pdf Accessed: March 27, 2015.

Etzioni, A. (1964). *Modern organizations.* Englewood Cliffs, NJ: Prentice-Hall.

Herzog, K. & Marley, P. (January 28, 2015). Scott Walker budget cut sparks sharp debate on UW system. *Milwaukee-Wisconsin Journal Sentinel.* Retrieved from: http://www.jsonline.com/news/education/scott-walker-says-uw-faculty-should-teach-more-classes-do-more-work-b99434737z1-290087401.html Accessed: March 22, 2015.

Jacobs, J.A. (November 22, 2009). Interdisciplinary hype. *The Chronicle of Higher Education.* Retrieved from: http://chronicle.com/article/Interdisciplinary-Hype/49191/ Accessed: March 30, 2015.

Jaschik, S. (March 16, 2005). Lost confidence. *Inside Higher Ed.* Retrieved from: https://www.insidehighered.com/news/2005/03/16/summers3_16 Accessed: March 29, 2015.

Jaschik, S. (January 2, 2015). Big union win. *Inside Higher Ed.* Retrieved from: https://www.insidehighered.com/news/2015/01/02/nlrb-ruling-shifts-legal-ground-faculty-unions-private-colleges Accessed: March 29, 2015.

Johnson, J., Kumar, A., & de Vise, D. (June 26, 2012). U-Va. board reinstates Sullivan as president. *The Washington Post.* Retrieved from: http://www.washingtonpost.com/local/education/u-va-leadership-crisis-mcdonnell-declines-to-take-sides/2012/06/26/gJQArOHU4V_story.html Accessed: March 29, 2015.

Lafer, G. (2013). *The legislative attack on American wages and labor standards, 2011–2012.* Washington, DC: Economic Policy Institute. Retrieved from: http://www.epi.org/publication/attack-on-american-labor-standards/ accessed: March 29, 2015.

Metzger, W. (1973). *Academic tenure in America: A historical essay.* Faculty Tenure: A Report and Recommendations by the Commission on Academic Tenure in Higher Education. San Francisco, CA: Jossey-Bass.

Mintzberg, H. (1979). *The structuring of organizations.* Englewood Cliffs, NJ: Prentice-Hall.

National Education Association (2015). Frequently asked questions: Collective bargaining in higher education. Retrieved from: http://www.nea.org/home/62147.htm Accessed: March 30, 2015.

Nelson, C. (December 21, 2010). Defining academic freedom. *Inside Higher Ed.* Retrieved from: https://www.insidehighered.com/views/2010/12/21/nelson_on_academic_freedom Accessed: March 28, 2015.

Pathe, S. (2014). Homeless professor protests conditions of adjuncts. *PBS News Hour.* Retrieved from: http://www.pbs.org/newshour/making-sense/homeless-professor-protests-conditions-adjuncts/ Accessed: March 27, 2015.

Quote Investigator (2013). Exploring the origins of quotes. Retrieved from: http://quoteinvestigator.com/2013/08/18/acad-politics/ Accessed: March 30, 2015.

Sav, G.T. (2012). *Does faculty tenure improve student graduation rates?* Wright State University CORE Scholar. Retrieved from: http://corescholar.libraries.wright.edu/cgi/viewcontent.cgi?article=1104&context=econ Accessed: March 27, 2015.

Schmidt, P. (March 9, 2015). Adjunct advocacy: Contingent faculty members are demanding—and getting—better working conditions. *The Chronicle of Higher Education.* Retrieved from: http://chronicle.com/article/Adjunct-Advocacy/228155/ Accessed: March 27, 2015.

Sherman, E. (March 21, 2015). College basketball coaches and their slam dunk salaries. *Fortune Magazine*. Retrieved from: http://fortune.com/2015/03/21/college-basketball-coaches-and-their-slam-dunk-salaries/ Accessed: March 25, 2015.

Smale, B. (March 9, 2015). Social-media skirmishes: More colleges are deciding how—and whether—to regulate faculty speech. *The Chronicle of Higher Education*. Retrieved from: http://chronicle.com/article/Social-Media-Skirmishes/228147/ Accessed: March 28, 2015.

Snyder, M. (January 25, 2015). Jim Harbaugh contract. *Detroit Free Press*. Retrieved from: http://www.freep.com/story/sports/college/university-michigan/wolverines/2015/01/23/jim-harbaugh-contract-michigan-football/22227589/ Accessed: March 24, 2015.

Taylor, M.C. (April 26, 2009). End the university as we know it! *New York Times*. Retrieved from: http://www.nytimes.com/2009/04/27/opinion/27taylor.html?pagewanted=all&_r=0 Accessed: March 30, 2015.

U.S. Supreme Court (1980). NLRB v. Yeshiva University. Retrieved from: http://caselaw.lp.findlaw.com/cgi-bin/getcase.pl?court=us&vol=444&invol=672 Accessed: March 29, 2015.

Wolf, B. (1997). Degrees of shame, part-time faculty: Migrant workers of the information economy. (Video). Retrieved from: http://search.library.wisc.edu/catalog/ocm39067615 Accessed: March 27, 2015.

4

HIGHER EDUCATION, DIGITAL TECHNOLOGY, AND INSTRUCTION

In 2014, Walter Isaacson published *The Innovators: How a Group of Hackers, Geniuses, and Geeks Created the Digital Revolution*. Isaacson has had a stellar career as a journalist, editor, CEO, and biographer. He started as reporter for *The Sunday Times of London* and then moved on to the *New Orleans Times-Picayune*. He joined *TIME* in 1978 and served as a political correspondent, national editor, and editor of new media before becoming the magazine's fourteenth editor in 1996. He became chairman and CEO of CNN in 2001 and then president and CEO of the Aspen Institute in 2003. He is the author of several best-selling biographies including *Steve Jobs* (2011), *Einstein: His Life and Universe* (2007), *Benjamin Franklin: An American Life* (2003), and *Kissinger: A Biography* (1992). His 2014 book starts with Charles Babbage and Ada Lovelace, who designed computer prototypes and a programming language in the mid-1800s but because of limited technology never were able to see the fruits of their creativity. It may be of interest to some readers that Ada Lovelace was the daughter of the eminent poet and fabled lothario, Lord Byron. Although abandoned just after birth and having never seen her father, Ada went on to lead a most interesting life and, ironically, just before her death, requested to be buried beside him (Markus, 2015). The remainder of Isaacson's book chronicles the lives of the men and women whose inventions, theories, and just plain hard work formed the foundation for much of the digital technology in use today. Most of these early pioneering men and women were affiliated with colleges and universities, and as you read their stories in Isaacson's book, a pattern emerges. While they had great ideas and visions, invariably they needed the support and funding from government and private industry in order to put them into working models and practice. External funding also helped bring these individuals together to pool their collective genius for the development of breakthrough technologies. As Isaacson concludes: "Most of the great innovations of the digital age sprang from an interplay of creative individuals (Mauchly, Turing, von Newmann, Aiken) with teams that knew how to implement ideas" (Isaacson, 2014, p. 92). As one reviewer commented, in many respects, the book could have been called "The Collaborators" (Bilton, 2014).

The work of Howard Aiken, John von Newmann, Grace Hopper, Alan Turing, John Mauchley, and others illustrates the enormous contribution that higher education and especially American higher education has made to the technological developments in our society, to say nothing of its status as one of the most important sectors of the world economy. At one time or another, most of the initial pioneering work and tinkering in technology was done by academics, professors, and researchers in small laboratories and faculty offices. Their freedom to think, to imagine, and to create was made possible by virtue of the fact that they had careers in our higher educational institutions. In the first part of this chapter, a brief examination of their work in the early development of digital technology will be presented. The second part of this chapter will look specifically at the early developments (pre-1990s) that laid the foundation for online education.

The Visionaries

American higher education has maintained a close relationship with digital technology development for the past seventy-plus years. College faculty and researchers at MIT, Harvard, Stanford, Princeton, and the University of Pennsylvania made critical contributions to the hardware, software, and communications technologies that form the foundation of the digital world in which we live today. Their stories provide important insights into how the search for knowledge evolves into everyday and not so everyday applications that serve to better our human existence.

Institute for Advanced Studies, Princeton: Alan Turing, John von Newmann, and Alonzo Church

In 2014, the award-winning movie *The Imitation Game* depicted the life of the mathematician Alan Turing, as based on the biography, *Alan Turing: The Enigma* by Andrew Hodges. The film begins in 1939 and traces the wartime development of a computer by Turing and a team of cryptologists to decode Germany's Enigma machine, which was being used to provide security for its wireless messages. The movie ends with the tragic death of Turing by suicide in 1954 two years after undergoing chemical castration following his arrest for sexual indecency and homosexual activity. In 2013, Turing was pardoned by Queen Elizabeth. In keeping with many Hollywood productions, a good deal of license was exercised and the historical accuracy of portions of the film has come under question. However, there is no doubt that Turing was instrumental in developing one of the early computers based on relay switches. The movie does not touch on any of his work in the 1930s. Turing worked at the University of Cambridge and the University of Manchester in the United Kingdom, but he completed his PhD at Princeton

University in 1938. While at Princeton he worked with John von Newmann and Alonzo Church at the Institute for Advanced Study (IAS) at Princeton.

The institute was endowed in 1930 by philanthropists Louis Bamberger and his sister Caroline Bamberger Fuld and was established in the vision of its founding director Abraham Flexner as a place where the greatest minds and thinkers in the world could share their ideas and collaborate with one another. To realize his vision in the 1930s, Flexner recruited a number of outstanding Eastern European scientists, including Albert Einstein, many of whom were Jewish and began to fear what was happening in Germany. Although independent, IAS had and continues to maintain close, collaborative ties with Princeton University (Institute for Advanced Study, 2015).

Turing is considered by some as the founder of computer science for his work with algorithms and computer programming. He designed a hypothetical Turing Machine in 1936 in which he described in great detail basic computer programming functions such as input, output, memory, coded programs, algorithms, compilers/interpreters, and central processing units. He described how paper tape could be encoded with instructions and data to program his machine. The Turing Machine was never built, but it established important principles about the future of computer programming that were realized in the future. He correctly identified several key components based on a systems model (input, process, output) that would be fundamental to all computer programs for decades to come. In the 1930s, these were revolutionary ideas. His work paved the way for many others in the 1940s and 1950s. Alonzo Church, his colleague at the Institute for Advanced Study, saw the importance of Turing's work and collaborated with him on subsequent designs. John von Newmann, a colleague of Church, was also interested in Turing's work. The following comments from von Newmann to Church in 1936 shed light on the nature of their interest in Turing:

> AM Turing here . . . was just about to send in for publication a paper in which he used a definition of "computable numbers" for the same purpose. His treatment, which consists in describing a machine which will grind out any computable sequence—is rather different from yours, but seems to be of great merit, and I think it of great importance that he should come and work with you next year if that is at all possible.

Newmann added:

> I should mention that Turing's work is entirely independent; he has been working without any supervision or criticism from anyone. That makes it all the more important that he should come into contact as soon as possible with the leading workers on this line, so that he should not develop into a confirmed solitary.

> *(Edwards, 2012)*

John von Newmann is generally considered the first to develop the architecture for a stored-computer program, described in his seminal paper, *First Draft of a Report on the EDVAC*. Electronic storage of programming information and data would eliminate the need for the more clumsy methods of programming, such as punched paper tape—a concept that characterized mainstream computer development at the time and directly derived from Turing's earlier design.

Harvard Computation Laboratory: Howard Aiken and Grace Hopper

Howard Aiken was an engineer, physicist, and mathematician who taught engineering and mathematics at Harvard University. In 1936, inspired by Charles Babbage's differential and analytical engines, he started thinking about building a calculator to assist in his mathematics teaching and research. However, funding for this project, estimated to cost several million dollars, was not readily available. In 1937, it was suggested that "he approach IBM for funding his calculator" (Cohen, 2000, p. 54). After meetings with IBM's senior engineer, James Bryce, and later with Thomas Watson, Sr., its president, a $5 million dollar contract was signed to build the calculator/computer at IBM's Endicott, New York, plant. Key collaborators with Aiken were Clair D. Lake, Benjamin M. Durfee, and Frank E. Hamilton, all employees of IBM. The machine was built in Endicott then disassembled and reassembled at Harvard in 1944 at the new Harvard Computation Laboratory. The computer, named by IBM as the *Automatic Sequence Control Calculator* (ASCC), was programed via pre-punched paper tape, could carry out addition, subtraction, multiplication, and division and reference previous results. It had special subroutines for logarithms and trigonometric functions and used twenty-three decimal places. Data was stored and counted mechanically using 3,000 decimal storage wheels, 1,400 rotary dial switches, and 500 miles of wire. Its electromagnetic relays classified the machine as a relay computer (Bellis, 2015). Aiken referred to the ASCC as Mark I. The difference in names illuminates a conflict between Aiken and IBM:

> The continued existence of an IBM name (ASCC) and an Aiken-Harvard name (Mark I) is symbolic of the long struggle over who invented the giant calculator: IBM or Harvard-Aiken.
>
> *(Cohen, 2000, p. xix)*

Regardless of the naming dispute, Aiken and IBM designed and built several more Mark/ASCC machines in the 1940s and early 1950s.

Grace Hopper received her master's degree in mathematics in 1931 from Yale University and shortly thereafter began teaching at Vassar College. In 1934, she was the first woman to earn a PhD in mathematics at Yale. In 1943, she joined the Navy Reserve and was assigned to work with the Bureau of Ordnance

Computation Project at Harvard University, where she learned to program the Mark I computer. As one of the lead programmers for the Mark I, she became a close colleague of Howard Aiken and assisted in the design of the Mark II and Mark III computers. Hopper's greatest contributions were in the field of computer programming. She popularized the term "computer bug" and helped advance the development of computer subroutines. The latter made computer programming far more efficient and provided for utilizing the same computer code over and over again. She is also credited with developing the concept of the compiler, which allows programs written on one machine to be easily converted to another machine. Mechanical relays would no longer need to be rewired and instead could receive a new set of instructions via paper tape. In sum, "By 1945, thanks largely to Hopper, the Harvard Mark I was the world's most easily programmable large computer" (Isaacson, 2014, p. 94).

After World War II, Hopper resigned from the Navy and left the academic world for private industry, where she continued her pioneering work in computer programming. She worked with J. Prescott Eckert and John Mauchly in designing new computers including Univac I and later coordinated the development of the Common Business Oriented Language (COBOL) which became the first machine-independent language and a mainstay of business applications for decades. In 1969, she was awarded the first ever Computer Science Man-of-the-Year Award from the Data Processing Management Association. In 1973, she became the first person from the United States and the first woman of any nationality to be made a Distinguished Fellow of the British Computer Society.

Moore School of Electrical Engineering, University of Pennsylvania: J. Prescott Eckert and John Mauchly

J. Prescott Eckert studied and worked at the Moore School of Engineering of the University of Pennsylvania in the 1930s. In 1941, John Mauchly took a course in wartime electronics at the Moore School, and a relationship developed between the two that was to last for decades. The Moore School was one of the major centers for wartime computing in the 1940s. It was there that Eckert and Mauchly had the idea for the design of the ENIAC (Electronic Numerical Integrator And Computer) that would give them their place in the history of computer technology. Although they had the idea for the design of ENIAC, they needed funding and support from others in order to actually develop and build it. It was the United States Army that would provide most of the funding for the project, and as a result, the first major ENIAC applications related to artillery firing tables and feasibility studies for the hydrogen bomb. ENIAC was a general-purpose decimal computer and could be programmed for a variety of applications. The project attracted a number of scientists and engineers of the time including John von Newmann, mentioned earlier in this chapter, in connection with his work on electronically stored computer programs. EDVAC (Electronic

Discrete Variable Automatic Computer), the successor to ENIAC, was designed by Eckert and Mauchly but incorporated most of von Newmann's ideas for stored programs. EDVAC was also a binary machine based on on-off circuits or "1s and 0s," which became the fundamental data and instruction set for computers that continues today.

Eckert and Mauchly left the Moore School in 1946 over an intellectual property dispute with the university. In that year, the University of Pennsylvania adopted a new patent policy to protect the intellectual purity of the research it sponsored. This policy would have required Eckert and Mauchly to assign all their future patents to the university. Rather than comply with the university's requirements, Eckert and Mauchly founded the Electronic Control Company and built the Binary Automatic Computer (BINAC), which among other things was able to store data on magnetic tape. The Electronic Control Company soon became the Eckert–Mauchly Computer Corporation and received an order from the National Bureau of Standards to build the Universal Automatic Computer (UNIVAC). In 1949, Grace Hopper, whom we met earlier in this chapter, became a full-time employee in charge of programming at the Eckert–Mauchly Computer Corporation. The first versions of Hopper's compilers were developed while working on UNIVAC. In early 1950, the Eckert–Mauchly Computer Corporation ran into financial troubles and was acquired by the Remington Rand Corporation. The UNIVAC I was completed on December 21, 1950.

UNIVAC became a major success, and forty-six of the machines were sold to government agencies and privates industries. Perhaps the event remembered most about UNIVAC occurred on election night in 1952. While various newspapers and poll watchers were predicting a close election between Dwight D. Eisenhower and Adlai Stevenson, CBS News Anchor Walter Cronkite described how UNIVAC would be used to predict the election as Presper Eckert explained UNIVAC'S workings. Days before, Grace Hopper and her programming team had written the code that would use previous election results to predict the outcome. With only 5 percent of the voting precincts reporting, UNIVAC correctly predicted that Eisenhower would win in a landslide. CBS News was not sure it could trust this information and held up reporting it for several hours.

> "The uncanny accuracy of UNIVAC's prediction during a major televised event sent shock waves across the nation," noted historian Kurt W. Beyer. . . . In the months that followed, "UNIVAC" gradually became the generic term for a computer.
>
> *(Lasar, 2011)*

While UNIVAC was capturing the public's attention in the 1950s, it was IBM that captured the market for general-purpose mainframe computers. Because of the expertise it gained from the Mark computers and also because it had large-scale production facilities, IBM was better able to develop, market, and sell many more computers than UNIVAC. IBM also developed a highly successful 700 series of computers that proved popular with its established data-processing customer base.

The three stories in this chapter illustrate that while internationally recognized scientists and engineers working in our universities were the knowledge leaders for many of the major developments in the early days of digital technology, it was government and private industry that provided the capital and business acumen to turn these ideas into practical applications that the world could enjoy. Leydesdorff (1995) referred to this integration of higher education with private industry and government as the "Triple Helix" of innovation. The universities provided fertile environments for ideas to be shared among colleagues through thought exchanges and small-scale experimentation, thus allowing larger projects and production to take root through funding and other support provided by the business and government sectors. The American universities of the 21st century continue to provide these environments in places such as the Kavli Nanotechnology Institute at the California Institute of Technology, the MIT Computer and Artificial Intelligence Lab, or the Cognitive and Neuro Systems Lab at Stanford University as well as in thousands of institutes, centers, and departments in our universities in many areas of inquiry including health, medicine, social sciences, and the humanities, all of which help make us understand and improve our society, our planet, and our being.

Leaders in Computer-Based Education

As noted earlier in this book, approximately 25 to 30 percent of all college students attend fully online courses, and millions more attend blended courses where some of the instruction is provided over the Internet. It is the university faculty, with the assistance of instructional designers, who are developing and teaching these courses. In the remainder of this chapter, some of the stories of faculty and other individuals who were actively involved in the early developments (pre 1990s) of instructional technology will be presented.

Harvard University, Ohio State, and Columbia University: B.F. Skinner, Sidney L. Pressey, and Edward L. Thorndike

> There are more people in the world than ever before, and a far greater part of them want an education. The demand cannot be met simply by building more schools and training more teachers. Education must become more efficient. To this end curricula must be realized and simplified, and textbooks and classroom techniques improved. In any other field a demand for increased production would have led at once to the invention of labor-saving capital equipment. Education has reached this stage very late, possibly through a misconception of its task. Thanks to the advent of [various technologies], . . . these tools are finding their way into American schools and colleges.

This commentary is the kind of narrative that one hears regularly today from those who promote the use of technology as a way to reach the masses around the world. Policymakers, MOOC providers, and corporate America have used this narrative as a rationale for infusing more online technology into teaching and learning. They see the technology as a cost-benefit that can greatly expand education opportunity. This quote, however, was taken from an article written by B.F. Skinner in 1958, and the various technologies to which he referred in the brackets were film projectors, television sets, phonographs, and tape recorders (Skinner, 1958).

Skinner was perhaps the best-known behavioral psychologist of the 20th century. He was a prolific writer who taught at the University of Minnesota and Indiana University but spent most of his career at Harvard University. Skinner was also a great believer in technology as a teaching aid and developed a teaching machine based on a number of sound instructional design principles. In the *Science* article quoted, he summarized the benefits of a teaching machine as:

> allowing each student to proceed at his own pace
> importance of immediate feedback
> a machine which permitted the student to play an active role
> there is constant interchange between program and student
> in addition to charts, maps, graphs, models, students would have access to auditory material.
>
> *(Skinner, 1958, pp. 969–972)*

All of the quotes from Skinner's article referred specifically to the work of Sidney I. Pressey, who designed his own teaching machine in the 1920s (Pressey, 1926). Pressey was a professor of psychology at The Ohio State University from 1921 to 1959. His machine incorporated the basic programmed instruction principles of self-paced learning using multiple-choice questions. Interestingly, Pressey credits Edward I. Thorndike for providing him with the insights to build his machine. Thorndike was a professor of psychology at Teachers College of Columbia University. He designed multiple-choice tests and teaching aids and wrote extensively about adult education. He also was a critic of textbooks. A common fault in textbooks, Thorndike wrote, is that "habits to be formed are stated but the reader does not have the chance to practice." In addition, textbooks do not give the reader a chance to think out conclusions for himself:

> If, by a miracle of mechanical ingenuity, a book could be so arranged that only to him who had done what was directed on page one would page two become visible, and so on, much that now requires personal instruction could be managed by print.
>
> *(Thorndike, 1912, pp. 164–165)*

Skinner, Pressey, and Thorndike made important contributions to our understanding of the use of instructional technology. Their principles were based on sound pedagogical practices that are still respected today by faculty, instructional designers, and commercial developers. In 2011, a new adaptive learning platform debuted at Arizona State University. The announcement in *The Chronicle of Higher Education* commented:

> Knewton is a new computerized-learning program that features immediate feedback and adaptation to students' learning curves. The concept can be traced back a half-century or so to a "teaching machine" invented by the psychologist B.F. Skinner, then a professor at Harvard University. Based on principles of learning he developed working with pigeons, Skinner came up with a boxlike mechanical device that fed questions to students, rewarding correct answers with fresh academic material; wrong answers simply got them a repeat of the old question. "The student quickly learns to be right," Skinner said.
>
> Fifty years later, that basic idea has evolved into a hot concept in education: adaptive learning. Programs like Knewton can pace an entire math course using sophisticated tracking of skill development, instant feedback, and help levels based on mastery of concepts, as well as something the Harvard students did not get: the enjoyment of a video-game-like interface.
>
> *(Fischman, 2011)*

Skinner and Pressey were recognized for their ideas and models, but the technologies of their eras were not robust enough to provide stimulating learning environments for the kinds of teaching machines that they envisioned. By the early 1960s, teaching machines generally were still considered "boring" and impersonal ways to learn and never really caught on in a major way at any level of education (Seattler, 2004, p. 303).

The Institute for Mathematical Studies in the Social Sciences, Stanford University: Patrick Suppes and Richard Atkinson

With the advent of computer technology in the mid-1960s, a number of projects at the University of Texas, Florida State University, the University of Pittsburgh, and the University of California at Santa Barbara converted the programmed instruction ideas of Skinner and Pressey to digital platforms. Perhaps the most extensive work in this area was carried out at the Institute for Mathematical Studies in the Social Sciences at Stanford University under the direction of Patrick Suppes and Richard Atkinson. Suppes received his PhD in philosophy from Columbia University in 1950. Atkinson received his PhD in psychology and mathematics from Indiana University and joined the faculty at Stanford in 1956. While Suppes continued at the Institute for most of his sixty-four-year career, Atkinson transitioned to administration in 1975, when he was appointed the Director of the National Science Foundation. He later served as chancellor of the University of California, San Diego, and then as president of the University of California system.

Suppes and Atkinson first partnered in developing what became known as computer-assisted instruction or CAI for teaching basic mathematics. The new digital technology of the 1960s and '70s afforded them more capability than the teaching machines of the earlier decades. Suppes and Atkinson were also able to attract a good deal of funding support from IBM, the National Science Foundation, the Carnegie Foundation, and the U.S. Department of Education. IBM in particular invested significant resources and developed the IBM 1500 instructional system in 1966 primarily for implementing CAI. Using either an IBM 1130 or IBM 1800 computer, the IBM 1500 supported 32 terminals and integrated what were at the time interesting audiovisual capabilities. Course materials for the IBM 1500 were developed by Science Research Associates, Inc., an IBM subsidiary. The programming on the IBM 1500 system was done in a specialized language called *Coursewriter*.

Just after the debut of the IBM 1500 instructional system, Suppes and Atkinson formed the Computer Curriculum Corporation (CCC) to develop drill and practice materials in mathematics, reading, and the language arts. CCC evolved into one of the most successful CAI companies of all time. It was bought by Simon & Schuster Publishing in 1990, which in turn was bought by Pearson Education, where it continues to develop and market CAI software and professional development programs for teachers under the Pearson umbrella. The work of Suppes and Atkinson had profound impact on CAI at the K–12 level and for remedial education at the college level.

Patrick Suppes died in 2014; his *New York Times* obituary noted:

> Patrick Suppes . . . sketched a vision of the democratic future of computerized education. "In a few more years," he predicted in 1966, "millions of schoolchildren will have access to what Philip of Macedon's son Alexander enjoyed as a royal prerogative: the personal services of a tutor as well informed and as responsive as Aristotle."
>
> *(Markoff, 2014)*

Loomis Laboratory/CERL, University of Illinois: Donald Bitzer

Donald L. Bitzer received his PhD in electrical engineering from the University of Illinois in 1960. He was professor of electrical and computer engineering at the University of Illinois from 1960 to 1989 when he retired to become a Distinguished University Research Professor in the computer science department at North Carolina State University. He is generally considered to be the "father" of the PLATO (Programmed Logic for Automatic Teaching Operations) software system developed at the University of Illinois at Urbana Champaign (UIUC). While Bitzer gets most of the credit for the development of PLATO, he was assisted by a number of colleagues at the Loomis Laboratory at UIUC including Daniel Alpert, Chalmers Sherwin, and Paul Tenczar. PLATO was conceived in 1959, and by 1960 a working model (PLATO I) was running on an ILLIAC I computer. It was designed to run on a network and can be considered the prototype for Internet-based online learning. Several versions of PLATO (II, III, IV) were developed in the 1960s and early 1970s, all of which added functionality. A most important feature of PLATO II was that it allowed a faculty member to design her/his own lesson modules using the TUTOR programming language, which was developed in 1967 by Paul Tenczar. Another unique feature was added in 1972 (PLATO IV): a plasma display terminal that provided far more interesting graphics than any other display at the time. Bitzer developed the plasma display and received a number of awards for his invention. A music synthesizer and limited speech recognition features were also added to a PLATO terminal in the 1970s. As a result, PLATO attracted a good deal of attention and, in turn, funding from both the federal government and private industry. The National Science Foundation, for instance, provided funding in 1967 for Bitzer to set up the Computer-Based Education Research Laboratory (CERL) dedicated essentially to developing and enhancing the PLATO system. PLATO no doubt set the standard for computer-assisted hardware and software in the early days of networked-based learning. It was considered a success and had several hundred customers operating on 1,000 or more terminals throughout the country at all levels of education by the mid-1970s. It should also be mentioned that much of the curriculum development on PLATO was for course modules, not entire online courses.

A most generous funder of PLATO was Control Data Corporation (CDC), which in the 1960s was one of the major manufacturers of large mainframe computers. William Norris, the CEO of CDC, donated several large mainframe computers to CERL to continue development and to provide the computer hub for the PLATO network. Norris's equipment donation helped to keep the costs for PLATO reasonable. This was critical because a single PLATO terminal cost $12,000. In addition, users paid for log-in hours. A PLATO lab of 25 terminals minimally cost $300,000 in start-up funds plus the ongoing costs for connectivity infrastructure, personnel, and training. Regardless, Norris was convinced of the future of PLATO and purchased its commercial rights in 1976. Over the next ten years, CDC would invest hundreds of millions of dollars into PLATO services, but CDC's timing was not good, as the industry moved away from mainframe computing to inexpensive microcomputers. In fact, by the 1980s, the entire large mainframe computer business pretty much collapsed as companies moved to distributed desktop computing devices. CDC was also involved in a well-publicized and costly lawsuit with IBM. CDC did try to market a mini version of PLATO to operate on microcomputer platforms, but it was too late. When asked about CDC's failure to make PLATO profitable, Donald Bitzer commented that the product was too expensive and driven by the need to keep itself profitable, resulting in higher user fees. In his opinion, they [CDC] "produced an inferior program at a very high cost" (Van Meer, 2003). By the end of the 1980s, CDC had sold off many of its assets including its PLATO business. The PLATO name is now associated with one of the online services sold by the company, Edmentum (http://www.edmentum.com/about/mission-values). The University of Illinois continued development of PLATO at CERL and eventually set up a commercial online service called NovaNET in partnership with University Communications, Inc. (UCI). CERL was closed in 1994, with the maintenance of the PLATO code passing to UCI. UCI was later renamed NovaNET Learning, which was bought by National Computer Systems (NCS). Shortly after that, NCS was bought by Pearson in 2000. A free, open-access version of PLATO is available online, of interest mostly as a nostalgia site for former users.

American Higher Education Prepares Society for a Digital World

The first department of computer science was established at Purdue University in 1962. Prior to this, colleges offered courses in computer science in the electrical engineering, physics, and mathematics departments. Since 1962, thousands of computer science programs have been developed around the country, and most universities offer undergraduate or graduate degrees in computer science. In addition, colleges offer degrees in information systems in schools of business and technology. Specialized programs are also offered in many professional programs designed to prepare students to be providers and leaders of technology services in education, health services, security, law enforcement, etc. American higher education has answered the call from a society and economy that require a well-trained technology workforce. In sum, the vast majority of computer programmers, web designers, database administrators, systems analysts, and other technology professionals receive their initial training in American colleges and universities. American universities will continue to make investments in these programs, many of which are expensive because equipment needs to be updated in response to a constantly changing technology environment. Colleges and universities are also being responsive to their markets. Students are interested in technology careers, and every indication is that they will continue to be. Colleges have revised their adult and continuing education programs to include offerings in technology-related courses and certificate programs.

There are also college educators who have made substantial investments of time and financial resources in technology-based education, not for the training of computer professionals but for students in general. Educators saw the impact that technology would have on all walks of human endeavor and began to require students to be knowledgeable of and literate in basic technology applications and functions. These educators also assisted other agencies and organizations such as schools, hospitals, libraries, and businesses to keep current on advances in technology. A brief look at some of the educators who led these initiatives would be a fitting close to this chapter.

Dartmouth College: John Kemeny and Thomas Kurtz

John Kemeny emigrated from Hungary with his family as a teenager in 1940. As were many Jewish émigrés, his father was concerned for his family's safety if they remained in Eastern Europe at the onset of World War II. Kemeny enrolled at Princeton University as an undergraduate and showed great promise in mathematics. He was invited to work on the Manhattan Project at Los Alamos, where he worked with a number of the country's leading mathematicians. He returned to Princeton, graduated, and entered a PhD program working with Alonzo Church at the Institute for Advanced Study. Upon receipt of his doctorate, he accepted a faculty position at Dartmouth College where he would stay for the remainder of his career. He became interested in administration and was president of Dartmouth from 1970 to 1981. Thomas Kurtz graduated with a PhD in mathematics from Princeton University in 1956 and immediately accepted a faculty position at Dartmouth College offered by John Kemeny, then the chairman of the mathematics department. The two mathematicians became close colleagues who collaborated on a number of projects, including the new and evolving computer technology.

Kemeny and Kurtz's most significant contribution was the development of the BASIC (Beginners All-Purpose Symbolic Instruction Code) programming language in 1964. The major purpose of BASIC was to make programming as easy as possible and to remove the mystique of providing instructions to a computer. At the time that Kemeny and Kurtz started this project, computer programming was done in assembler code, which was very difficult to understand even for trained programmers, or in several higher level languages such as COBOL (Common Business-Oriented Language) and FORTRAN (Formula Translator), which required a good deal of training and practice to master. They built several features into BASIC that were ahead of their time. For instance, they develop BASIC as an interpreter rather than a compiler of instructions. At the time, programmers would compile all the instructions of a program (usually supplied on punched cards) into the language translation program at one time. The language translation program's compiler would review all the instructions for syntax as well as for certain logic constructs. After the review, all detected errors were identified and printed out for the programmer to correct and then to resubmit. BASIC took a much different approach by utilizing an instruction by instruction interpreter. The BASIC interpreter reviewed each instruction as it was being submitted and required the programmer to make corrections immediately. This was far more efficient and easier for the programmer to understand. In order to provide the instant review, BASIC programmers worked on a time-share system where they submitted their instructions on a terminal. The instruction set in BASIC was also very streamlined, with just the "basic" computer-programming functions. It proved to be immensely successful and popular. When microcomputers arrived in the 1970s, most of the operating systems or overall system software packages provided BASIC as their standard programming language. BASIC received a significant boost in popularity when Microsoft Incorporated decided to include it as part of the DOS (Disk Operating System), which became the most commonly used operating system on microcomputers in the 1970s and 1980s.

Kemeny and Kurtz also took an unprecedented step forward by requiring that students be familiar with BASIC. They persuaded the faculty to make a working knowledge of BASIC a core curriculum requirement for all students at Dartmouth. In the 1980s, other colleges and high schools followed suit and began to offer computer literacy courses, which frequently included an introduction to BASIC. As a result, BASIC became by far the most popular programming language ever developed up to that time. It is still used extensively today on a good deal of computer equipment.

MIT Media Lab: Seymour Papert

Seymour Papert was born in Pretoria, South Africa, and completed a doctor of philosophy program in mathematics at the University of Witwatersrand (Johannesburg) and at Cambridge University. He held several faculty appointments at European universities before accepting a position at MIT in 1963, where he remained for much of his career. Papert made a number of contributions to the study of artificial intelligence and cognition but is most associated with the development of the Logo programming language, used mostly by children. Working with colleagues, Daniel G. Bobrow, Wally Feurzeig, and Cynthia Solomon, Logo was developed in 1967. The original intent of the Logo project was to develop a way to teach artificial intelligence and used LISP, derived from "LISt Processing," as its developmental programming tool. However, Papert, influenced by the work of Jean Piaget, converted the project into designing a programming language that could be used by children. Papert's philosophy behind the design was based on experiential and discovery learning, which at the time had little if any relationship to computer programming. Papert (1980), who lived and studied with Jean Piaget, believed that children were able to benefit from computer technology at a very early age. The fundamental Logo concept of manipulating a friendly turtle icon was directed specifically at the young learner and is derived from Piaget's theories on cognitive development. Though children develop cognitively at different rates, Piaget (1952) proposed that logical thinking, at least as applied to physical reality, begins at approximately 7 to 11 years of age. *Logo* and its derivatives, such as *Microworlds*, and many other software programs directed at the young learner have been used successfully in many elementary school programs. While offered as a content area in which children learn about computer technology, *Logo* is also commonly integrated with other curriculum activities such as mathematics and problem solving. The success of *Logo* and other software packages designed for young children also suggests that many children of elementary school age are indeed cognitively ready to use and benefit from technology experiences.

Papert's work with *Logo* is important for higher education for several reasons. First, it pushed higher education and specifically colleges of education to start thinking about how digital technology could be extended to the K–12 environment, which until then was never considered as an arena for instructional technology. Second, Papert was among the first to integrate theories of cognitive development and learning with computer programming. This influenced many faculty at colleges and universities to consider the same as they moved forward in artificial intelligence, cognitive science, and learning theory. No longer was computer programming considered the domain of electrical engineers and mathematicians focused on physical processes but came to be considered a fundamental tool in studying and promoting social, psychological, and cultural development.

Logo reached the height of its popularity in the 1980s with the advent of microcomputers. K–12 schools had precious few software programs available for children. *Logo*, however, provided teachers with a software platform that could relate to younger children's learning. A major issue was that teachers were not trained well enough to use technology in pedagogically meaningful ways and had little experience in integrating technology into curriculum. In addition, *Logo* required a good deal of hands-on computer time in order for students to learn the language and to develop projects. In addition, many schools did not have enough computer workstations in their schools to support an intensive technology activity. As a result, *Logo* proved difficult to implement broadly throughout K–12 schools. Regardless, *Logo* continued to evolve and is available today for both home and school use in several forms, including a version that works with robotics and another that uses the popular children's Lego building blocks.

Stanford University: Norman Nie, C. Hadlai Hull, and Dale Bent

One of the most useful tools ever developed for the social sciences and for the teaching of research methods is a package called SPSS (Statistical Package for the Social Sciences). The project to build this software package was started at Stanford University in the 1960s by three graduate students: Norman Nie, Dale Bent, and C. Hadlai Hull. As described at the SPSS website:

> The initial work on SPSS was done at Stanford University with the intention to make it available only for local consumption and not international distribution. Nie, a social scientist and Stanford doctoral candidate, represented the target audience and set the requirements; Bent, a Stanford University doctoral candidate in operations research, had the analysis expertise and designed the SPSS system file structure; and Hull, who had recently graduated from Stanford with a master of business administration degree,

programmed. After graduate school in 1969, Nie joined the University of Chicago's National Opinion Research Center. The University of Chicago considered SPSS an important intellectual property and encouraged Nie's continuing development of the software system. Nie was successful in recruiting Hull to join him at the University of Chicago by encouraging him to take a position as the head of the University's Computation Center. Bent, a Canadian, decided not to join Nie and Hull in Chicago, and returned to Canada where he had an academic appointment at the University of Alberta.

(About SPSS, Inc., 2009)

The speed with which SPSS caught on was nothing short of amazing. Prior to its advent, social science researchers doing data analysis typically were using manual equipment and calculators. Frequently, social science researchers relied on other experts who knew the specifics of statistical procedures and had great dexterity in using manual equipment. It was one thing to add a sum of numbers on a calculator, it was quite another to do an analysis of variance. Nie and Hull decided to give the software away for the cost of making make a duplicate set of the program, which initially consisted of a tray of punched cards. However, Nie, Bent, and Hull came to realize that SPSS users would need instructions or a manual to use the software properly. The original version of the SPSS manual published in 1970 has been described as one of "sociology's most influential books" for allowing ordinary researchers to do their own statistical analysis (Wellman, 1998). The manual became a best seller, and tens of thousands of social scientists took charge of their own research destinies as they learned the basics as well as the nuances of doing data analysis. SPSS provided the classic environment of learning by doing. The software, with the aid of the manual, was very user friendly, and a conscientious student learned the statistical procedures as well as the SPSS coding to conduct the analysis.

It is difficult to assess SPSS's impact on the entire field of data analysis, but in less than a decade it became the mainstay of faculty for teaching introduction to statistics in all of the disciplines. Furthermore, it also opened up data analysis to collecting larger sample sizes because the drudgery of running statistical routines disappeared once the data were converted into electronic form. Students and researchers could now collect sample sizes numbering in the thousands. Government agencies could collect sample sizes in the hundreds of thousands and make the data available in SPSS format free to other researchers. SPSS set the standard for a number of other statistical packages, such as SAS and Stata, which were to follow. It was SPSS that changed the way statistical research is conducted. Agencies such as NASA and the Census Bureau, as well as corporate America, became regular users of the software. Versions of SPSS were made available for all the major computer hardware platforms (IBM, Univac, Burroughs, GE). A whole style of research evolved based on collecting large quantities of data without necessarily having specific hypotheses or research questions and then searching the data for relationships and patterns. This approach has evolved into the era of "big data."

In 1975, Nie and Hull incorporated SPSS into a company and began to sell SPSS commercially. To its credit, SPSS, Inc., always provided student versions at substantial discounts. In 2003, SPSS, Inc., also developed predictive analytics products that were especially popular for marketing applications. In 2009, SPSS, Inc., was acquired for $1.2 billion by IBM, which continues to market it under the SPSS brand.

Summary

This chapter tells the story of how American higher education played a critical role in developing and designing pivotal elements of the digital technology evolution that commenced in the 20th century and continues today. The chapter began with stories of academic visionaries who foresaw and modeled computer hardware and software that would usher in technologies for all aspects of our societal endeavors. The chapter then focused on education leaders who envisioned technology as a tool in teaching and learning. Computer-based education owes a lot to these individuals, even though early CAI applications proved to be limited. The chapter closed with the stories of three developments outside of computer-based education that nonetheless resulted in major contributions on the part of American higher education.

References

About SPSS, Inc. (2009). Corporate history. Retrieved from: http://www.spss.com.hk/corpinfo/history.htm Accessed: April 8, 2015.

Bellis, M. (2015). *Inventors of the modern computer.* About.com Inventors. Retrieved from: http://inventors.about.com/library/weekly/aa052198.htm Accessed: April 3, 2015.

Bilton, N. (October 1, 2014). The women tech forgot: 'The Innovators' by Walter Isaacson: How women shaped technology. *New York Times.* Retrieved from: http://www.nytimes.com/2014/10/02/fashion/the-innovators-by-walter-isaacson-how-women-shaped-technology.html Accessed: April 2, 2014.

Cohen, I.B. (2000). *Howard Aiken: Portrait of a computer pioneer.* Boston: Massachusetts Institute of Technology Press.

Edwards, J.R. (2012). *A history of early computing at Princeton: Turing centennial celebration.* Princeton: Princeton University. Retrieved from: http://www.princeton.edu/turing/alan/history-of-computing-at-p/ Accessed: April 2, 2015.

Fischman, J. (May 8, 2011). The rise of teaching machines. *The Chronicle of Higher Education.* Retrieved from: http://chronicle.com/article/The-Rise-of-Teaching-Machines/127389/ Accessed: April 5, 2105.

Institute for Advanced Study (2015). Mission and history. Retrieved from: https://www.ias.edu/about/mission-and-history Accessed: April 2, 2015.

Isaacson, W. (2014). *The innovators: How a group of hackers, geniuses, and geeks created the digital revolution.* New York: Simon & Schuster.

Lasar, M. (2011). UNIVAC: The troubled life of America's first computer. *Ars Technica.* Retrieved from: http://arstechnica.com/tech-policy/2011/09/univac-the-troubled-life-of-americas-first-computer/1/ Accessed: April 4, 2015.

Leydesdorff, L. (1995). The Triple Helix—university-industry-government relations: A laboratory for knowledge-based economic development. *EASST Review, 13*(1), 14–19.

Markoff, J. (December 2, 2014). Patrick Suppes, pioneer in computerized learning, dies at 92. *New York Times.* Retrieved from: http://www.nytimes.com/2014/12/03/us/patrick-suppes-pioneer-in-computerized-learning-dies-at 92.html?emc=edit_th_2014 1203&nl=todaysheadlines&nlid=1596194&_r=1 Accessed: April 6, 2014.

Markus, J. (2015). *Lady Byron and her daughters.* New York: W.W. Norton and Company.

Papert, S. (1980). *Mindstorms: Children, computers, and powerful ideas.* New York: Basic Books.

Piaget, J. (1952). *The origins of intelligence in children.* New York: Norton.

Pressey, S.L. (1926). A simple apparatus which gives tests and scores and teaches. *School and Society, 23*, 373–376.

Seattler, P. (2004). *The evolution of American educational technology.* Charlotte, NC: Information Age Publishing.

Skinner, B.F. (1958). Teaching machines. *Science, 128*(3330), 969–977.

Thorndike, E.L. (1912, published 1923). *Education: A first book.* New York: Macmillan Co.

Van Meer, E. (November 3, 2003). PLATO: From computer-based education to corporate social responsibility. *Iterations: An Interdisciplinary Journal of Software History.* Retrieved from: http://www.cbi.umn.edu/iterations/vanmeer.html Accessed: April 7, 2015.

Wellman, B. (1998). Doing it ourselves: The SPSS manual as sociology's most influential recent book." In D. Clawson (Ed.), *Required reading: Sociology's most influential books* (pp. 71–78). Amherst: University of Massachusetts Press.

SECTION II
Online Education

5

THE FIRST WAVE

Beginnings (1993–1999)

The evolution of online learning technology can be viewed as five waves starting in 1993 and continuing through the 2020s. The metaphor of waves representing evolutionary stages is not new. A number of authors, including Alvin Toffler (1970, 1984, 1991), have used waves to designate or demark periods of time. Toffler is an apt comparison in that he deals with information technology. His waves, however, occur over millennia and encompass mega issues associated with the evolution of man as well as information technology. The use of the wave metaphor in this book, although apt, is far more modest than Toffler's.

The focus of this chapter is the first wave of online education, which began in the early 1990s with the advent of the ubiquitous Internet. While the Internet touched practically every field of human endeavor, its relationship to higher education is unique. First, universities were integral to the development of digital technology, including data communications systems. Many of the major breakthroughs were as a result of collaborations among faculty who had a vision of what technology could do for humankind. Second, before the Internet existed, there was a well-established distance education community in colleges and universities that used mostly passive technologies such as television, radio, and course packs. This community immediately saw the benefits of an interactive technology like the Internet. J.C. Taylor (2001) referred to online education as the new generation of distance education. Third, American higher education had already established closed online education networks (i.e., PLATO) and had some expertise and experiences in delivering online learning. The Internet provided the facility to open up these education networks to the masses.

The Internet

The Idea for an Internet

Joseph C.R. Licklider, the only son of a Baptist minister, came from modest beginnings in a small, rural Missouri town. He was a bright child and enrolled at Washington University in St. Louis and graduated with a BA degree majoring in physics, mathematics, and psychology in 1937. He received a master's degree in psychology in 1938 from Washington University. In 1942, he completed a PhD in psychoacoustics from the University of Rochester. He held teaching positions at Harvard University and MIT until 1957, when he became a vice president at Bolt, Beranek, and Newman, Inc.

In the 1950s, Licklider became convinced that the future of computing technology would center on a digital time-sharing network that would be user friendly and capable of storing large amounts of information in an online environment. Licklider envisioned small personal computers that would link up to the larger computers that were typical of the era to share information. In 1960, he wrote an article titled *Man-Machine Symbiosis*, which has been described as "one of the most influential papers in the history of postwar technology" (Isaacson, 2014, p. 226). In this article, he described a real-time computer network where people could make inquiries and access large databases for information and assistance in solving problems.

> It seems reasonable to envision, for a time 10 or 15 years hence, a 'thinking center' that will incorporate the functions of present-day libraries together with anticipated advances in information storage and retrieval.
>
> The picture readily enlarges itself into a network of such centers, connected to one another by wide-band communication lines and to individual users by leased-wire services. In such a system, the speed of the computers would be balanced, and the cost of the gigantic memories and the sophisticated programs would be divided by the number of users.
>
> *(Licklider, 1960, p. 7)*

In October 1962, Licklider was appointed head of the Information Processing Techniques Office (IPTO) at DARPA, then called ARPA, the United States Department of Defense Advanced Research Projects Agency. In that same year, he delivered a paper with W.E. Clark titled *On-Line Man-Computer Communication,* wherein he elaborated on his thoughts on people working online on small computers linked to a larger network. In 1963, he sent a memorandum to his colleagues at ARPA titled, "Memorandum for Members and Affiliates of the Intergalactic Computer Network." In this memorandum, he further explored the early challenges associated with establishing a time-sharing network of computers, given the software of the era. Licklider's vision would lead to development of ARPANET, the precursor of the Internet in use today.

In 1999, Robert Taylor, who succeeded Licklider at ARPA, received the National Medal of Technology for his more than thirty years of service and "for visionary leadership in the development of modern computing technology, including initiating the ARPAnet project—forerunner of today's Internet—and advancing groundbreaking achievements in the development of the personal computer and computer networks" (Softky, 2000). Yet, if you asked Taylor about ARPANET and the Internet, he would say that Licklider "was really the father of it all" (Isaacson, 2014).

The Roots of the Internet (1960s–70s)

It has been well documented that the roots of the Internet can be traced to the U.S. Department of Defense in the 1960s. Concerned about establishing and maintaining a worldwide communications system in the event of a major disaster such as nuclear war, the department engaged engineers and scientists from Rand, UCLA, and MIT to design a data communications system that would be decentralized and capable of functioning regardless of whether any single node or point in the network was no longer available. This design was a departure from the common centralized data communications systems that required a hub or center point to control the entire network. Dozens of technology and communications specialists, researchers, and faculty were involved with the design and implementation, which took twenty years to finalize before the Internet as we know it evolved. Key organizations involved with its development included the U.S. Department of Defense, the Rand Corporation, Bolt Beranek and Newman (BBN), MIT, and UCLA. Paul Baran, a key figure at Rand Corporation in the1960s who conceived of packet switching, was quoted as stating: "the Internet is really the work of a thousand people" (Isaacson, 2014, p. 245). Some of the important milestones in its development were as follows.

In 1969, the Pentagon's Advanced Research and Projects Agency established the first node of this new network—called Advanced Research and Projects Agency Network (ARPANET)—at UCLA. Throughout the 1970s, the ARPANET grew but was used essentially by government officials, engineers, and scientists connected with research for the U.S. Department of Defense. The major applications were email, file transfer, and discussion groups such as USENET. The underlying key feature of the Internet was the concept of packet switching, which took messages and broke them down into small chunks or packets. This was a major change from previous message switching technology, which essentially transmitted entire messages regardless of length. The packet switching technique was much faster and reduced queuing problems that might result with long messages. In addition, the paths for individual packets, even though they might have the same origin, did not have to go through the same routes of the network but could use different routes as long as they all got to their destination in the proper sequence. The protocol made for a highly efficient and fast distribution of messages that took full advantage of the available network resources.

The Internet Takes Shape (1980s)

In 1983, the military segment of ARPANET developed a separate network called MILNET, and access to ARPANET was expanded to include other computer networks worldwide that used its protocol or method of transferring data. By 1985, there were over 5,000 host computers on ARPANET. In the 1980s, other international networks were being established in the higher education, government, and research communities. Because It's Time Network (BITNET) was established by the City University of New York, Yale University, and IBM to link university mainframe computers. Computer Science Network (CSNET) was funded by the U.S. National Science Foundation (NSF) to provide data communications facilities for industry, government, and university groups engaged in computer science research. Later, several U.S. agencies—namely, the NSF, the National Aeronautics and Space Agency (NASA), and the U.S. Department of Energy—funded and established networking facilities that eventually would be used to enhance the aging ARPANET system. By the late 1980s, all of these major networks were communicating with one another, either using or converting to the standard protocol (Transfer Control Protocol/Internet Protocol (TCP/IP) established on ARPANET: hence the birth of the Internet as we know it today. A protocol in data communications is the way one computer node greets and alerts another node about the message that is being delivered. The construction of the Internet's TCP/IP is a datagram that has two components: a header and a payload. The IP header is tagged with the source (sending node) IP address, the destination (receiving node) IP address, and other meta-data needed to route and deliver the datagram. The payload is the data message itself that is being transported.

By 1990, there were over 300,000 host computers, and the ARPANET ceased to exist, having fully evolved into what became known as the Internet. In 1991, Paul Lindner and Mark P. McCahill from the University of Minnesota developed the first user-friendly, menu-driven interface for the Internet and named it "gopher." It was entirely text-based but made sending and receiving files and messages much simpler than the previous command-driven method. The next major breakthrough for the Internet would come later in the same year with the development of the World Wide Web.

The World Wide Web (1990s)

While the Internet resulted from a large-scale collaboration of American government, private industry, and higher education, the development of the World Wide Web (WWW) was a European creation of the *Conseil Européen pour la Recherche Nucléaire* (CERN), established in Geneva, Switzerland. As mentioned in Chapter Three, in the 1950s, I.I. Rabi of Columbia University has been credited with giving the European physicist community the idea for establishing a European-wide laboratory or center patterned after similar facilities established in the United

States. Tim Berners-Lee and Robert Cailliau, who were researchers at CERN, are the two individuals most associated with developing the WWW. Berners-Lee and Cailliau built all the software tools necessary to allow the Internet to use hypermedia, including the HyperText Transfer Protocol (http), the Hyper-Text Markup Language (HTML), and the first Web browser (named World Wide Web). Fundamental to the WWW is its hypermedia capability, which allows the transfer and display of various media (text, images, video) that are processed via the HTML coding language. The first browser developed by Berners-Lee and Cailliau was text-based. In 1993, Mosaic, the first graphic interface for the WWW, was developed at the University of Illinois and made available to the public. Marc Andreessen and Eric Bina, graduate students working at the National Center for Supercomputing Applications at the University of Illinois at Urbana-Champaign, were the developers of Mosaic, which became a global success and was credited with making the Internet available to the masses. In 1993, there were 2 million Internet hosts. By 1997, there were 19.5 million.

The Internet Today—Expansion and Concerns

The Internet is the most impressive medium ever developed. It provides fast multimedia communications worldwide, and it is free. Users have to pay Internet service providers a fee to make the connection, but the Internet itself is a free resource. It was estimated that the Internet reached its first billion users world-wide in 2005, the second billion in 2010, the third billion in 2014. In the United States, it was estimated that in 2015, almost 280 million people, or 87 percent of the population, had access to the Internet (Internet Live Stats (2015). Such a medium cannot be ignored. To the contrary, it has been embraced by all segments of the world population including higher education, which played a vital role in its development. However, concerns exist about how the Internet has changed many aspects of the human condition, especially its psychological, social, and cultural dimensions.

Nicholas Carr, the *New York Times* best-selling author of *The Shallows: What the Internet Is Doing to Our Brains*, acknowledges that the Internet may be the "single most powerful mind-altering technology" that has ever come into general use. He also cautions that it is an environment that promotes "cursory reading, hurried and distracted thinking, and superficial learning" (Carr, 2014, p. 116). Carr also refers to the work of Antonio Damasio, who expresses concern that the immediate access to information provided by the Internet can damage our ability to deal with deep psychological and social situations. Carr suggests that the Internet is "rerouting our vital paths and diminishes our capacity for contemplation and is altering the depth of our emotions as well as our thoughts" (Carr, 2014, p. 221). He concludes that we are becoming too dependent upon the Internet for our memory and that our culture needs to be sustained by our collective memories. To remain vital, "culture must be renewed in the minds of the members of every generation. Outsource memory and culture withers" (Carr, 2014, p. 196). Andrew Keen, author of *The Internet is Not the Answer,* goes further than Carr in his criticism:

> The more we use the contemporary digital network [Internet], the less economic value it is bringing to us. Rather than promoting economic fairness, it is a central reason for the growing gulf between rich and poor and the hollowing out of the middle class. Rather than generating more jobs, this digital disruption is a principal cause of our structural unemployment crisis. . . . . Rather than making us happy, it is compounding our rage.
>
> *(Keen, 2015, p. iv)*

Without a doubt the Internet has its issues, and there are justifiable concerns. Nevertheless, it remains the most significant communications invention of humankind to date and has become indispensable to many of our endeavors.

The Alfred P. Sloan Foundation and Anytime, Anyplace Learning

Colleges and universities serve as effective incubators of ideas. However, in order to translate the ideas of faculty and researchers into reality (products and services), resources, especially funding, are typically needed from external sources. The same is true of online education. College faculty were experimenting with the facilities provided by the Internet and World Wide Web in their teaching in the 1990s, and many could demonstrate successes in individual courses or modules within courses. But in order to scale up, outside funding was needed. The Alfred P. Sloan Foundation filled this need.

Ralph Gomory received his PhD in mathematics from Princeton University in 1954. After serving in the U.S. Navy from 1954 to 1957, he held an appointment as Higgins lecturer and assistant professor at Princeton University from 1957–59. In 1959, he joined IBM's Research Division. At IBM, he helped establish that company as one of the major research institutions in the world. In 1970 he was named director of research. He continued in a leadership role for the next twenty years as director of research and eventually IBM senior vice president for science and technology. During his tenure, IBM's research division made many fundamental contributions to advanced technology in such areas as the single-transistor memory cell, high-density storage devices, silicon processing methods, and the invention of the relational database and the RISC computer architecture. His researchers also won two successive Nobel Prizes in physics as well as a number of other rewards (Gomory, 2015).

On reaching the mandatory retirement age of 60 for corporate officers at IBM in 1989, Gomory became president of the Alfred P. Sloan Foundation. The Alfred P. Sloan Foundation is a philanthropic, not-for-profit grant-making institution established in 1934 by Alfred Pritchard Sloan, Jr., then-president and chief executive officer of the General Motors Corporation. The foundation has a distinguished history of making grants to support original research and broad-based education in the areas of science, technology, and economics. The foundation is an independent entity and has no formal relationship with the General Motors Corporation (Alfred P. Sloan Foundation Website, 2015). During Gomory's eighteen years as president, the Foundation sponsored research relevant to a number of national issues. However, in the early 1990s, he established the *Learning Outside the Classroom/Anytime, Anyplace Learning Program*, based on his vision that students could learn in their homes, places of business, or just about anywhere or anytime they could connect to a digital network. Joel Hartman, vice provost for information technologies and resources at the University of Central Florida, commented that "Dr. Ralph Gomory and the Foundation were way ahead of their time in promoting digital teaching and learning especially considering that the Internet as we know it did not exist" (Interview, Picciano, 2013, p. 2). The vast majority of households in the United States did not have connections to digital networks, and no one was predicting that within a decade the populace would be willing to pay for high-speed communications lines to use the vast information resources of the Internet, including access to online courses and degrees.

In 1992, the Alfred P. Sloan Foundation formally funded the *Learning Outside the Classroom Program* and began accepting grant proposals. The purpose of the program was to explore educational alternatives for people who wanted to pursue higher education but who could not easily attend regularly scheduled college classes. The name was changed in 1993 to the *Anytime, Anyplace Learning Program*. This grant program promulgated a major development in pedagogical practice referred to as the asynchronous learning network or ALN. The Foundation chose the ALN acronym to indicate that its grant program would favor proposals for asynchronous access to education with a faculty member leading the class (asynchronously) over a computer-based learning network. The over-arching goal was that ALNs would allow teaching and learning to transcend time and space in order to provide access to a quality higher education.

Over the twenty-year life-span of the *Anytime, Anyplace Learning Program,* 346 grants totaling $72,197,965 were awarded. Of that total, $40 million of the grants were awarded to just twenty-two institutions (Picciano, 2013). Major distance and adult learning providers such as the University of Maryland–University College, the Penn State World Campus, Rio Salado Community College, and Northern Virginia Community College were early grantees. Following on the heels of these institutions, large mainstream public university systems such as the University of Illinois, the State University of New York, the University of Massachusetts, and the University of Central Florida also received funding. In the early 2000s, large urban universities in New York, Chicago, and Milwaukee were funded to develop and expand blended learning environments. The awarding of grants to public university systems and community colleges was not an accident, but by design, as confirmed by Frank Mayadas, the Sloan Foundation program officer for the *Anytime, Anyplace Learning Program*:

> In discussing the focus on large public universities with Frank Mayadas, it becomes clear that the foundation's early attempts to work with elite institutions such as MIT, Cornell, and Brown did not yield tangible results, with the exception of Stanford University. . . . So early on, we gained the conviction that if the ALN program was to succeed, it needed to direct grant resources to academic programs at the large public university systems. These institutions were an excellent fit for the ALN program, and most (e.g., SUNY Learning Network, Penn State World Campus, UMASS Online) formalized their grant programs into major university operations involving traditional departments.
>
> *(Interview, Picciano, 2013, p. 29)*

Public institutions represent approximately 76 percent of all student enrollments in American higher education, and many of them, especially the community colleges, focus on the importance of access to higher education. The strategy of the foundation to support the public sector made sense and enabled it to penetrate the largest segment of American higher education.

The foundation also developed a strategy wherein individual faculty or administrators initially received small or modest grants to demonstrate the capability of establishing larger ALN projects at their institutions. If successful, they were then encouraged to apply for larger grants. Examples of this approach were evident at the University of Illinois, SUNY Learning Network, and the University of Massachusetts. Eric Fredericksen of the State University of New York described the concept as follows:

> a three-phase progression from small proof-of-concept projects to larger university-wide proof-of-scale projects and finally to full expansion and proof-of-sustainability projects. The smaller initial projects brought in "early-adopter" faculty and administrators who then formed a "grassroots" base of individuals willing to support the larger, system-wide effort. The larger system-wide efforts brought ALN to scale, and the grassroots base that supported these efforts gave credence to the overall scaling-up of ALN.

Fredericksen also emphasized that the proposals submitted to the Sloan Foundation focused on "doing or accomplishing something with tangible results" (Interview, Picciano, 2013, p. 22).

The *Anytime, Anyplace Learning Program* lasted twenty years, but its importance really stems from the early years of online education in the 1990s. At the time, there was widespread belief that online education represented low-quality instruction and would breed "digital diploma mills" (Noble, 2003). The investment of the foundation gave online education credibility and built a community of educators and scholars devoted to promoting good education practice and careful pedagogical design.

The Sloan Consortium (now the Online Learning Consortium)

One of the most significant initiatives of the *Anytime, Anyplace Learning Program* was the establishment of the Sloan Consortium of Colleges and Universities, now known as the Online Learning Consortium. Originally an informal organization of *Anytime, Anyplace Learning Program* grantees, the consortium incorporated in 2008 as a nonprofit, 501(c)(3) organization. The Sloan Consortium became the largest recipient of funding from the *Anytime, Anyplace, Learning Program*, receiving in excess of $15 million over the course of the grant program's lifetime (1992–2012) to fill several important roles for the grantees and other institutions interested in online education.

First and most important, it established a community of administrators, faculty, and instructional designers whose purpose was to share knowledge and practices. In the 1990s, no comparable community existed. There were centers focused on generic distance education at the University of Wisconsin-Madison and Penn State that provided research and other information services. However, at that time, distance education and online education were very different entities. Traditional distance education had a long history of colleges, universities, and correspondence schools providing academic programs using various modalities (i.e., television, radio, course packs). The Sloan Consortium focused exclusively on Internet-based online education, which in the 1990s was a brand new entity with an uncertain future.

Second, the Sloan Consortium focused on integrating online education into mainstream higher education and not necessarily as something distinct and apart from the regular academic programs.

Third, from the beginning, the consortium sought to promote quality in the development and delivery of online education, which in its early years was viewed skeptically by many segments of higher education. The consortium's *Five Pillars of Quality Online Learning* was the first formal framework to specify goals, objectives, and metrics for evaluating online programs. These pillars focused on the following:

- Student access to higher education
- Learning effectiveness
- Student satisfaction
- Faculty satisfaction
- Cost-effectiveness

This framework continues to be widely used today and is frequently cited by a variety of practitioners and education policy makers (OLC Quality Framework, 2015).

Fourth, the consortium saw itself as an important information resource to its community and others. In 1996, it published the first edition of the *Journal of Asynchronous Learning Networks* (JALN). JALN was the first refereed free online journal devoted exclusively to online education. Many of the most important researchers and thinkers in the field of online education (i.e., James Duderstadt, Karen Swan, Ray Schroeder, Chuck Dziuban, Randy Garrison, Eric Fredericksen, Peter Shea, Terry Anderson, Burks Oakley, Katrina Meyer, and Gary Miller) have published in it over its twenty-year existence. The consortium also sponsored annual national surveys of chief academic officers and their perceptions of online education. These surveys were conducted by Elaine Allen and Jeff Seaman and represented the most comprehensive collection of longitudinal data on online education in American colleges and universities that ever existed.

The Sloan Consortium changed its name in 2014 after funding from the Alfred P. Sloan Foundation ended by mutual agreement. It is now known as the Online Learning Consortium and is still the leading professional organization devoted to online education in American colleges and universities.

The Asynchronous Learning Network Model

The interactive asynchronous learning network (ALN) model was the dominant pedagogical approach used for online education in the 1990s. As mentioned earlier, this model was made popular through the Alfred P. Sloan Foundation's emphasis on anytime and anyplace learning, the underlying concept being that there was little need for faculty and students to log on at the same time for instruction. Students could participate at times most convenient for them (i.e., after work, after the children were put to bed, etc.). It also fit the approaches used by most distance education providers at the time, who relied on passive technologies such as television and radio. However, another rationale for using the ALN model was that home connectivity to the Internet was largely based on slow-speed, dial-up modem lines. Even where available, most students could not afford higher-speed Internet connections. So while a college or a business might have high-speed lines, it made little sense to develop instructional approaches that took advantage of this type of connectivity, which would only frustrate students who had slower speed access to the Internet in their homes. In addition, digital multimedia was difficult and time-consuming to develop and required a good deal of bandwidth to download. As a result, many of the earliest online learning courses were text-based and relied heavily on asynchronous learning. However, this was not necessarily a major hindrance for teaching and learning. The digital media that did exist on the Internet was rudimentary and frequently displayed on a small window. There were also problems synching the audio and video. Standard video file formats for the Internet were just evolving, and there was no guarantee that student computers had the required software viewers to view media developed by faculty or instructional designers. Software such as learning/course management systems were also rudimentary, so a number of schools had to develop their own course-delivery platforms. For example, the SUNY Learning Network established its entire platform on Lotus Notes.

The text-based ALN model relied on several well-proven approaches that were understood by faculty in schools of education and anyone else who had an introduction to pedagogy and curriculum. One of the more popular design frameworks for developing online courses was a community of inquiry (COI) model that focused on three common elements of social presence, cognitive presence, and teaching (Garrison, Anderson, & Archer, 2000). COI was grounded in constructivist learning theory made popular by John Dewey, Lev Vygotsky, and others (Swan, Garrison, & Richardson, 2009). For example, the ALN model was and remains very conducive to reflective practice by teachers and learners, which utilizes time to think about what is being taught and presented. The benefits of reflection in instruction were promoted by John Dewey in the early 1900s. The basic threaded discussion board used in online classes for posing questions and responses also simulates the Socratic Method. When combined with time for reflection, it might be considered more educationally beneficial than traditional face-to-face class meetings, where time limits the amount of discussion that can ensue. In addition, threaded discussion board lists allow students to review over and over again how a discussion evolved. This is rarely if ever possible in a traditional class. The discussion board also allows for greater participation by all students, because discussions could go on for days. Perhaps the most important aspect of the text-based discussion board is that it is a simple technology, easy for both faculty and students to utilize in the early, pioneering days of online education.

There were some drawbacks to the text-based ALN model. Certain subject areas and disciplines rely on media and demonstrations to illustrate concepts. For example, the sciences do not teach biological or chemical processes such as the cardiovascular system or molecule formation through reading about them but by using video, simulations, and laboratory activities. The early Internet, because of slow connectivity and the expense of developing media, was not mature enough to develop and deliver quality instructional materials for these subject areas. Another concern was the time required for active participation on a threaded list because, while it was excellent for reflective practice, it also meant that students and faculty might be spending excessive amounts of time on class activities. It is one thing for a faculty member to respond to a question in a traditional class with a quick sixty-second response. It is quite another to compose an answer to the same question for a discussion board; that may require ten, fifteen, twenty minutes or more. The issue of lurking received some attention as well. In a traditional class, students did not have to participate if they did not want to. In the ALN model, all students were expected to participate even if they did not have much to offer. There was sometimes a proliferation of "me too" responses that did not add very much other than reading time to the overall lesson activity. The technology of the early Internet also made it difficult to do assessments. Faculty could not know who was taking exams and tests. There was a well-recognized credibility problem with any short-answer type of assessment. Lastly, the early Internet was not friendly enough for students with certain special needs. Assistive technologies were nonexistent or rudimentary and did not provide an appropriate learning environment for many special need students. Many of the concerns raised about the text-based ALN model were resolved as Internet technology evolved and became more sophisticated. And the basic discussion board or its text-based progenies such as blogs and wikis still continue to be dominant pedagogical tools used today in many online courses.

The ALN model ushered in online education in the 1990s. Data on the growth of online education during this period is sketchy at best and nonexistent at worst. The first systematic study, conducted in 2002, estimated that there were 1.6 million students enrolled in at least one fully online course in the public and nonprofit private sectors of higher education (Allen & Seaman, 2014, p. 15). Little is known about online student enrollments in the private, for-profit sector during this period.

Online Education and the Ascent of For-Profit Colleges

The 1990s was a pivotal decade for the private, for-profit sector of American higher education. Kevin Kinser (2006), in *From Main Street to Wall Street: The Transformation of For-Profit Higher Education*, likens this transformation to small mom-and-pop businesses that expand into national business chains. For-profit higher education has a long history in this country, but it never played a major role until the end of the 20th century. The vast majority of the institutions in this sector were not degree-granting but offered certificates concentrating on career education. Students enrolling in their programs could expect a credential within several months and could apply for licenses issued by the states. The subjects of these certificate programs varied significantly from personal grooming/cosmetology to large-equipment operation. While these certificate schools still dominate the number of postsecondary, for-profit institutions in this sector, major changes occurred in the 1990s. First, a small number of these institutions decided to expand and to offer degrees. Second, they incorporated and became publicly held corporations, which gained them substantial new financing while also making them more accountable to Wall Street investors. And finally, they used their new financing to expand their operations, especially in the area of online education. Perhaps the best example of this development was the University of Phoenix (UOP).

In 1973, John Sperling opened the Institute for Community Research and Development, specializing in adult education, in Phoenix, Arizona. Shortly thereafter it became the Institute for Professional Development (IPD), which, in 1976, established a second entity, the University of Phoenix (University of Phoenix, 2015). In 1981, Sperling created the Apollo Group, which became the parent company of UOP. Under the aegis of the Apollo Group, UOP focused on creating degree-granting programs by establishing small local education centers to provide professional development opportunities for corporate clients. In 1994, the Apollo Group made a public offering, and at that time enrolled 27,000 students (including about 2,000 distance education students) at sixty IPD and UOP locations. Flushed with new capital from the public offering, the Apollo Group grew within ten years to over 200 locations all over the world, enrolling 228,000 students, of which 100,000 were online learners. The investment in online learning, although not the only reason for its growth, certainly was a major factor. Several other for-profit colleges such as Kaplan Higher Education, Corinthian Colleges, American Public University System, and Devry expanded their operations in the 1990s and invested in online program development, resulting in sizeable increases in student enrollments.

The UOP primarily used the ALN model of online education. In addition, it tightly controlled its curricula and scripted most of its courses, designed by a small cadre of full-time faculty. Their online courses had several interesting features including a small class size of no more than thirteen students per section. Their courses did not follow the traditional fifteen-week semester calendar but instead could be completed in eight weeks. Most courses were taught by part-time faculty who were hired on a course-by-course basis. UOP has had one of the highest percentages of part-time faculty of any higher education institution (private or public, nonprofit or for-profit) in the world. One estimate had the percentage of courses taught at UOP by part-time faculty at 97.9 percent (Kinser, 2006, p. 91). The use of part-time faculty combined with the online delivery mode significantly reduced its instructional costs, and with increased student enrollments, its profits soared. By the early 2000s, UOP evolved to become one of the largest private, for-profit or nonprofit universities in the world and became the face of large, publicly held, for-profit higher education. However, in the late 1990s, several questions about UOP practices had emerged regarding recruitment of students and federal financial aid. There were also several vocal critics of the way UOP expanded. Senator Tom Harkin (Democrat, Iowa), during a series of congressional hearings held by the U.S. Senate's Health, Education, Labor and Pensions (HELP) Committee in 2012, was quoted as stating:

> When the school [UOP] was founded in 1976 it had a "pretty good model . . . ." "They started out as a college completion school," says Harkin. Many of the students were successful. But then the school "kept expanding and expanding and expanding, and so it kind of morphed into this behemoth that it is now."
>
> *(Hanford, 2012)*

The University of Phoenix is the nation's largest private university. Its enrollment peaked in 2010 with 470,800 students, more than in all the universities of the Big Ten Conference combined. But according to the HELP Committee investigation, more than 60 percent of the students who started degrees at the University of Phoenix in 2008–2009 ended up leaving by the middle of 2010 without a degree. The students who quit had been enrolled for a median of four months. Harkin believes the University of Phoenix went wrong in 1994 when it became a publicly traded company.

> "I think what really turned this company is when they started going to Wall Street," he says. "[They] started raising hedge fund money, and then they had to meet quarterly reports, and all they were interested in, basically, was 'How much money ya makin'?'"
>
> *(Hanford, 2012)*

The move to online education changed the nature of UOP as well as a number of other for-profit institutions. It changed their scale but their character as well as they sought to use the technology to aggressively compete worldwide for students. The issue of the accountability of the for-profit colleges will be discussed further in the next chapter, which deals with the evolution of online education in the early 2000s.

New Higher Education Model—Western Governors University

Online education also provided the vehicle for new or expanded models of public and nonprofit higher education. For example, the Penn State World Campus was created in 1998 and quickly became dependent upon online technology after 100 years of offering distance education via television, radio, and other media. Athabasca University, the open university of Canada, also went through a similar transformation. One of the more interesting new models was the Western Governors University (WGU), conceived in 1995 when nineteen members at a meeting of the Western Governors Association decided to establish a university that would be competency-based and would offer programs that would be fully online. Utah Governor Mike Leavitt is generally credited with having the foresight to realize that distance learning technologies had the power to tackle one of the Western states' most pressing problems: rapid population growth confronted by limited public funds for educational services (Western Governors University, 2015).

WGU was chartered in 1996, incorporated as a private, nonprofit university in 1997, and began accepting students in 1999. WGU is a totally online university. It operates out of an office complex in Salt Lake City, Utah. In addition to its fully online nature, WGU is unique in that its programs are all competency-based rather than seat-time based. Students only need to demonstrate competency in a subject to receive credit for a course. It has a full-time teaching faculty who follow scripted course materials developed by master teachers and administrators. WGU also makes extensive use of faculty advisers for course, career, and personal student services. State funding was used for the creation of WGU, but it has evolved into a self-supporting institution dependent upon tuition, gifts, and grants. Using mostly an ALN model, WGU has flourished, serving more than 55,000 online students from all 50 states. In addition, a number of other states including Indiana, Texas, Missouri, Tennessee, and Washington have created state-affiliated WGUs that offer the same programs and curricula as WGU.

WGU has not been without its critics and has come under scrutiny for a number of issues. For instance, in a CBS *Money Watch* ranking of best and worst college completion rates, WGU was ranked as having the lowest graduation rate, at 6.5 percent (O'Shaughnessy, 2012). WGU also has a very high student to faculty ratio of 47:1 (Career Index, 2015). Johann Neem, in an op-ed piece for the *Seattle Times*, criticized WGU's basic premise:

> WGU does not offer a college education. A college education is about going through a process that leaves students transformed. That's why it takes time. Learning is hard—brain research demonstrates that real learning requires students to struggle with difficult material under the consistent guidance of good teachers. WGU denies students these opportunities. In fact, its advertisements pander to prospective students by offering them credit for what they already know rather than promising to teach them something new.
>
> *(Neem, 2011)*

WGU's role may be to provide a nonprofit alternative to for-profit higher education. Gravois (2011), in an article titled "The College For-Profits Should Fear," makes the case that many students who might have enrolled in an online program at a for-profit college find WGU a much more viable alternative. It is less expensive, it provides credit for life experience, and it has fairly good advisement services. Gravois commented:

> The school's enrollment was verging on 25,000 students—up from just 500 in 2003—and its yearly revenues had climbed from $32 million to $111 million. And if 2010 was the worst of years for the for-profits, it was among WGU's best.
>
> *(Gravois, 2011)*

WGU is an interesting model, and the fact that it is being emulated in a number of other universities gives credence to its approach. In fact, the concept of competency-based online education is receiving a good deal of attention across the country. Southern New Hampshire was a struggling university with 2,000 residential students in 2009. A new president initiated a competency-based online program, and enrollments grew to almost 40,000 in five years (Kahn, 2014). It may be that this approach is more appropriate for a niche population of older students who are interested in earning a degree as quickly as possible. Regardless, WGU was made possible by the online education technology movement of the 1990s and has made its mark.

Online Education Opens a Number of Policy Issues

The emergence of online education in the 1990s forced colleges and universities to revisit a number of existing bylaws, governance documents, and collective bargaining contracts to ensure that institutional policies related to curriculum approval, workload, copyright, intellectual property, accreditation compliance, and faculty observations and evaluation were not being bypassed or infringed upon. If a college had already developed a substantial distance education program, some of these policy issues may have been addressed. However, those colleges mounting new online education initiatives found themselves needing to review both internal as well as external compliance policies.

Intellectual property, for instance, received new attention when faculty started to move course materials from their brick-and-mortar classrooms to online delivery platforms. Course content delivered in a physical classroom is not easily duplicated, while online materials in electronic form can easily be used by others. As a result, there was renewed interest on the part of both administration and faculty in determining which party owned these materials. This was especially the case where administration provided incentives (i.e., release time, stipends, new equipment) to encourage faculty to develop online courses. While most cases were handled amicably, it took time for some intellectual property policies to be resolved. In the City University of New York, for example, a moratorium on any online distance learning development was declared in June 1997 by the Professional Staff Congress, the faculty union, over a number of issues including intellectual property rights. Although a temporary memorandum of understanding was agreed to in 1998, it took approximately five years of negotiations for a final agreement on a new intellectual property policy to be enacted.

A review of copyright infringement laws became important as well. The facility with which the Internet made it possible to copy and paste and to download files and media had made many institutions vulnerable to copyright infringement. In addition, having materials online and open to the public also made it easier for infringement to be detected by copyright owners. While the principle of fair use provided for some flexibility, instructional designers and faculty needed to be aware of what was allowed before a copyright infringement occurred and to ensure that online materials were in compliance. The much debated Digital Millennium Copyright Act of 1998 clarified a number of issues and allowed certain exemptions for nonprofit library, archive and educational institutions, but it was not a carte blanche to completely bypass copyright laws.

Accreditation of online programs also became an important issue as colleges converted or added entire programs for online delivery. In 1998, the regional accreditation bodies began joint meetings to discuss issues of accreditation of online learning programs. In 2001, they adopted a common set of broad standards to determine if a college is well suited to offer online courses and if it is using the best practices to deliver them (Kelderman, 2011). Those guidelines, which were revised in 2006, recommended, for example, that colleges show evidence that faculty members who teach online courses have been appropriately trained to use the medium and that student-support services were sufficient. Initially, in addition to the regular cycle of accreditation evaluation, new cycles were developed for distance education. Eventually, evaluation criteria developed for online programs were integrated into the traditional accreditation criteria.

There has also been an ongoing debate about the accreditation of fully online, for-profit colleges, some of which were never accredited for a variety of reasons associated with a lack of support services, high percentages of part-time faculty, and low program completion rates. Many of these colleges remain unaccredited by any of the major regional accreditation bodies.

A number of other policy issues have evolved since the initiation of online education and became more prominent after the 1990s. These will be discussed in more detail in later chapters.

Summary

This chapter described the first wave of online and blended learning that occurred in the 1990s. Internet technology, which was born in the 1960s and 1970s, evolved as a result of the collaboration of government, private enterprise, and higher education. By the 1990s, Internet technology ushered in new approaches for most enterprises, including higher education. The first colleges and universities interested in online learning development during this decade were those that had well-established distance education programs using other modalities such as television, radio, and course packs. Public institutions such as Athabasca University, the Penn State World Campus, the SUNY Learning Network, and the University of Maryland–University College were early leaders in the development of online education programs. For-profit colleges such as the University of Phoenix, a subsidiary of the Apollo Education Group, also invested heavily in developing fully online education programs. The most common technology of the first wave was based on slow-speed, dial-up modem lines. As a result, many of the earliest online learning courses were text-based and relied heavily on asynchronous learning. The main pedagogical model of the time was an interactive, asynchronous learning network (ALN) made popular by the Alfred P. Sloan Foundation's grant program, titled *Anytime/Anyplace Learning*. Online education also provided the vehicle for new or expanded models of higher education. One of the more interesting new models was the Western Governors University (WGU) which was conceived in 1995 when nineteen members of the Western Governors Association decided to establish a university that would be competency-based and would offer programs that were fully online. By the end of the 1990s, online education began to move into mainstream higher education. Policy issues related to intellectual property, copyright, and accreditation emerged as online education migrated to mainstream public and private colleges and universities.

References

Alfred P. Sloan Foundation Website (2015). Retrieved from: http://www.sloan.org Accessed: April 13, 2015.

Allen, E. & Seaman, J. (2014). *Grade change: Tracking online education in the United States.* Needham, MA: Babson College Survey Research Group.

Career Index (2015). *Western Governors University.* Career Index Website. Retrieved from: http://www.educationnews.org/career-index/western-governors-university/ Accessed: April 18, 2015.

Carr, N. (2014). *The shallows: What the Internet is doing to our brains.* New York: W.W. Norton and Company.

Digital Millennium Copyright Act (December 1998). *U.S. Copyright Office Summary.* Washington, DC: U.S. Copyright Office. Retrieved from: http://www.copyright.gov/legislation/dmca.pdf Accessed: April 19, 2015.

Garrison, D.R., Anderson, T., & Archer, W. (2000). Critical inquiry in a text-based environment: Computer conferencing in higher education. *The Internet and Higher Education, 2*, 87–105.

Gomory, R. (2015). Ralph Gomory Website. Retrieved from: http://www.ralphgomory.com Accessed: April 10, 2015.

Gravois, J. (September/October 2011). The college for-profits should fear. *Washington Monthly.* Retrieved from: http://www.washingtonmonthly.com/magazine/september october_2011/features/the_college_forprofits_should031640.php?page=all Accessed: April 18, 2015.

Hanford, E. (2012). The case against for-profit colleges and universities. *American Public Media, RadioWorks.* Retrieved from: http://americanradioworks.publicradio.org/features/tomorrows-college/phoenix/case-against-for-profit-schools.html Accessed: April 17, 2015.

Internet Live Stats (2015). Internet Live Stats Website. Retrieved from: http://www.internetlivestats.com/internet-users/ Accessed: April 11, 2015.

Isaacson, W. (2014). *The innovators: How a group of hackers, geniuses, and geeks created the digital revolution.* New York: Simon & Schuster.

Kahn, G. (January 2, 2014). The Amazon of higher education. *Slate.* Retrieved from: http://www.slate.com/articles/life/education/2014/01/southern_new_hampshire_university_how_paul_leblanc_s_tiny_school_has_become.html Accessed: April 18, 2015.

Keen, A. (2015). *The Internet is not the answer.* New York: Atlantic Monthly Press.

Kelderman, E. (November 6, 2011). Online programs face new demands from accreditors. *The Chronicle of Higher Education.* Retrieved from: http://chronicle.com/article/Online-Programs-Face-New/129608/ Accessed: April 20, 2015.

Kinser, K. (2006). *From Main Street to Wall Street: The transformation of for-profit higher education.* San Francisco: Jossey-Bass.

Licklider, J.C.R. (1960). Man-machine symbiosis. *IRE Transactions on Human Factors in Electronics, HFE-1,* 4–11, March 1960.

Licklider, J.C.R. (1963). Memorandum for members and affiliates of the intergalactic computer network. Retrieved from: http://www.kurzweilai.net/memorandum-for-members-and-affiliates-of-the-intergalactic-computer-network Accessed: April 14, 2015.

Licklider, J.C.R. & Clark, W.E. (May 1962). On-line man-computer communication." In *AFIPS Proceedings, 1962 Spring Joint Computer Conference* (vol. 21, pp. 113–128). New York: Spartan Books.

Neem, J. (April 1, 2011). Online university doesn't offer 'real college education.' *Seattle Times*. Retrieved from: http://www.seattletimes.com/opinion/online-university-doesnt-offer-real-college-education/ Accessed: April 18, 2015.

Noble, D. (2003). *Digital diploma mills: The automation of higher education*. New York: Monthly Review Press.

OLC Quality Framework (2015). The Online Learning Consortium Website. Retrieved from: http://onlinelearningconsortium.org/5-pillars/ Accessed: April 14, 2015.

O'Shaughnessy, L. (2012). Fifty colleges with the best and worst graduation rates. *CBS Money Watch Website*. Retrieved from: http://www.cbsnews.com/news/50-private-colleges-with-best-worst-grad-rates/ Accessed: April 18, 2015.

Picciano, A.G. (2013). *Pioneering higher education's digital future: An evaluation of the Alfred P. Sloan Foundation's Anytime, Anyplace Learning Program* (1992–2012). Unpublished monograph January 12, 2013. New York: Graduate Center of the City University of New York. Available at: http://aalp-sloan-report.gc.cuny.edu/pdf/Evaluation%20of%20Anytime%20Anyplace%20Learning%20Program.pdf.

Softky, M. (October 11, 2000). Building the Internet: Bob Taylor won the National Medal of Technology "for visionary leadership in the development of modern computing technology." *The Almanac*. Retrieved from: http://www.almanacnews.com/morgue/2000/2000_10_11.taylor.html Accessed: April 13, 2015.

Swan, K., Garrison, R., & Richardson, J. (2009). A constructivist approach to online learning: The community of inquiry framework. In C.R. Payne (Ed.), *Information technology and constructivism in higher education: Progressive learning frameworks* (pp. 43–57). Hershey, PA: IGI Global.

Taylor, J.C. (2001). Fifth generation distance education. *Instructional Science and Technology*, 4(1), 1–14. Retrieved from: http://eprints.usq.edu.au/136/ Accessed: May 1, 2015.

Toffler, A. (1970). *Future shock*. New York: Bantam Books.

Toffler, A. (1984). *The third wave*. New York: Bantam Books.

Toffler, A. (1991). *Powershift: Knowledge, wealth and violence at the edge of the 21st century*. New York: Bantam Books.

University of Phoenix (2015). About the University of Phoenix Website. Retrieved from: http://www.phoenix.edu/about_us/about_university_of_phoenix/history.html Accessed: April 17, 2015.

Western Governors University (2015). The unique history of Western Governors University. Retrieved from: http://www.wgu.edu/about_WGU/WGU_story Accessed: April 18, 2015.

6

THE SECOND WAVE

Blending Into the Mainstream (Early 2000s)

By the early 2000s, the majority of people in the United States were able to afford high-speed connectivity to the Internet using cable modems or digital subscriber lines (DSL). This enhanced connectivity opened up the possibility of incorporating multimedia (pictures, sound, video) into online learning development. Social media such as blogs, wikis, podcasts, YouTube, and Facebook also came on the scene, allowing for greater interaction. Faculty from around the world began sharing learning tools and objects in digital depositories such as Merlot. Perhaps the most important development of this second wave was that Internet technology was no longer seen solely as a vehicle for distance education providers but could be used in mainstream education in almost any class and for teaching any subject matter. Course/learning management systems were acquired by the vast majority of colleges and universities. It was estimated in 2003 that more than 80 percent of the universities and colleges in the United States were utilizing CMS/LMS (Harrington, Gordon, & Shibik, 2004). If these systems were not purchased, institutions contracted out for cloud-based CMS/LMS services. The predominant pedagogical model of this wave was blended learning, as faculty began to use online facilities to enhance their courses and to replace seat time in regular face-to-face courses. This was particularly true in the public and nonprofit private sectors. Courses were designed to take pedagogical advantage of the best of the fully online and face-to-face modalities. In the for-profit sector, fully online courses continued to dominate program offerings.

Three Scenarios

Scenario One

J.S. taught an introduction to sociology course (three credits/three hours) at a large public urban university. He considered himself a good lecturer and tried to provide material that provoked questions on the part of the students. When he first started teaching this course in 1991, the average enrollment was about twenty students. By 2007, as the overall college enrollment increased while budgets stagnated, his section sizes grew to thirty-five to forty students. He was frequently frustrated because he would run out of class time and was not always able to answer all the students' questions. He sometimes curtailed the time he took to answer questions in order to cover the material for the day's lesson. He read about the idea of flipping or inverting a class, wherein more of his lecturing would be provided by videos and more class time would be devoted to discussions of the content. He met with an instructional designer and developed a series of short videos (twelve to fifteen minutes) on the key topics of his course. Rather than meeting for three hours, his classes were reduced to meeting for two hours in a traditional face-to-face session, but students were required to have viewed one or more of his videos and read assigned material before class. His two hours of class time were devoted extensively to discussions of the video topics and answering student questions. He found he had much more control and could use his class time for more in-depth question and answer activities. Students were also able to view the videos multiple times if needed to improve understanding of the material.

Scenario Two

D.G. is an associate professor at a small community college where she teaches chemistry. In 2005, she applied for and received a grant from her college's instructional technology initiative to develop an online course. Previously, she had used a learning management system to develop some online materials, including several simulations of chemical lab experiments. As part of her grant, she refined her online course materials and developed an entire course in organic chemistry. The most difficult part of her online course development was simulating complex experiments that normally were conducted in "wet" laboratories. To solve this problem, D.G. decided to use commercially available software to supplement her own "home-grown" simulations. D.G. offered the fully online organic chemistry course for two semesters, and while she was happy with the result, she also was conflicted: perhaps students would be better served by doing lab experiments in face-to-face situations. When the grant expired, she decided that she preferred to teach part of the course online and part (the lab component) face-to-face.

Scenario Three

C.S., the program coordinator of a fully online masters of business administration (MBA) at a college specializing in adult and distance learning brought her full-time faculty together in 2003 to consider offering a variation of the program that would require students to meet face-to-face. Although the fully online MBA program was well enrolled and considered successful, evaluations of the program indicated that students would like opportunities to meet with their course mates. The faculty were well experienced in online learning but tended to agree with C.S.'s suggestion. A small committee was formed to work out the logistics and details. One year later a "blended" version of the online MBA program was offered in which students met once a month on Saturdays in face-to-face mode at the college. During the Saturday meetings, three hours in the morning were reserved for traditional face-to-face classroom instruction, and the rest of the day including lunch was reserved for group work, project presentations, and student socializing/bonding. The new "blended" program has been very successful, especially among students who live within a 150-mile radius of the college. While the enrollment in the fully online MBA program has decreased, the number of students in the blended program has more than made up for the loss. In fact, in a survey of new students, many of them would have enrolled in the fully online program but liked the idea of meeting face to face once a month.

These three scenarios represent different approaches to using online technology to supplement or replace some aspect of instruction. While very different in design, they all come under the common concept of blended learning. With the proliferation of CMS/LMSs, there was also a growing acceptance of the use of these tools for supplementing traditional classes, with no intention of replacing face-to-face time. Web-enhanced courses developed and grew at most institutions. Some of this development increased faculty "efficiency"—making it easier to share a syllabus or course readings while at the same time leading to greater faculty understanding of these systems. During this period, student enrolments in blended learning courses soared, but accurate data was impossible to collect mainly because a generally accepted definition of blended learning did not and still does not exist. It is safe to say that many millions of students were enrolled in courses that used online technology in one form or another.

Blended Learning Definition

Given its multifaceted evolution, blended learning defies definition. There is not even agreement on the nomenclature. Terms used interchangeably include blended learning, hybrid learning, web-enhanced courses, mixed-mode learning, technology-mediated instruction, and flipped classes. At its core, blended learning is the practice of using both online and in-person learning experiences when teaching students. However, this definition is generally considered too simplistic and does not reflect the variety of blended learning approaches.

Blended learning comes in many different flavors, styles, and applications. It means different things to different people. The word "blended" implies a mixture more than a combination of components. When a picture is pasted above a paragraph of text, a presentation is created that may be more informative to the viewer or reader, but the picture and text remain intact and can be individually discerned. On the other hand, when two cans of different colored paints are mixed, the new paint will look different from either of the original colors.

In fact, if the paint is mixed well, neither of the original colors will continue to exist. Similar situations exist in blended learning. The mix can be a simple separation of part of a course into an online component. For instance, in a course that meets for three weekly contact hours, two hours might meet in a traditional classroom while the equivalent of one weekly hour is conducted online. The two modalities for this course are carefully separated, and although they may overlap, they can still be distinguished from one another. In other forms of blended courses and programs, the modalities are not so easily differentiated. Consider an online program that offers three online courses in a semester that all students are required to take. The courses meet for three consecutive five-week sessions. However, students do a collaborative fifteen-week project that overlaps the courses. The students are expected to maintain regular communication with one another through email and group discussion boards. They also are required to meet face-to-face once a month on Saturdays, where course materials from the online courses are further presented and discussed, and some sessions are devoted to group project work. These activities begin to blur the modalities in a new mixture or blend where the individual parts are not as discernable as they once were. Add to this the increasing popularity of integrating videoconferencing, podcasting, YouTube videos, wikis, blogs, and social media into class work, and the definition of blended learning becomes very fluid. In the broadest sense, blended learning can be defined or conceptualized as a wide variety of technology/media integrated with conventional, face-to-face classroom activities (see Figure 6.1). However, this conceptualization serves as a guideline and cannot be viewed as an absolute, limiting declaration. Also, while the term "blended learning" was developed to refer specifically to courses, it also can apply to entire academic programs.

In an article titled "Can Blended Learning Be Redeemed?" Oliver and Trigwell (2005) contended that the term "blended"—when associated with learning—should be abandoned or reconceived, especially as applied to research. They further stated that the multiple definitions in the literature were not at all helpful but rather quite confusing and redundant. They summarized the crux of their argument as follows:

> The term "blended learning" is ill-defined and inconsistently used. Whilst its popularity is increasing, its clarity is not. Under any current definition, it is either incoherent or redundant as a concept. Building a tradition of research around the term becomes an impossible project, since without a common conception of its meaning, there can be no coherent way of synthesizing the findings of the studies, let alone developing a consistent theoretical framework with which to interpret data.
>
> *(Oliver & Trigwell, 2005, p. 24)*

In sum, a definition of blended learning was and continues to be elusive.

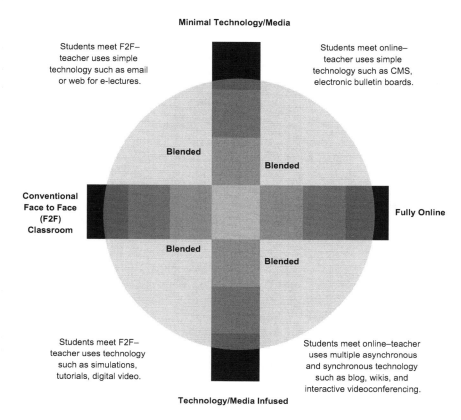

Minimal Technology/Media

Students meet F2F–
teacher uses simple
technology such as email
or web for e-lectures.

Students meet online–
teacher uses simple
technology such as CMS,
electronic bulletin boards.

Blended

Blended

**Conventional
Face to Face
(F2F)
Classroom**

Fully Online

Blended

Blended

Students meet F2F–
teacher uses technology
such as simulations,
tutorials, digital video.

Students meet online–teacher
uses multiple asynchronous
and synchronous technology
such as blog, wikis, and
interactive videoconferencing.

Technology/Media Infused

FIGURE 6.1 Blended Learning Conceptualization

Source: Picciano, A.G. (2009). Blending with purpose: The multimodal model. *Journal of the Research Center for Educational Technology*, 5(1). Kent, OH: Kent State University.

Blended Learning Models

Just as there has been little agreement on a definition for blended learning, there has also been little agreement on design models. In one review of blended learning models, Moskal, Dziuban and Hartman (2013) concluded:

> Blended learning models may be found in higher education (Kaur & Ahmed, 2005), industry (Executive Conversation, 2010), K–12 education (Keller, Ehman, & Bonk, 2004), the military (Bonk, Olson, Wisher, & Orvis, 2002) and in many other sectors. There are formulations based on organizational infrastructures (Khan, 2001) that concern themselves with such things as development time, program combinations, cost factors, multiple locations and institutions, and landscape considerations. Learning environment approaches (Norberg, Dziuban, & Moskal, 2011) foster such issues as

interaction, constructivism, communication, learning communities, learning enhancements, cognition and performance support, as well as synchronicity. Added value constructs (Graham, 2006) deal with elements such as enhancement, presence, access, reusability, transformation, replacement and process emphasis. Graham (2006) uses this approach to define enabling blends that increase access, enhancing blends that incrementally improve pedagogy, and transforming blends that create fundamental paradigm shifts. Mayadas and Picciano (2007) took the notion one step further coining the term "localness" as an amalgam of locations, courses, and course modalities (blended, online, face-to-face, and lecture capture) affording students the opportunity to avail themselves of comparable educational opportunities whether they are on campus, near campus or far from campus by blending those elements. All these approaches are definitional in some respects but differ in their emphasis. Most of them assert that blended learning offers potential for improving the manner in which we deal with content, social interaction, reflection, higher order thinking and problem solving, collaborative learning, and more authentic assessment.

(Moskal et al., 2013, p. 16)

Among the models reviewed, it may be worthwhile to examine Graham's (2005) three categories of blending learning models, which he labeled:

- Enabling blends
- Enhancing blends
- Transforming blends

Enabling blends primarily focused on issues of access and convenience for students, for example, allowing students to take some of their coursework asynchronously and at times more accommodating to their work schedules or family obligations, with little changes to course materials or pedagogical approaches. Many of the early enabling blends focused on making course content available online. Enhancing blends provided for modest changes to course materials or pedagogical approaches but did not radically change the way teaching and learning occurs. In some of these cases, faculty and instructional designers supplemented existing course material used for traditional, face-to-face courses with online delivery of course materials and added pedagogical features, such as the use of discussion boards or blogs for student exchanges and collaborative activities. Transforming blends provided for a major change of the pedagogical approach and a redesign of course materials to take advantage of "the best of the both worlds" of online and face-to-face modalities. All aspects of course content as well as pedagogy approaches are reconsidered and redeveloped as needed. Multiple online features such as blogs, wikis, and media are considered. There is also an emphasis on providing students with the facilities to develop their own knowledge rather than simply receiving information from an instructor. To some degree, the three models represent a progression of blended learning models in terms of the extent of pedagogical redesign that go into a blended program. In the final analysis, Graham's categories of models appropriately found that blended learning was based on pedagogical approaches rather than on distance education, student access, or cost-beneficial considerations.

Blending with Pedagogical Purpose

Figure 6.2 depicts a model, Blending With Pedagogical Purpose, in which pedagogical objectives and activities drive the approaches that faculty use in designing blended learning courses. The model also suggests that blending objectives, activities, and approaches within multiple modalities might be most effective for and appeal to a wide range of students. This model typifies many of the design approaches that evolved during the second wave (Blending Into the Mainstream) of online education. It served as the focus and theme for a conference on blended learning hosted by the University of Illinois-Chicago in 2008. The model presents six basic pedagogical objectives/activities and approaches for achieving them. It is

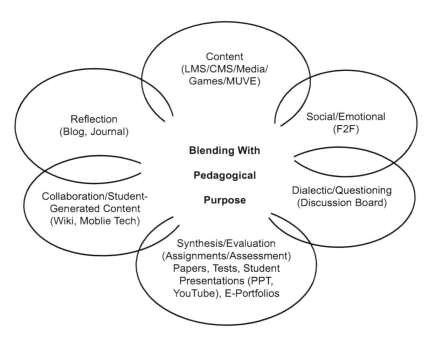

FIGURE 6.2 Blending With Pedagogical Purpose (The Multimodal Model)

Source: Picciano, A.G. (2009). Blending with purpose: The multimodal model. *Journal of the Research Center for Educational Technology*, 5(1). Kent, OH: Kent State University.

a given that other objectives can be added where appropriate. The most important feature of this model is that instructors need to carefully consider their objectives and understand how to apply the technologies and approaches that will work best for their students. A quick review of the objectives used in the model and their concomitant technology would be helpful in understanding the overall model.

Content is one of the primary drivers of instruction, and there are many ways in which content can be delivered and presented. While much of what is taught is delivered linguistically (teacher speaks—students listen; or teacher writes—students read), this does not have to be the case either in face-to-face or online environments. Certain subject areas such as science are highly dependent upon using visual simulations to demonstrate processes and systems. The humanities, especially art, history, and literature, can be greatly enhanced by rich digital images. Increasingly, course management systems such as *Blackboard* or *Moodle* provide basic content delivery mechanisms for blended learning. CMS software easily handles the delivery of a variety of media including text, video, and audio. Multiuser virtual environments (MUVEs) and gaming are also evolving and playing a larger role in providing instructional content. In providing and presenting content, the Blending with Pedagogical Purpose model suggests that multiple technologies and media be utilized.

The Blending with Pedagogical Purpose model posits that instruction is not always just about learning content or a skill but is also about supporting students *socially and emotionally*. Perhaps more readily recognized for younger K–12 students, social and emotional development is an important part of anyone's education. Faculty who have taught advanced graduate courses know that the students, even at this advanced level, frequently need someone with whom to speak, whether for understanding a complex concept or providing advice on career and professional opportunities. While fully online courses and programs have evolved to the point where faculty can provide some social and emotional support in blended courses and programs, this might best be provided in a face-to-face mode.

Dialectics or questioning is an important activity that allows faculty to probe what students know and to help refine their knowledge. The Socratic Method remains one of the major techniques used in instruction, and many successful teachers are proud of their ability to stimulate discussion by asking the "right" questions to help students think critically about a topic or issue. These questions serve to refine and narrow a discussion to very specific "points" or aspects of the topic at hand and are not meant to be open-ended "anybody can say anything at any time" activities. For dialectic and questioning activities, a simple-to-use threaded electronic discussion board is as or more effective than most other approaches. Research has continuously shown that asynchronous online discussion boards are the most prominent mechanism for supporting learning in an online environment (Rovai, 2007; Darabi, Liang, Suryavanshi, & Yurekli, 2013; Thomas, 2013). A well-organized discussion board activity generally seeks to present a topic or issue and have students respond to questions and provide their own perspectives while evaluating and responding to the opinions of others. The simple, direct visual of the "thread" also allows students to see how the entire discussion or lesson has evolved. In sum, for instructors wishing to focus attention and dialogue on a specific topic, the main vehicle has been and continues to be the electronic discussion board.

Incorporating *reflection* can be a powerful pedagogical strategy under the right circumstances. There is an extensive body of scholarship on the "reflective teacher" and the "reflective learner." While reflection can be a deeply personal activity, the ability to share one's reflections with others can be most beneficial. Pedagogical activities that require students to reflect on what they are learning and to share their reflections with their teachers and fellow students extend and enrich reflection. Blogs and blogging, whether as group exercises or as individual journaling activities, are evolving as appropriate tools for students to reflect on their learning and other aspects of course activities.

The *collaborative learning* concept has been evolving for decades. In face-to-face classes, group work has grown in popularity and become commonplace in many courses. Many professional programs such as business administration, education, health science, and social work rely heavily on collaborative learning for group problem solving. In the past, the logistics and time needed for effective collaboration in face-to-face classes were sometimes problematic. However, email and other electronic communications alleviated some of these logistical problems. More recently, wikis have grown significantly in popularity and are becoming a staple in group projects and writing assignments. Furthermore, unlike group work, which typically ends up on the instructor's desk when delivered in paper form, wikis allow students to generate content that can be shared with others during and beyond the end of a semester. Papers and projects developed with wikis can pass seamlessly from one group to another and from one class to another.

Finally, perhaps the most important component of the Blending With Pedagogical Purpose model is *synthesizing, evaluating, and assessing* learning. CMS/LMSs and other online tools provide a number of mechanisms for assisting in this area. Papers, tests, assignments, and portfolios are among the major methods used for assessing student learning and are increasingly being done electronically. Essays and term projects can pass back and forth between teacher and student without ever being printed on paper. Oral classroom presentations are giving way to YouTube videos and podcasts. The portfolio is evolving into an electronic multimedia presentation of images, video, and audio that goes far beyond the three-inch paper-filled binder. Weekly class discussions that take place on discussion boards or blogs provide the instructor with an electronic record that can be reviewed over and over again to examine how students have participated and progressed over time. They are also most helpful to instructors in assessing their own teaching and in reviewing what worked and what did not work in a class. In sum, online technology allows for a more seamless sharing of evaluation and assessment activities and provides an ongoing record that can be referred to over and over again by both students and teachers.

The six components of the model as described should blend together in an integrated manner that appears as seamless as possible for students. As mentioned earlier in this chapter, blending should be more a mixture of different colors of paint to create new colors or new learning environments rather than cutting and pasting visibly separate combinations of images, text, and other media or material. Furthermore, not every course must incorporate all of the activities and approaches of the model. The pedagogical objectives of a course should drive the activities and hence the approaches. For example, not every course needs to require students to do group work or rely on reflective activities. Finally, beyond examining individual courses, faculty and instructional designers should consider examining their entire academic program to determine which components of the model best fit which courses to cohesively serve overall programmatic goals and objectives.

The Efficacy of Blended Learning

In 2007, the United States Department of Education (U.S. DOE) contracted with SRI International to conduct a meta-analysis of the effects of online learning on student achievement. Barbara Means led the project team of more than twenty individuals. The project was completed and a report prepared in 2009 and revised in 2010. As part of its work, the project team conducted a systematic search of the research literature published from 1996 through July 2008.

The overall finding of the meta-analysis was that classes with online learning (whether taught completely online or blended) on average produce stronger student learning outcomes than classes with solely face-to-face instruction. The mean effect size for all 50 contrasts was $+0.20, p < .001$ (U.S. DOE, p. 18). It is important to keep in mind that an effect size of $+0.20$ is considered small but is nonetheless positive. However, the researchers for the meta-analysis went a step further by separating the findings for fully online versus blended learning. To quote:

> The conceptual framework for this study, which distinguishes between purely online and blended forms of instruction, calls for creating subsets of the effect estimates to address two more nuanced research questions:
>
> 1. *How does the effectiveness of online learning compare with that of face-to-face instruction?*
>
> Looking only at the 27 Category 1 effects that compared a purely online condition with face-to-face instruction, analysts found a mean effect of $+0.05, p = .46$.
>
> This finding is similar to that of previous summaries of distance learning (generally from pre-Internet studies), in finding that instruction conducted entirely online is as effective as classroom instruction but no better.

2. *Does supplementing face-to-face instruction with online instruction enhance learning?*

For the 23 Category 2 contrasts that compared blended conditions of online plus face-to-face learning with face-to-face instruction alone, the mean effect size of +0.35 was significant ($p < .0001$). Blends of online and face-to-face instruction, on average, had stronger learning outcomes than did face-to-face instruction alone.

A test of the difference between Category 1 and Category 2 studies found that the mean effect size was larger for contrasts pitting blended learning against face-to-face instruction ($g+ = +0.35$) than for those of purely online versus face-to-face instruction ($g+ = +0.05$); the difference between the two subsets of studies was statistically significant ($Q = 8.37, p < .01$).

(U.S. DOE, p. 12)

This study was one of the first well-financed, large-scale research projects to examine the efficacy of face-to-face, fully online, and blended learning. Its conclusion, that the effect size comparing blended learning and face-to-face instruction is much stronger, at +0.35, gave significant credibility to the blended learning movement in higher education. Its general acceptance supported the insights of many faculty using blended learning techniques. However, there was one small caveat in the findings. The researchers commented later in the study that some of the difference in the effects of blended learning might be attributed to more time on task than in fully-online or face-to-face instruction. This too resonated with faculty and instructional designers working in blended learning environments. In many cases, the blended course designs did require more time for participation on the part of both teachers and students. This has not been studied carefully, but there is probably some truth to the speculation that faculty and instructional designers were adding additional components to blended courses that resulted in more time on instructional tasks.

Before concluding this section, it might also be appropriate to comment on research that compares modalities of learning. The U.S. DOE report recognized the important work of Richard Clark (1983, 1985, 1989), who proposed in 1983 that technology, or any medium, was basically a vehicle carrying an instructional substance and that real improvement in achievement only comes with improving the substance, not the vehicle. Unlike Marshall McLuhan's thesis that the "medium is the message," Clark posited that in education the message or content is what matters. Clark's position has been challenged over the years by a number of researchers such as Robert Kozma (1991, 1994a, 1994b) and Jack Koumi (1994), who see the medium as integral to the delivery of instruction. The two differing opinions on this issue remain to this day, and the "great debate" continues. As an indication of the ongoing nature and importance of this debate, a search of "Clark vs. Kozma" on Google provides over a million URLs, many of which refer to websites and blogs created in the past several years. Anyone interested in the effects of technology on learning would be well served by reading and rereading the cited articles by Clark, Kozma, and Koumi. Most recently, the tide seems to be shifting against Clark, mainly because his position was developed during the 1980s and '90s, when instructional technology was much less sophisticated than it is today.

Online Education Spurs Policy and Regulation Issues!

As online and blended learning became more prevalent at the beginning of the 21st century, policy considerations came to the fore. Higher education policy can evolve in many different ways, mainly because no single agency in the United States has complete jurisdiction. Two major policy developments that evolved in the early 2000s focused on accreditation and providing greater access to online education.

Accreditation

The main purpose of accreditation is to ensure and improve the quality of higher education. In addition to quality assurance, Judith Eaton (2012), president of the Council of Higher Education Accreditation (CHEA), identifies three main functions of accreditation as:

1. Enable students to transfer credits from one institution to another.
2. Provide access to federal and state funding.
3. Engender private sector confidence.

How well the accreditation system in the United States has fulfilled its purpose is the subject of a good deal of debate, with some supporting the current processes that are independent of government or political influences while others believe the processes are broken and require more governmental oversight and involvement. The issues are complex and require lengthy examination beyond the scope of this chapter. Readers are encouraged to review these issues as presented by Paul Gaston (2014) in *Higher Education Accreditation: How it is Changing, Why it Must.*

Unlike most other countries where the accreditation of higher education is conducted by a governmental agency, in the United States it is conducted by several independent accrediting bodies. First, regional accreditation agencies accredit all degree-granting public and most nonprofit private institutions and some for-profit private institutions. Second, there are specialized accreditation organizations that accredit programs in specific disciplines, usually in professional areas such as health and nursing. Third, there are national accrediting organizations that accredit institutions and programs that are primarily career oriented. These tend to be mostly small, for-profit colleges. The vast majority of accrediting agencies are recognized by the Council of Higher Education Accreditation (CHEA) and the U.S. Department of Education. As online education entered the 21st century, a number of new issues related to academic quality arose for these accrediting bodies.

Judith Eaton, in an article in 2000 directed at "presidents, chancellors, other college and university administrators, and trustees," called on administrators to become informed on quality issues related to distance learning. She defined distance learning as, "online teaching and learning, as well as academic support and student support services that are electronically delivered" (Eaton, 2000). In the article, she went on to state:

> In the fluid and sometimes volatile environment created by distance learning, we at the Council for Higher Education Accreditation (CHEA)—the national coordinating body for national, regional, and specialized accreditation— struggle to bring some order to the avalanche of information about both distance learning and quality assurance.
>
> *(Eaton, 2000)*

Eaton was highlighting concerns that evolved as a result of significant enrollment increases in online education at the same time that policymakers and others questioned their academic quality. The major American accreditation organizations started adopting standards for online education programs that closely mirrored those established for traditional face-to-face programs; however, there were concerns that these standards were not accomplishing their purpose.

First, accreditation standards had been developed with the assumption that instruction was centered within a physical entity identified as a classroom in which a group of students and a teacher met for so many hours per week in a place called a college. Online learning and virtual environments did not operate in physical places or at specific times but in the electronic world of the Internet and World Wide Web. Basic questions arose such as:

- How do hours spent in online activities equate to time normally spent in a physical classroom?
- How does a professor know who is responding to a question on a discussion board?
- How often do students need to respond online to participate effectively or in a sense be "present" for online course activities?

These questions did not have simple answers and served to require policy makers including accreditation bodies to explore venues for agreement among the various stakeholders.

Second was the issue of whether academic program goals and objectives were being adequately met in online education environments and student outcomes were being properly assessed. The meta-analysis commissioned by the U.S. Department of Education and conducted by Barbara Means et al. in 2010, cited earlier in this chapter, supported the premise that learning experiences in online environments were comparable to those in face-to-face classes. This study, however, was conducted ten years after Eaton's comments. In the early 2000s, it was recognized that online learning presented challenges to doing proper assessment of student outcomes while also providing new opportunities. For example, testing and other forms of summative evaluations frequently used to assess student learning were problematic in an online mode. As a result, many online education providers established policies that written tests be conducted in proctored, face-to-face environments to ensure the identities of the students taking the tests. On the other hand, it was becoming apparent to those who taught online that the electronic medium also provided opportunities for enhancing and extending assessment activities. Online education environments that relied on programmed or self-paced instruction generally had built-in assessment of student mastery. A complete record of student progress including ongoing formative testing was a common element of this type of instruction and could meet the needs of many assessment programs. Even in more highly interactive, asynchronous online models where students were expected to communicate ideas, comments, and responses to questions via written electronic bulletin boards, instructors had a complete record of student participation in class activities. Instructors could integrate assessment into electronic group discussions that resulted in a complete record of the activity. Most of the popular course management software systems used in online learning allowed for the entire course to be archived. An instructor could simply add comments on his assessment of the students and create a complete record for future reference. This was not possible in most face-to-face class situations unless videotaping, audiotaping, or some other form of recording technique were used. In sum, online education environments posed challenges but also provided opportunities for doing assessment of student outcomes in new ways. The approach faculty and administrators were taking was to provide multiple means for doing assessment of learning in online mode while not necessarily changing the goals and objectives of their academic programs because of the different delivery formats.

Third, perhaps the most significant issue for policy makers concerned with the accreditation and program quality of online education was the increasing number of providers, some of questionable quality. David Noble, mentioned in Chapter Five, popularized the term "digital diploma mill" to characterize the less-than-scrupulous online education providers that essentially provided online degrees with minimum or no academic requirements. While no one questions that such institutions should be closed down for their fraudulent operations, they caused problems for legitimate online education providers who needed to accredit their programs. For example, Athabasca University, a well-respected, publicly supported Canadian open university with physical campuses in Athabasca, Edmonton, and

Calgary, Alberta, enrolled online students from around the world. It sought and received accreditation in the United States from the Middle States Association of Colleges and Schools in order to establish its legitimacy, to increase its appeal to American students, and to distance itself from the diploma mills. However, many unscrupulous distance education providers sought to avoid the accreditation process altogether. A whole industry of "fake accreditation agencies" evolved that catered specifically to granting accreditation to online diploma mills. By the end of the decade, a consumer group, GetEducation.com, listed more than sixty unrecognized or "fake" accreditation organizations (Get Educated.com, 2009).

Athabasca University was significantly different from the traditional not-for-profit public and private colleges that American accreditation agencies had typically served. The accreditation agencies were being challenged to develop appropriate evaluation procedures while policy makers questioned whether national, regional, and specialized accreditation as we knew it could assure quality in online programs. Many policymakers remained skeptical of the existing accreditation practices. Eaton (2000) concluded her article with a warning that CHEA as well as the accreditation agencies needed to provide more organization and coherence to the "plethora" of information and issues involved with quality assurance in online education and that "the price for misunderstanding . . . is very, very high." Such a misunderstanding could lead to greater involvement of governmental agencies in accreditation and other issues of accountability in higher education.

John Boehner, the chair of the U.S. Congress House Committee on Education and the Workforce during the rewriting the Higher Education Act (HEA), conducted hearings and raised several critical issues that were addressed as part of the reauthorization process for HEA. Among these issues were:

1. Accreditation policies
2. Transfer credit issues
3. Financial aid for distance learning students

He specifically recommended that:

> federal student aid programs must include more [distance learning] students and [that Congress] wanted to work with . . . accrediting organizations to assure the quality of these expanding programs.
>
> *(Boehner, 2005)*

Boehner's statement expressed concern over the quality of distance learning programs while opening up the possibility of expansion. Eaton's "price of misunderstanding" was greater involvement by the federal government in an attempt to ensure quality either directly or indirectly through accreditation. While the federal government did become more involved in attempts to assure academic quality, it left it to the private accrediting agencies to come up with new accreditation standards. As a result, there were extensive reviews, resulting in the developments of new accreditation standards that were subsequently integrated into the overall existing accreditation processes. Readers may wish to refer to the accreditation standards developed by one or more of the regional accrediting agencies. As an example, the Middle States Commission on Higher Education developed new accreditation standards in 2006 and revised them again in 2011 to identify hallmarks of quality and "to reflect the new distance education and correspondence education requirements of the Higher Education Opportunity Act of 2008" (Middle States Commission on Higher Education, 2006). Pages 57–60 specifically refer to distance education programs, an excerpt of which appears here:

> An accredited institution is expected to possess or demonstrate the following attributes or activities:
>
> - distance education or correspondence education offerings that meet institution-wide standards for quality of instruction, articulated expectations of student learning, academic rigor, and educational effectiveness;
> - consistency of the offerings via distance education or correspondence education with the institution's mission and goals, and the rationale for the distance education delivery;
> - planning that includes consideration of applicable legal and regulatory requirements;
> - demonstrated program coherence, including stated program learning outcomes appropriate to the rigor and breadth of the degree or certificate awarded;
> - demonstrated commitment to continuation of offerings for a period sufficient to enable admitted students to complete the degree or certificate in a publicized time frame;
> - assurance that arrangements with consortial partners or contractors do not compromise the integrity of the institution or of the educational offerings;
> - validation by faculty of any course materials or technology-based resources developed outside the institution;
> - a system of student identity verification that ensures that the student who participates in class or coursework is the same student who registers and receives academic credit; that students are notified at the time of registration or enrollment of any additional student charges associated with the verification of student identity; and that the identity verification process protects student privacy;
> - available, accessible, and adequate learning resources (such as a library or other information resources) appropriate to the offerings at a distance;
> - an ongoing program of appropriate orientation, training, and support for faculty participating in electronically delivered offerings;

- adequate technical and physical plant facilities, including appropriate staffing and technical assistance, to support electronic offerings; and
- periodic assessment of the impact of distance education on the institution's resources (human, fiscal, physical, etc.) and its ability to fulfill its institutional mission and goals.

(Middle States Commission on Higher Education, 2006, pp. 57–58)

The document goes on to establish acceptable evidence and criteria for evaluating these attributes.

Federal Policy Changes the Landscape of Online Higher Education

In 2006, the U.S. Congress lifted the "50 Percent" Rule that limited the number of distance education credits a student could take and qualify for financial aid. This change had the most significant impact on the evolution of online higher education of any other federal, state, or local policy. The biggest beneficiary of this change was the for-profit, higher education industry. The Education Trust estimated that the for-profit higher education sector in the United States grew 236 percent from 1998 to 2008, while the public and nonprofit sectors grew 21 percent and 17 percent, respectively (Lynch, Engle, & Cruz, 2010, p. 1). This increase in the enrollments in the for-profit colleges can be attributed largely to the change in the 50 Percent Rule. A brief review of how this policy evolved will provide insight into education policy development in what some have termed the "American education-industrial complex" (Picciano & Spring, 2013).

In 1992, the U.S. Congress enacted what became known as the 50 Percent Rule that required all colleges to deliver at least half their credits on a campus instead of online or via distance education in order to qualify for federal student aid. This rule was established after investigations showed that some for-profit trade schools were little more than diploma mills intended to harvest federal student loans (Dillon, March 1, 2006). In 2006, by adding eight lines of language as part of an 82,000-word budget bill, the U.S. Congress eliminated the 50 Percent Rule and allowed colleges, regardless of the number of courses held on campus or online, to qualify for federal student aid (Kirkham, July 29, 2011). Sam Dillon, two-time Pulitzer prize-winning reporter for the *New York Times*, characterized the passage of this bill as follows:

The Bush administration supported lifting the restriction on online education as a way to reach nontraditional students. Nonprofit universities and colleges opposed such a broad change, with some academics saying there was no proof that online education was effective. But for-profit colleges sought the rollback avidly.

"The power of the for-profits has grown tremendously," said Representative Michael N. Castle, Republican of Delaware, a member of the House

Education and Workforce Committee who has expressed concerns about continuing reports of fraud. "They have a full-blown lobbying effort and give lots of money to campaigns. In 10 years, the power of this interest group has spiked as much as any you'll find."

Sally L. Stroup, the assistant secretary of education who is the top regulator overseeing higher education, is a former lobbyist for the University of Phoenix, the nation's largest for-profit college, with some 300,000 students.

Two of the industry's closest allies in Congress are Representative John Boehner of Ohio, who just became House majority leader, and Representative Howard P. McKeon, Republican of California, who is replacing Mr. Boehner as chairman of the House education committee.

And the industry has hired well-connected lobbyists like A. Bradford Card, the brother of the [George W. Bush] White House chief of staff, Andrew H. Card Jr.

(Dillon, March 1, 2006)

Stroup was in a pivotal position to support or not to support this legislation. She authored a series of reports outlining an imperative to lift the online learning restrictions—a major impetus for Congress to ultimately scrap the 50 Percent Rule (Kirkham, July 29, 2011). Dillon characterized Stroup's evaluation as follows:

In a 2004 audit, the Education Department's inspector general said a 2003 report she provided to Congress on the program "contained unsupported, incomplete and inaccurate statements.

(Dillon, March 1, 2006)

Most were assertions that online education was working as well or better than traditional methods, with little risk. The inspector general, citing the collapse of one participant in the program, the Masters Institute in California, chided the Education Department for reporting that it had found "no evidence" that the rule change could pose hazards. Stroup formally disagreed with the inspector general. In an interview, she said a subordinate had written the report, although she had signed off on it. In a later report to Congress, the department [later] acknowledged "several possible risk factors" (Dillon, March 1, 2006).

Stroup started as a staffer on the House Education and Workforce Committee, then took a "$220,000-a-year job as a lobbyist for the Apollo Group, the parent company for the University of Phoenix and was then appointed by Bush as assistant secretary for post-secondary education . . . overseeing the central interest of her previous employer" (Kirkham, July 29, 2011).

While a number of congressmen, both Democrats and Republicans, received campaign funds from the for-profit lobby organizations, significant campaign donations were distributed to Boehner, Senator Mike Enzi (R-Wyoming), and

Representative Howard "Buck" McKeon (R–Calif.), the men who controlled the Education committees in the House and the Senate.

> McKeon held and sold stock for Corinthian Colleges Inc., . . . during the time he was crafting policies for the industry on the House Education committee, according to his required personal financial disclosure forms. . . . For the three election cycles between 2002 and 2006, those three lawmakers and their political action committees alone took in nearly one-fifth of the money donated to federal candidates and committees by the for-profit college industry.
>
> *(Kirkham, July 29, 2011)*

The result of the change in the 50 Percent Rule was dramatic. As mentioned earlier in this chapter, the for-profit higher education sector in the United States grew 236% from 1998 to 2008 (Lynch et al., 2010, p. 1). Enrollments soared at a number of for-profit colleges. For example, Bridgeport Inc. of San Diego purchased a small, failing college in Iowa and grew enrollment from fewer than 350 students in 2005 to more than 76,000 students by the end of 2010. Grand Canyon Education Inc. grew online enrollments from 3,000 in 2003 to more than 42,000 by the beginning of 2011. In general, approximately 25 percent of the revenue accrued by the for-profit industry from 2007 through 2011 was probably as a result of the change to the 50 Percent Rule. "Most of the large publicly traded institutions would not be able to exist the way they do today if that rule had not been taken away," said Kevin Kinser, an associate professor at the University at Albany who studies the history of for-profit higher education. "You have an entirely new revenue source that's been open to these institutions. . . . The cost goes down, the revenue goes up, and that's a pretty attractive investment vehicle" (Kirkham, July 29, 2011).

Summary

In this chapter, the second wave of online and blended learning in the early 2000s was presented. Online education evolved rapidly and moved into the mainstream. A variety of blended learning models that mixed and matched online and face-to-face modalities had a special appeal to traditional colleges and universities. Social media blossomed throughout the Internet world and was embraced by higher education, as well. In 2007, the United States Department of Education (U.S. DOE) contracted with SRI International to conduct a meta-analysis of the effects of online learning on student achievement. It was one of the first major studies to examine student outcomes across modalities (face-to-face, full online, and blended learning). The project was completed and a report prepared in 2009 and revised in 2010. The overall finding of the meta-analysis was that classes with online learning (whether taught completely online or blended) on average produce stronger student learning outcomes than did classes with solely face-to-face instruction. However, upon further analysis, the blended model had the highest positive effects on student learning. The chapter concluded with an examination of two major education policy developments related to accreditation and the elimination of the 50 Percent Rule, which greatly expanded student enrollments in online education, especially for many of the for-profit colleges and universities.

References

Boehner, J. (February 4, 2005). *Keynote address made at the 2005 CHEA Conference in Phoenix, AZ.* Source: CHEA Update, No. 18. Retrieved from: http://www.chea.org/Government/HEAupdate/CHEA_HEA18.htm Accessed: May 9, 2015.

Clark, R. (1983). Reconsidering research on learning from media. *Review of Educational Research, 53*(4), 445–459.

Clark, R. (1985). Evidence for confounding in computer-based instruction studies. *Educational Communications and Technology Journal, 33*(4), 249–262.

Clark, R. (1989). Current progress and future directions for research in instructional technology. *Educational Technology Research and Development, 37*(1), 57–66.

Darabi, A., Liang, X., Suryavanshi, R., & Yurekli, H. (2013). Effectiveness of online discussion strategies: A meta-analysis. *American Journal of Distance Education, 27*(4), 228–241.

Dillon, S. (March 1, 2006). Online colleges receive a boost from Congress. *New York Times.* Retrieved from: http://www.nytimes.com/2006/03/01/national/01educ.html?pagewanted=all Accessed: May 7, 2015.

Eaton, J.S. (2000). Assuring quality in distance learning. *The CHEA Chronicle, 3*(3). Retrieved from: http://www.chea.org/Chronicle/vol3/no3/focus.html Accessed: May 16, 2015.

Eaton, J.S. (2012). *An overview of United States accreditation.* Washington, DC: Council for Higher Education Accreditation.

Gaston, P. (2014). *Higher education accreditation: How it is changing, why it must.* Sterling, VA: Stylus Publications.

GetEducated.com (2009). List of fake college degree accreditation agencies. Retrieved from: http://www.geteducated.com/college-degree-mills/204-fake-agencies-for-college-accreditation Accessed: May 10, 2015.

Graham, C.R. (2005). Blended learning systems: Definition, current trends, and future directions. In C.J. Bonk & C.R. Graham (Eds.), *Handbook of blended learning: Global perspectives, local designs* (pp. 3–21). San Francisco, CA: Pfeiffer Publishing.

Harrington, C.F., Gordon, S.A., & Shibik, T.J. (Winter, 2004). Course management system utilization and implications for practice: A national survey of department chairpersons. *Online Journal of Distance Learning Administration, 8*(4). Retrieved from: http://www.westga.edu/~distance/ojdla/winter74/harrington74.htm Accessed: May 16, 2015.

Kirkham, C. (July 29, 2011). John Boehner backed deregulation of online learning, leading to explosive growth at for-profit colleges. *Huffington Post.* Retrieved from: http://www.huffingtonpost.com/2011/07/29/john-boehner-for-profit- colleges_n_909589.html?page=1 Accessed: May 7, 2015.

Koumi, J. (1994). Media comparison and deployment: A practitioner's view. *British Journal of Educational Technology, 25*(1), 41–57.

Kozma, R. (1991). Learning with media. *Review of Educational Research, 61*(2), 179–211.

Kozma, R. (1994a). Will media influence learning? Reframing the debate. *Educational Technology Research and Development, 42*(2), 7–19.

Kozma, R. (1994b). A reply: Media and methods. *Educational Technology Research and Development, 42*(3), 11–14.

Lynch, M., Engle, J., & Cruz, J.L. (2010). *Subprime opportunity: The unfulfilled promise of for-profit colleges and universities.* Washington, DC: Education Trust.

Middle States Commission on Higher Education (2006). *Characteristics of excellence: Requirements of affiliation and standards for accreditation.* Philadelphia, PA: Middle States Commission on Higher Education. Retrieved from: http://www.msche.org/publications/CHX-2011-WEB.pdf Accessed: May 10, 2015.

Moskal, P., Dziuban, C., & Hartman, J. (July, 2013). Blended learning: A dangerous idea? *The Internet and Higher Education, 18*, 15–23. Retrieved from: http://www.uws.edu.au/__data/assets/pdf_file/0020/530336/Reading7_BlendedLearning-ADangerousIdea.pdf Accessed: May 3, 2015.

Oliver, M. & Trigwell, K. (2005). Can 'blended learning' be redeemed? *E-Learning, 2*(1), 17–26.

Picciano, A.G. (2009). Blending with purpose: The multimodal model. *Journal of the Research Center for Educational Technology, 5*(1). Kent, OH: Kent State University. Retrieved from: http://www.rcetj.org/index.php/rcetj/article/view/11 Accessed: May 3, 2015.

Picciano, A.G. & Spring, J. (2013). *The great American education-industrial complex.* New York: Routledge/Taylor & Francis.

Rovai, A.P. (2007). Facilitating online discussions effectively. *Internet and Higher Education, 10*(1), 77–88.

Thomas, J. (2013). Exploring the use of asynchronous online discussion in health care education: A literature review. *Computers & Education, 69*, 199–215.

U.S. Department of Education (U.S. DOE), Office of Planning, Evaluation, and Policy Development (2010). Evaluation of evidence-based practices in online learning: A meta-analysis and review of online learning studies, Washington, DC. Retrieved from: http://www2.ed.gov/rschstat/eval/tech/evidence-based-practices/finalreport.pdf

7

THE THIRD WAVE

The MOOC Phenomenon (2008–2013)

The term *MOOC* (massive open online course) was coined in 2008 by Dave Cormier and Bryan Alexander to describe an online course led by George Siemens (Athabasca University) and Stephen Downes (National Research Council). Whether this course, *Connectivism and Connective Knowledge* (CCK08), was the first MOOC is debatable. The Humanities, Arts, Science, and Technology Alliance and Collaborative (HASTAC) offered a MOOC in 2006–2007 (although the term was not in use then) that reached well over 100,000 students (Davidson, 2013). Shimon Schocken and Noam Nisan developed a freely available, open-source, self-paced program for learning applied to computer science, *The Elements of Computing Systems*, in 2005, which also evolved into a free, open online course (DeNeen, 2012).

On November 2, 2012, the *New York Times* ran an article declaring 2012 as "The Year of the MOOC." Interviews were held with several of the major MOOC developers. "This has caught all of us by surprise," said David Stavens, who co-founded the MOOC company Udacity with Sebastian Thrun and Michael Sokolsky. "A year ago [2011] we were three guys in Sebastian's living room and now we have 40 employees full time" Sokolsky said. "I like to call this the year of disruption," said Anant Agarwal, president of edX, a nonprofit MOOC provider (Pappano, 2012). Two months later, on January 26, 2013, world-renowned *New York Times* columnist Tom Friedman devoted his column to MOOCs as the "revolution" that would transform higher education. He wrote:

> Nothing has more potential to unlock a billion more brains to solve the world's biggest problems. And nothing has more potential to enable us to reimagine higher education than the massive open online course, or MOOC,

> platforms that are being developed by the likes of Stanford and the Massa-
> chusetts Institute of Technology and companies like Coursera and Udacity.
>
> *(Friedman, 2013)*

In sum, MOOCs captured the imagination of educators, the media, and investors like no other instructional technology had ever done.

In the spring of 2013, the results of a high-profile MOOC initiative at San Jose State University were publicized showing relatively poor results for students using Udacity's course materials. This produced great concern over the efficacy of MOOCs. Sebastian Thrun, the face of the MOOC movement at the time, opened up the flood gates for criticism in an interview with *Fast Company*. He was quoted as saying that he was throwing in the towel and that "we [Udacity] have a lousy product. . . . We don't educate people as others wished, or as I wished" (Chafkin, 2013). While the popular media followed Thrun's proclamation with a series of "I told you so" articles, it was too early to predict that the end was near for MOOCs (Kolowich, November 27, 2013).

Society has evolved so that media are used to influence activity like never before. Marshall McLuhan's "the medium is the message" is well understood and in play. Mass media such as television, the Internet, and social networks like Facebook have contributed significantly to this trend. Technology hardware and software have always been closely associated with media hype. At its extreme, the term "vapor-ware," coined in the 1980s, was applied to technology products that were all hype but really did not exist, or at least did not exist in the form advertised. Products like the Apple Lisa, Windows Vista Operating System, Microsoft Zune, and Linden Labs' Second Life are examples of technologies that never lived up to their hype. In educa-tion, as well, there has been hyping of new approaches or "silver bullets" that have never fulfilled expectations. MOOCs were lauded by the media and the technology business sectors as a brand new approach that was going to change higher educa-tion. It would have been impossible for MOOCs to live up to these expectations, and while they took a serious fall, they did have a lot to offer higher education.

The focus of this chapter is the third wave of online education and specifically the MOOC phenomenon, which started approximately in 2008 and lasted through 2013. The term *MOOC* was adopted to identify an online course that was capable of enrolling and delivering instruction to tens of thousands of students at a time. In 2011 Stanford University offered several MOOCs, one of which, led by Sebastian Thrun and Peter Norvig, enrolled more than 160,000 students. Thrun shortly there-after started Udacity, a for-profit company designed to provide MOOC materials to colleges and universities. A few months later, Andrew Ng and Daphne Koller, both from Stanford University, launched Coursera, another for-profit MOOC provider. Both Udacity and Coursera received extensive start-up funding from Silicon Val-ley investors. The third major player in MOOC development was edX, a nonprofit provider funded initially by Harvard University and the Massachusetts Institute of

Technology. The MOOC models were grounded in improving student access to higher education and cost effectiveness by facilitating "massive" course enrollments while relying extensively on well-developed course content.

MOOC Definition and Models

The term MOOC (massive open online course) is self-descriptive. A MOOC is capable of enrolling large numbers of students, literally tens of thousands or more. In its original form, a MOOC was free (open) and did not require the payment of tuition or fees. This changed as colleges and universities began to charge for participation in MOOC courses. The early MOOCs were also envisioned as being primarily fully online rather than blended (online and face-to-face) experiences. This too changed as mainstream higher education began to integrate or blend MOOC content into traditional course approaches. The concept of the MOOC "course" also changed, as many colleges and universities used MOOC technology for recruitment, professional development, and alumni outreach.

Some institutions (Daniels, 2013) have altered the term MOOC to develop what they call POOCs, or highly participatory open online courses. POOCs emphasize "participation" rather than "massive" and attempt to engage with people both inside and outside the academy.

There has not been general agreement on the types or models of MOOCs. For example, Clark (2013) identified eight different MOOC models as follows:

- transferMOOCs—take existing courses and transfer them into a MOOC.
- madeMOOCs—take innovative approaches to the creation of course material.
- synchMOOCs—have fixed start and end dates and deadlines for assignments.
- asynchMOOCs—do not have fixed start and end dates and deadlines for assignments.
- adaptiveMOOCs—use adaptive algorithms to present personalized learning experiences.
- groupMOOCs—emphasize group work among students.
- connectivistMOOCS—rely on connectivity as afforded by digital networks that focus on knowledge creation and generation rather than content delivery.
- miniMOOCSs—course and module activity that lasts for short periods of time (days, weeks) rather than entire semesters (Clark, 2013).

There can be a good deal of overlap within these models. For instance, a MOOC could easily include transfer, synch, adaptive, and group characteristics.

Perhaps the most common difference between MOOCs is based on the terms cMOOC and xMOOC (Lugton, 2012; Bates, 2014; Kesim & Altınpulluk, 2014).

CMOOCs are based on connectivist theory, as promoted by George Siemens (2004), and focus on the development and creation of knowledge by the interactions of students in a network environment such as an online course (Kop, 2011). Individuals are responsible for their own learning and for establishing their own learner structures. The cMOOC provides the environment, but students are responsible for making the connections that are most important to their learning and the construction of their knowledge. CMOOCs use pedagogical approaches that are highly interactive; students develop their own subgroups of individuals with common goals and interests. While interesting and even provocative, it will take a while for connectivism to be accepted by the majority of faculty and students. Many students, for instance, are not necessarily interested in developing their own learning groups and would rather have a structured environment with a teacher and content-driven course.

An xMOOC allows for a variety of learning theories but focuses on providing quality content in the form of media, promoting student interaction, and assessing student progress. An xMOOC typically takes existing course material, converts it to a new medium (i.e., video, simulations), and integrates it with the interactive facilities that the online environment provides. In comparing the cMOOC and xMOOC models, the xMOOC is by far the more commonly used, mainly because most faculty are interested initially in converting their existing course materials or relating their content to other content developed by a MOOC provider (Bates, 2014).

MOOC Providers

By 2015, there were dozens of MOOC providers, with the number of new players increasing every year. It is likely that the future of MOOCs will play out in a highly competitive market that will see companies enter and companies fold. In the third wave, however, the three major MOOC providers were Udacity, Coursera, and edX.

Udacity is a for-profit MOOC provider founded in 2011 by Sebastian Thrun, David Stavens, and Mike Sokolsky, all of whom had affiliations with Stanford University. Udacity grew out of MOOC courses that Thrun, Stavens and Sokolsky developed in computer science and artificial intelligence. Udacity received a good deal of start-up funding from venture capitalists including Charles River Ventures and Andreessen Horowitz, Inc. Udacity's initial focus was on higher education and partnering with colleges and universities, but it moved away from these to focus on providing MOOCs for major technology companies such as Google, AT&T and Facebook. Udacity had a well-publicized problematic partnership with San Jose State University, which will be discussed in more detail later on in this chapter. While willing to partner with others, Udacity has come to see itself as its own university that is the major provider of professional development for the technology industry. Its homepage states that education is no longer a one-time event but a lifelong experience. Udacity pioneered what it called "nanodegree" programs and credentials designed mainly for technology professionals such as web developers, data analysts, and mobile developers.

Coursera was founded in 2012 by Stanford University professors Andrew Ng and Daphne Koller. Coursera is a for-profit company that, like Udacity, received substantial funding from a number of investors. In one fiscal year (2012–2013), it raised $65 million in venture capital. *Time* magazine included Coursera's two co-founders on its 2013 list of "The 100 Most Influential People in the World," and *Inc.* magazine named Coursera one of its "25 Most Audacious Companies" in 2013 (Weiner, 2013). Coursera made a big splash among the media, especially those that follow Wall Street investment developments. Stanford, Princeton, Duke, the California Institute of Technology, and the University of Illinois at Urbana-Champaign are among its college partners. Typical Coursera courses were free and ran anywhere from four to ten weeks. The courses were heavily dependent upon video lectures followed by multiple choice tests and other assessments. In many ways, they followed a computer-assisted instruction model pioneered by Patrick Suppes in the 1960s and reviewed in Chapter Four of this book. The difference in the Coursera approach was that it had at its disposal a far more powerful, media-rich Internet technology that was not available in the early days of CAI development. Coursera also marketed to an international clientele, especially in countries with developing economies and where higher education opportunities were limited.

EdX is a nonprofit MOOC provider founded in 2012 and funded by Harvard University and the Massachusetts Institute of Technology. Anant Agarwal, a professor of electrical engineering at MIT, is the CEO and taught the first edX course on circuits and electronics, which drew 155,000 students from 162 countries. EdX has attracted a number of college and university partners including California-Berkeley and the University of Texas as well as foreign institutions such as the Sorbonne, Australian National University, and the University of Hong Kong. EdX organizes its courses around weekly topics and makes extensive use of short instructional video clips followed by student participation activities and assessments. Much of its material, especially the video clips, has begun to be used in blended courses. EdX has been active in collecting data on student interactions during its courses and has published a number of important studies on student performance in MOOC courses. EdX maintains a website on its research at https://www.edx.org/about/research-pedagogy. One study reporting on two years of data on students enrolled in edX courses has received a good deal of attention (Ho et al., 2015).

As competition increases from other MOOC providers, the top positions enjoyed by Udacity, Coursera, and edX may not be sustainable. Udacity and Coursera, especially, need to become profitable companies, and their investors will expect a return on their investments. Intense competition frequently leads to financial problems for new technology pioneers. It is likely that the current expansion of MOOC companies will lead to shakeouts and mergers in the not-too-distant future.

MOOC Performance, Reactions, and Research

The extensive media coverage of MOOC technology served as a catalyst for discussions on university campuses about teaching and learning in general—and online learning in particular. However, the major interest in MOOC technology was not its pedagogical benefits but its scale. Without a doubt, courses that were enrolling hundreds of thousands of students attracted deserved attention. In addition, some big name institutions such as Stanford University, Harvard, and the Massachusetts Institute of Technology had become associated with the MOOC phenomenon. MOOCs were promoted by their founders at Udacity, Coursera, and edX as the technological revolution that would change higher education. Significant investments of capital were made mostly by private investors and venture philanthropies into MOOC companies. Education policymakers and university trustees took notice and thought they had found a solution to their education funding woes and pushed for major new MOOC initiatives. With this attention, MOOCs came under closer scrutiny in terms of their efficacy in delivering higher education.

San Jose University/Udacity Study

As the MOOC phenomenon took off, a closer examination of the pedagogy of this technology was made by faculty and instructional technologists, many of whom were experienced online learning developers. The greatest concerns revolved around their extremely high student dropout rates, frequently as high as 90 percent. These were not isolated cases but pervaded many MOOC courses. The CAI style of early MOOCs based on high-tech "read, watch, listen and repeat" course materials was questioned by experienced online learning developers who relied on socially constructed pedagogical approaches that emphasized extensive interaction among students and faculty. There were also serious questions about whether the MOOC approach was really appropriate for all students, especially those who had basic skills needs. Daphne Koller, co-founder of Coursera, in November 2013, commented at the Sloan Consortium's Annual Conference that students who have remediation or other learning needs and who lack the basic skills of reading, writing, and arithmetic would probably better be served by face-to-face instruction (Koller, November, 2013).

A high-profile research initiative at California's San Jose State University in 2012–13 became the poster-child for MOOC efficacy. Six basic courses in mathematics and statistics were carefully planned and offered at San Jose State using MOOC materials developed by Udacity. Course enrollments were limited and similar in size to traditional, face-to-face courses. Personnel from Udacity were highly-involved with the faculty in the development and subsequent teaching of the courses. The results were not very positive. The average pass rate across all six courses was 33.3 percent and ranged from a low of 11.9 percent to a high of 54.3 percent. These pass rates were considerably lower than those in the same courses taught in traditional, face-to-face modes in previous years, where average pass rates were closer to 75 percent and ranged from 30.4 percent to 80.4 percent (Collins, 2013). An important aspect of this study was the diverse characteristics of the student participants and the controls for matriculation status, age, gender, underrepresented minority (URM), and PELL eligibility. A criticism of many other freely available MOOC courses was that they appealed to a certain population of mainly older male students who already had college credentials. Of the 213 student participants in the San Jose University study, 54 percent were nonmatriculants, 79 percent were under the age of 24, 51 percent were female, 40 percent were URM, and 31 percent were Pell eligible. As a side note, 274 students originally enrolled in the MOOC courses at San Jose State University; 249 students remained in the study sample after data cleaning. In addition, 36 students were removed who withdrew from the course or received a final grade of Incomplete, leaving a study sample of 213 students (Collins, 2013).

Elitism

Another significant anti-MOOC sentiment appeared in 2013, when concerns were expressed by educational leaders and faculty that colleges would use course materials developed by the faculty at Ivy League and other highly selective universities to replace efforts directed at a broader student base. To the contrary, some faculty and administrators saw the Ivy League partnerships as elitism and arrogance on the part of the MOOC providers. At a meeting of MOOC developers sponsored by MIT and Harvard University, Bill Bowen, former president of Princeton University, reminded the audience that they occupied a privileged position,

> that they occupied "really rarefied air" in deciding how they might want to use online education. But professors who are serious about reaching the masses online, he said, will have to think about innovation and design with a broader, more diverse audience in mind. . . . "I would humbly suggest that the kinds of assessment and standards and all the rest that I'm sure are appropriate at MIT and Harvard and so forth," Mr. Bowen said, "have very little relevance for the large parts of American higher education, particularly in the state systems, that are under genuine siege."
>
> *(Kolowich, March 4, 2013)*

Faculty at San Jose State University were asked to pilot an edX MOOC titled *JusticeX*. In an open letter to Professor Michael Sandel, the professor at Harvard

University who had developed the course, they stated that the course undermines their university and that:

> Professors who care about public education should not produce products that will replace professors, dismantle departments, and provide a diminished education for students in public universities.
>
> *(Open Letter from the Philosophy Department at*
> *San Jose State University, April 29, 2013)*

The "elitism" label resounded among many educators and was used by critics to depict MOOCs as an ill-conceived technology for the masses while the colleges of the privileged would continue to be taught in modest-sized, face-to-face classes led by faculty.

University of Pennsylvania and Coursera

As mentioned earlier, concern existed about the success and completion rates in many of the early MOOC courses. An important study was conducted of sixteen Coursera courses taught by University of Pennsylvania faculty between June 2012 and July 2013. This study examined success as defined by a final grade of "80% or higher" and retention rates as defined by the number of students who accessed a lecture in the last module divided by the number who accessed a lecture in the first module. The authors of the study also collected data on students who progressed sequentially through a course versus those who opted to progress nonsequentially or as they wished. They defined

> sequential movement as the progression of a user through a course in the sequential order identified by the instructor. The second [non-sequential] "user-driven" approach considered the share of users who accessed a lecture in any course module, ignoring the order or sequencing of lecture access or whether the user accessed any other lecture. This second approach recognized that a user may choose whether and when to access learning materials.
>
> *(Perna et al., p. 424)*

The percentage of students who successfully completed a course with an 80 percent or above ranged from 0 percent to 12 percent. Retention rates ranged from 11 percent to 39 percent. There were not significant differences between sequential and nonsequential or user-driven students. The authors of the study concluded:

> Additional research is needed to understand how course design characteristics and pedagogical practices influence user outcomes. Some portion of the low completion rates in this study is likely attributable to the failure of these first-generation courses to adequately engage students in the course content or utilize

effective instructional practices. Future research should consider whether these outcomes reflect insufficient interaction with students, the absence of effective pedagogical approaches, and/or failure to motivate students to learn.

(Perna et al., p. 429)

The pedagogical issues raised in this study were well-known to faculty and instructional designers who had experience in developing online learning courses and materials going back to the 1990s. The fundamental model promoted in the early years (1990s–early 2000s) of online learning was the highly interactive, asynchronous learning network (ALN) made popular by the Alfred P. Sloan Foundation's *Anytime, Anyplace Learning Program.* The results of the University of Pennsylvania study gave credence to the concern that many of those involved in MOOC development at companies like Coursera did not pay enough attention to the nuances involved in developing online learning materials. In addition, the size of MOOC courses, enrolling tens of thousands of students, made meaningful interaction with faculty difficult at best and impossible at worst. This study, however, provided important new insights into the concept of "sporadic participation": students proceeding and progressing through course material nonsequentially at their own pace (Haggard, 2013). These students may not complete or do well in a course, but they still derive meaningful learning experiences by accessing portions of the course content. It might have been their intention all along to simply study and learn from one or two modules and not the entire course. In addition, it supports the concept that self-regulated or self-determined learning may be at play (Wiebe, Thompson, & Behrend, 2015). As the authors of the University of Pennsylvania study concluded, the future of MOOCs may lie in supporting other types of learning rather than providing entire courses:

> Future research should consider how user outcomes vary for MOOCs that are specifically targeted to such groups as individuals seeking personal enrichment, adult learners needing vocational or occupational training, currently enrolled college students seeking supplemental learning resources, secondary school students looking to improve academic readiness for college, and prospective college students considering whether college is right for them.
>
> *(Perna et al., p. 429)*

Research at edX

One of the most comprehensive reviews of MOOC technology was conducted by Ho et al. as a collaboration between the HarvardX Research Committee at Harvard University and the Office of Digital Learning at MIT. The study was based on data collected over two academic years (2012–13 and 2013–14) from sixty-eight edX courses, 1.7 million participants, 10 million participant hours, and

1.1 billion logged events. Two of the major foci of the study were examinations of student characteristics and performance, defined as those who received certificates of completion.

Among the key student demographic, data findings were as follows:

- 30 percent of the students were female;
- 69 percent had bachelor's degrees;
- The median age was 28;
- 29 percent resided in the United States (Ho et al., 2015, p. 10).

This study supported earlier research that established that many MOOCs appealed to older male students who already held bachelor degrees. It also supported the fact that many MOOCs had great appeal to students in other countries where there were limited opportunities for higher education.

Certificates of completion were awarded to 7 percent of the students in 2012–13 and 8 percent in 2013–14. These findings supported other studies such as Perna et al. (2014). The study also surveyed student intentions when registering for a MOOC, and the results indicated that a range of 19 percent to 57 percent intended to earn a certificate. It was concluded that large percentages of students had no intention of completing or receiving a certificate. The authors stated that the certification rate was a poor indicator of course efficacy and student performance, but that, without any other agreed-upon measure, would have to do. Earlier in this chapter, we saw that in the study at the University of Pennsylvania, a retention rate measure was used as an indication of course efficacy, but this was not a generally agreed-upon measure either. Study of the efficacy of MOOC technology continued, but many of the findings indicated weak completion rates whatever the definition. It may be that, in the future, a major role for MOOCs may be providing resources such as videos, assessment tools, and online delivery platforms in addition to complete courses. It would give faculty the option of making best use of these materials. It would also allow students to access these materials to meet their own self-directed learning needs.

MOOC Finances and Branding

In preceding parts of this chapter, several aspects of MOOCs have been examined, including massive enrollments, major providers, online learning designs, and student performance. An important element of MOOCs not yet discussed is their financial positions. With the exception of edX, the major MOOC providers are private companies (i.e., Udacity, Coursera) funded by investors for the long term with the goal of returning profits in years to come. EdX was the major exception and, as a nonprofit, received its funding from Harvard University and MIT. None of the big three companies is public, so hard numbers are difficult to come by. It appears, though, that at the time they were established, capital investments were significant. For example, Coursera received $85 million in capital funding between 2011 and 2014 (Shah, 2014). A critical question is when and how these MOOC providers are expected to demonstrate that they are profitable. While they generate millions of student enrollments, most of their courses have had free or significantly reduced tuition. In fact, while low or no tuition of most MOOCs has been a major driver of their large enrollment numbers, they cannot just keep giving the courses away. MOOCs also have to be careful that they are not seen as the McDonalds or Burger Kings of higher education, the providers of low-quality, mass-produced courses. Jason Lane and Kevin Kinser of SUNY-Albany have warned of the "McDonaldization of Higher Education," with centralized production of cookie-cutter content for distribution around the world (Wildavsky, 2014, p. 76). Eventually competition becomes very keen in new technologies, and the major MOOC providers will have to be very cognizant of their costs of production, the pricing of their services, and their customer base. It also needs to be noted that at the time of this writing (2015), most MOOC courses did not count for formal college credit and are more akin to noncredit continuing education units.

During the early days of MOOC development, the major providers established partnerships with colleges and universities with high-end reputations. While many of these partnerships involved developing complete courses, a modification of this approach began with MOOC providers offering modules and services rather than developing entire courses. As noted earlier, this may serve the MOOC providers well. MOOCs may rebrand themselves as high-quality content providers rather than as full course providers and developers. Another possibility might be finding a particular niche and becoming the provider of courses and content for certain student populations. Udacity took this approach by positioning itself as the major MOOC provider of content and professional development courses for technology-related companies. Udacity also began to charge for career services by identifying and matching exceptional students with available positions in client companies. Another market that is wide open and where MOOCs are having success is the global education market. Many countries, especially those with developing economies, have limited higher education opportunities. To have courses available under American college and university auspices has appeal. But even here McDonaldization is of concern. As stated by Jason Lane and Kevin Kinser:

> Few would argue against the potential of MOOC's to open up higher education to the masses. More than a million people have enrolled in the courses (though their completion rate remains quite low). Being available online and free makes MOOC's accessible to folks all over the world, including in remote regions lacking capacity for high-quality university education. As long as one has Internet service and a device to access it, MOOC's provide the missing content (though certifying the learning is still problematic).
>
> But, let's be clear what this means: thousands of students across the world taking the same course, with the same content, from the same instructor. And

that is the problem. MOOC's are now at the forefront of the McDonaldization of higher education.

In an era when higher education is making significant advances in becoming global and helping to build educational capacity within developing nations, MOOC's play the center against the periphery. They strengthen the ivory towers by enabling a few elite institutions to broadcast their star courses to the masses from the comfort of their protected perches.

(Lane & Kinser, 2012)

Financial and branding issues are not easy to resolve, and the major MOOC providers have yet to figure out how to develop financial models that will work for them. However, with the cushion of well-situated funders and endowments, they have a good chance at succeeding. Lastly, there is a theory about technology that supports the concept of winner take all (Ford, 2015). Consider the corporations (Google, amazon.com, or Facebook) that have prospered as a result of capturing the vast majority of a market for a new technology application and apply it to MOOC technology. It is possible that only one or two companies will still be in business in the not-too-distant future.

Policy Issues in the Third Wave

The period of the third wave (2008–2013) saw policy issues related to online education evolving at all levels—federal, state, and local—including college shared governing bodies.

At the Local Level

Colleges and universities continued to review their policies regarding the development of online education, paying attention to issues such as program/course quality, faculty personnel issues, funding and tuition. The case that probably drew the most attention during the third wave occurred at San Jose State, when the president decided to enter into a contract with Udacity to develop six courses in basic mathematics and statistics. (A review of the performance of these courses was provided earlier in this chapter.) As the MOOC implementation unfolded at San Jose, the university's Academic Senate became involved with a number of issues but was especially concerned about how the contract to Udacity was awarded. The major point of concern was that faculty were not consulted about the MOOC contract. In November 2013, and after several months of discussion, academic leaders voted overwhelmingly in favor of a resolution asking the chancellor of the entire California State University system to review governance at San Jose. The resolution cited "a series of conflicts over the past year" that have highlighted "communication and transparency" issues and "opened serious rifts in our shared sense of community." The Academic

Senate passed the resolution by a vote of 38 to 2, with five abstentions (Kolowich, November 19, 2013).

After several months of discussion, in an open letter to the campus, California State University Chancellor Timothy White (2014) cited Mohammad H. Qayoumi, president of San Jose State, as acknowledging that faculty, staff, and students had become frustrated and angered by the fast-paced actions "taken by me and members of my administration." Qayoumi said that, in trying to make progress on a series of goals for the university, he had "stepped on longstanding SJSU consultation practices and, as a result, harmed our practice of collegial shared governance." "For this," he continued, "I am regretful." Mr. Qayoumi pledged to "honor the consultative process" and said he was "committed to moving slowly where necessary," allowing for consultation with a variety of groups (DeSantis, 2014).

San Jose State University adopted a new policy in 2014 on how the creation and implementation of "technology-intensive, hybrid, and online courses" may be created and run on its campus. The new policy stated:

> "The university will not agree in a contract with any private or public entity to deliver technology-intensive, hybrid, or online courses or programs without the prior approval of the relevant department," using the "same department procedure" that is currently used to review changes in traditional courses.
> *(Kolowich, 2014)*

While San Jose received the most attention regarding governance and the implementation of MOOCs and other forms of online education, similar discussions were being held in faculty governing bodies throughout the country.

U.S. Department of Education Moves for State Authorization

The U.S. Department of Education issued a controversial state authorization policy in 2010 that focused on institutions that offer postsecondary education through distance education to students in a state in which it is not physically located or in which it is otherwise subject to state jurisdiction. The policy was particularly aimed at online education providers (and not necessarily MOOC developers) that operated nationally and across state borders. Under state authorization guidelines, an online college or university whose physical home was in one state would need to apply for and receive authorization in each of the other forty-nine states in order to enroll students from those states in its academic programs. This put a bureaucratic burden on online education providers because common operational standards or authorization application procedures were nonexistent, and each state had its own set of requirements. The U.S. DOE policy required an institution's ability to offer federal financial aid to the institution to be authorized in the student's state. The regulation was subsequently "vacated" by a federal court ruling in 2011. However, many of the states moved forward under their own jurisdictional powers to enforce state authorization of distance or online education providers. The application process was cumbersome, lengthy, and costly for all distance education providers. As of this writing and five years later, the U.S. Department of Education was rewriting its state authorization regulations and was in the process of reinstating them. WCET (WICHE Cooperative for Educational Technologies [a division of the Western Interstate Commission for Higher Education]) maintains an excellent informational website on state authorization issues at: http://wcet.wiche.edu/learn/issues/state-authorization.

Federal Government Tries to Rein in For-Profit Colleges

To its credit, the for-profit sector provided educational opportunities for large numbers of adult learners, minority students, students who needed flexible place and time schedules, online learners, and military personnel. Figure 7.1 illustrates that in 2008, for-profit institutions enrolled the largest percentage of minority students of any of the higher education sectors. Approximately 48 percent of students in for-profit colleges were nonwhite. This is a full seven percentage points higher than the next highest sector, public two-year colleges, which enrolled 41 percent.

While the for-profit sector was to be commended for providing higher education opportunities for nontraditional and minority students, the quality of their programs had come under question. The Education Trust is an advocacy organization whose mission is:

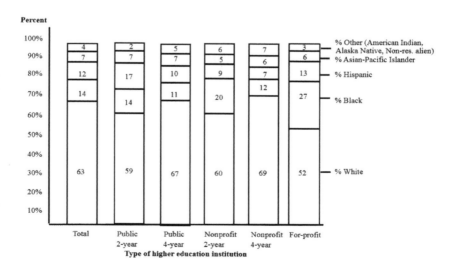

FIGURE 7.1 Percentage Distribution of Enrollment in Degree-Granting Institutions by Sector and Race/Ethnicity: Fall 2008

To promote high academic achievement for all students at all levels—pre-kindergarten through college. Our goal is to close the gaps in opportunity and achievement that consign far too many young people—especially those from low-income families or who are black, Latino, or American Indian—to lives on the margins of the American mainstream.

(Education Trust Website, 2015)

In 2010, the Trust issued a report that looked at the success of students in for-profit colleges. Using data from the National Center for Education Statistics and some other sources, the report titled, *Subprime Opportunity: The Unfulfilled Promise of For-Profit Colleges and Universities*, found:

In the 2008–09 academic year, for-profit colleges received $4.3 billion in Pell Grants—quadruple the amount they received just ten years earlier—and approximately $20 billion in federal student loans. As a result of this large federal investment, the average for-profit school derives 66 percent of its revenues from federal student aid, and 15 percent of institutions receive 85 to 90 percent of their revenue from Title IV. The behemoth that is the University of Phoenix brought in over one billion dollars in Pell Grant funding alone in 2009–10 . . . risks exceeding federal limits by deriving over 90 percent of revenues from federal financial aid. The rapid growth and record profit levels reported by these institutions might be acceptable if students were succeeding at record rates. But they are not. . . . Low-income students and students of color are getting access, but not much success.

(Lynch, Engle, & Cruz, 2010, p. 2)

This finding was especially true for students in the four-year for-profit institutions, where the data indicated that only 20.4 percent of the students graduate within six years, while the graduation rates at the public four-year and private nonprofit colleges were 55.7 percent and 65.1 percent, respectively. The entire University of Phoenix system had a six-year graduation rate of 9 percent, and the University of Phoenix Online program had a graduation rate of 5 percent (Lynch et al., 2010). Furthermore, most of these low-income and minority students, even those who graduated, were incurring significant debt that would take them years to pay off. The median debt for students who graduated with a baccalaureate degree at a for-profit college was $31,190, compared to $7,960 for a public college and $17,040 at a private, nonprofit college (Lynch et al., 2010, p. 6).

The report's conclusion was that:

For-profit colleges argue that they are models of access and efficiency in America's overburdened higher education system. But instead of providing a solid pathway to the middle class, they are paving a path into the subbasement of the American economy. They enroll students in high-cost degree programs . . . that saddle the most vulnerable students with more debt than they could reasonably manage to pay off, even if they do graduate.

(Lynch et al., 2010, p. 7)

As the name suggested, the Education Trust report drew comparisons to the collapse of the housing market in the U.S. in 2008 caused by unregulated subprime mortgage companies. It concluded that for-profit colleges provided access to higher education but delivered little more than crippling debt. This report set off a flurry of policy-related activity on the part of the federal government.

In 2009, the U.S. General Accountability Office (GAO) conducted an undercover operation to gather information at fifteen for-profit colleges. On August 4, 2010, Gregory D. Kutz, managing director of Forensics, Audits and Special Investigations, gave testimony before the U.S. Senate Committee on Health, Education, Labor, and Pensions. His testimony included the following summary:

> Undercover tests at 15 for-profit colleges found that 4 colleges encouraged fraudulent practices and that all 15 made deceptive or otherwise questionable statements to GAO's undercover applicants. Four undercover applicants were encouraged by college personnel to falsify their financial aid forms to qualify for federal aid—for example, one admissions representative told an applicant to fraudulently remove $250,000 in savings. Other college representatives exaggerated undercover applicants' potential salary after graduation and failed to provide clear information about the college's program duration, costs, or graduation rate despite federal regulations requiring them to do so. For example, staff commonly told GAO's applicants they would attend classes for 12 months a year, but stated the annual cost of attendance for 9 months of classes, misleading applicants about the total cost of tuition. Admissions staff used other deceptive practices, such as pressuring applicants to sign a contract for enrollment before allowing them to speak to a financial advisor about program cost and financing options. However, in some instances, undercover applicants were provided accurate and helpful information by college personnel, such as not to borrow more money than necessary.
>
> In addition, GAO's four fictitious prospective students received numerous, repetitive calls from for-profit colleges attempting to recruit the students when they registered with Web sites designed to link for-profit colleges with prospective students. Once registered, GAO's prospective students began receiving calls within 5 minutes. One fictitious prospective student received more than 180 phone calls in a month. Calls were received at all hours of the day, as late as 11 p.m.
>
> Programs at the for-profit colleges GAO tested cost substantially more for associate's degrees and certificates than comparable degrees and certificates at public colleges nearby. A student interested in a massage therapy certificate costing $14,000 at a for-profit college was told that the program was a good

value. However the same certificate from a local community college cost $520. Costs at private nonprofit colleges were more comparable when similar degrees were offered.

(Kutz, August 4, 2010)

This report and the subsequent testimony of its authors before the U.S. Senate committee touched off calls around the country for increased regulation of for-profit colleges. The names of the fifteen colleges were not made public.

Senator Tom Harkin (Democrat–Iowa), chair of the U.S. Senate Health, Education, Labor and Pensions (HELP) Committee, conducted hearings for almost three years and released a report in July 2012 based on a comprehensive investigation of thirty of the largest for-profit college companies. It's full of stark revelations about this sector.

In this report, you will find overwhelming documentation of exorbitant tuition, aggressive recruiting practices, abysmal student outcomes, taxpayer dollars spent on marketing and pocketed as profit, and regulatory evasion and manipulation. . . . These practices are not the exception—they are the norm. They are systemic throughout the industry, with very few individual exceptions.

(U.S. Senate Health, Education, Labor, and Pensions Committee Report,
July 2012)

A *New York Times* article commented:

Over the last 15 years, enrollment and profits have skyrocketed in the [for-profit] industry. Until the 1990s, the sector was made up of small independent schools offering training in fields like air-conditioning repair and cosmetology. But from 1998 to 2008, enrollment more than tripled, to about 2.4 million students. Three-quarters are at colleges owned by huge publicly traded companies—and, more recently, private equity firms—offering a wide variety of programs.

Enrolling students, and getting their federal financial aid, is the heart of the business, and in 2010, the report found, the colleges studied had a total of 32,496 recruiters, compared with 3,512 career-services staff members.

Among the 30 companies, an average of 22.4 percent of revenue went to marketing and recruiting, 19.4 percent to profits and 17.7 percent to instruction.

Their chief executive officers were paid an average of $7.3 million, although Robert S. Silberman, the chief executive of Strayer Education, made $41 million in 2009, including stock options.

Presently [2012], there is a stalemate in Washington on holding this industry accountable, because the big money that it spends on lobbying, lawyering, and campaign contributions has bought the allegiance of many congressional Republicans and Democrats and has thwarted federal regulations. Thus determined reform efforts by the Obama Administration, and principled leaders like Senators Harkin, Dick Durbin (D-IL), and Kay Hagan (D-NC), and Representatives Elijah Cummings (D-MD), Maxine Waters (D-CA), and Keith Ellison (D-MN), have largely been blocked.

(Lewin, 2012)

As a result of the Education Trust, GAO, and U.S. Senate Committee Report, the U.S. Department of Education drafted a set of regulations related to higher education outcomes and especially to institutional claims of gainful employment that was highlighted as one of the more egregious come-ons on the part of for-profit colleges.

Summary

In this chapter, the third wave (The MOOC Phenomenon—2008–2013) of online education was presented. The term *MOOC* (Massive, Open, Online Course) was coined in 2008 by Dave Cormier and Bryan Alexander to describe an online course led by George Siemens and Stephen Downes. The course enrolled more than 2,000 students. With this course, the third wave of online learning development began in earnest. In 2011 Stanford University offered several MOOCs, one of which, led by Sebastian Thrun and Peter Norvig, enrolled more than 160,000 students. The MOOC model was grounded in improving student access to higher education and cost effectiveness. The emphasis was surely on "massive" enrollments, and courses that were enrolling hundreds of thousands of students attracted deserved attention. The media went into a frenzy, and the *New York Times* declared 2012 as "The Year of the MOOC."

By the end of 2013, the media's infatuation with MOOCs had ended as well. A major development that spurred the backlash took place at California's San Jose State University, where, in a well-publicized experiment, several blended learning courses in mathematics and statistics were developed by Udacity. In comparing completion rates and grades, students taking the MOOC courses did not fare as well as students in previous years' face-to-face courses. Subsequently, in December 2013, Sebastian Thrun, the founder of Udacity, opened himself and his company up to criticism in an interview with *Fast Company*, where he was quoted as saying that he was throwing in the towel and that "we [Udacity] have a lousy product."

The chapter reviewed several major studies on courses developed by the three major MOOC providers (Udacity, Coursera, and edX). This was followed by a section examining finance and branding issues.

The chapter concluded with a review of several policy developments during this period, including the federal government's investigations of financial aid abuses at several for-profit colleges.

References

Bates, T. (2014). Comparing xMOOCs and cMOOCs: Philosophy and practice. Blog posting: *Online and Distance Education Resources*. Retrieved from: http://www.tonybates.ca/2014/10/13/comparing-xmoocs-and-cmoocs-philosophy-and-practice/ Accessed: May 17, 2015.

Chafkin, M. (December 2013). Udacity's Sebastian Thrun: Godfather of free online education, changes course. *Fast Company*. Retrieved from: http://www.fastcompany.com/3021473/udacity-sebastian-thrun-uphill-climb Accessed: May 12, 2015.

Clark, D. (2013). MOOCs: Taxonomy of 8 types of MOOCs. Blog posting: *Plan B*. Retrieved from: http://donaldclarkplanb.blogspot.co.uk/2013/04/moocs-taxonomy-of-8-types-of-mooc.html Accessed: May 17, 2015.

Collins, E.D. (2013). *Preliminary summary: SJSU+ augmented online learning environment pilot project*. Research and Planning Group for California Community Colleges (RP Group) in collaboration with the Office of Institutional Effectiveness and Analytics at San José State University (SJSU). Retrieved from: http://www.sjsu.edu/chemistry/People/Faculty/Collins_Research_Page/AOLE%20Report%20-September%2010%20 2013%20final.pdf Accessed: May 20, 2015.

Daniels, J. (2013). MOOC to POOC: Moving from massive to participatory. Blog posting: *Just Publics*. Retrieved from: http://justpublics365.commons.gc.cuny.edu/2013/02/05/mooc-to-pooc-moving- from-massive-to-participatory/ Accessed: May 17, 2015.

Davidson, C. (September 27, 2013). *What was the first MOOC?* HASTAC. Retrieved from: http://www.hastac.org/blogs/cathy-davidson/2013/09/27/what-was-first-mooc Accessed: May 13, 2015.

DeNeen, J. (October 15, 2012). Simon Schocken on the first MOOC. *InformED*. Retrieved from: http://www.opencolleges.edu.au/informed/trends/shimon-schocken-on-the-first-mooc/ Accessed: May 13, 2015.

DeSantis, N. (May 13, 2014). San Jose State U. chief vows reforms after clashes over governance. *The Chronicle of Higher Education*. Retrieved from: http://chronicle.com/blogs/ticker/san-jose-state-u-s-president-vows-reforms-after-clashes-over-campus-governance/77543 Accessed: May 23, 2015.

Education Trust Website (2015). About the Education Trust. Retrieved from: http://www.edtrust.org/dc/about Accessed: May 15, 2015.

Faculty in the Philosophy Department at San Jose State University (April 29, 2013). Open letter to Professor Michel Sandel. Retrieved from: http://chronicle.com/article/The-Document-an-Open-Letter/138937/ Accessed: May 20, 2015.

Ford, M. (2015). *Rise of the robots*. New York: Basic Books.

Friedman, T. (January 26, 2013). Revolution hits the universities. *New York Times*. Retrieved from: http://www.nytimes.com/2013/01/27/opinion/sunday/friedman-revolution-hits-the-universities.html?_r=0 Accessed: May 12, 2015.

Haggard, S. (2013). *The maturing of the MOOC: Literature review of massive open online courses and other forms of online distance learning*. London, UK: Department for Business, Innovation and Skills.

Ho, A.D., Chuang, I., Reich, J., Coleman, C.A., Whitehill, J., Northcutt, C.G., Williams, J.J. Hansen, J.D., Lopez, G., Petersen, R. (March 30, 2015). HarvardX and MITx: Two years of open online courses Fall 2012-Summer 2014. Retrieved from: http://ssrn.com/abstract=2586847 Accessed: May 18, 2015.

Kesim, M. & Altınpulluk, H. (2014). *A theoretical analysis of MOOC types from a perspective of learning theories*. Presentation at the 5thWorld Conference on Learning, Teaching and Educational Leadership (WCLTA 2014). Retrieved from: http://www.academia. edu/9403509/A_Theoretical_Analysis_of_MOOCS_Types_From_a_Perspective_of_ Learning_Theories Accessed: May 17, 2015.

Koller, D. (November, 2013). *Online learning: Learning without limits.* Keynote presentation at the 19th Annual Sloan Consortium Conference on Online Learning. Orlando, FL. http://www.irrodl.org/index.php/irrodl/article/view/882/1823 Accessed: May 17, 2015.

Kolowich, S. (March 4, 2013). Online education may make top colleges more elite, speakers say! *The Chronicle of Higher Education.* Retrieved from: http://chronicle. com/blogs/wiredcampus/researchers-push-mooc-conversation-beyond-tsunami- metaphors/48911?cid=at&utm_source=at&utm_medium=en Accessed: May 20, 2015.

Kolowich, S. (November 19, 2013). Citing a series of conflicts, San Jose State U. asks for governance review. *The Chronicle of Higher Education.* Retrieved from: http://chronicle. com/article/As-MOOC-Debate-Simmers-at-San/139147/ Accessed: May 23, 2015.

Kolowich, S. (November 27, 2013). Academics to Udacity founder: Told ya! *The Chronicle of Higher Education.* Retrieved from: http://chronicle.com/blogs/wiredcampus/academics- to-udacity-founder-told-ya/48667?cid=wc&utm_source=wc&utm_medium=en Accessed: May 20, 2015.

Kolowich, S. (January 31, 2014). San Jose State U. adopts new policy for online and 'hybrid' courses. *The Chronicle of Higher Education.* Retrieved from: http://chronicle. com/blogs/wiredcampus/san-jose-state-u-adopts-new-policy-for-online-and-hybrid- courses/50029 Accessed: May 23, 2015.

Kop, R. (2011). The challenges to connectivist learning on open online networks: Learn- ing experiences during a massive open online course. *International Review of Research in Open and Distance Learning, 12*(3). Retrieved from: http://nparc.cisti-icist.nrc-cnrc. gc.ca/eng/view/accepted/?id=2d83ddb7-b3cd-45cd-8371-92a94e5dd349 Accessed: June 8, 2016.

Kutz, G.A. (August 4, 2010). *Testimony before the Committee on Health, Education, Labor, and Pensions, U.S. Senate.* Based on a report: For-Profit colleges: Undercover testing finds colleges encouraged fraud and engaged in deceptive and questionable marketing practices. Washington, DC: United States Government General Accountability Office. Retrieved from: http://www.gao.gov/new.items/d10948t.pdf Accessed: May 13, 2015.

Lane, J. & Kinser, K. (September 28, 2012). MOOC's and the McDonaldization of global higher education. *The Chronicle of Higher Education.* Retrieved from: http://chronicle. com/blogs/worldwise/moocs-mass-education-and-the-mcdonaldization-of-higher- education/30536 Accessed: May 23, 2015.

Lewin, T. (July 29, 2012). Senate committee report on for-profit colleges condemns costs and Practices. *New York Times.* Retrieved from: http://www.nytimes.com/2012/07/30/ education/harkin-report-condemns-for-profit-colleges.html?_r=2&nl=todaysheadline s&emc=tha24_20120730 Accessed: May 25, 2015.

Lugton, M. (2012). *What is a MOOC? What are the different types of MOOCs?* xMOOCs and cMOOCs. Retrieved from: http://reflectionsandcontemplations.wordpress. com/2012/08/23/what-is-a-mooc-what-are-the-different-types-of-mooc-xmoocs- and-cmoocs/ Accessed: May 17, 2015.

Lynch, M., Engle, J., & Cruz, J.L. (2010). *Subprime opportunity: The unfulfilled promise of for- profit colleges and universities.* Washington, DC: Education Trust.

Pappano, L. (November 2, 2012). The year of the MOOC. *New York Times.* Retrieved from: http://www.nytimes.com/2012/11/04/education/edlife/massive-open-online-courses- are-multiplying-at-a-rapid-pace.html Accessed: May 12, 2015.

Perna, L.W., Ruby, A., Boruch, R.F., Wang, N., Scull, J., Seher, A., & Evans, C. (December, 2014). Moving through MOOCs: Understanding the progression of users in massive open online courses. *Educational Researcher, 43*(8), 421–432.

Shah, D. (2014). How does Coursera make money? Blog posting: *edSurge*. Retrieved from: https://www.edsurge.com/n/2014–10–15-how-does-coursera-make-money Accessed: May 23, 2015.

Siemens, G. (2004). *Connectivism: A learning theory for the digital age*. Elearnspace. Retrieved from: http://www.elearnspace.org/Articles/connectivism.htm Accessed: May 17, 2015.

U.S. Senate Health, Education, Labor and Pensions (HELP) Committee report (July 30, 2012) For profit higher education: The failure to safeguard the federal investment and ensure student success, Washington, DC. Retrieved from: http://www.gpo.gov/fdsys/browse/committeecong.action?collection=CPRT&committee=health&chamber=senate&congressplus=112&ycord=0 Accessed: May 24, 2015.

Weiner, J. (September 23, 2013). Inside the Coursera hype machine. *The Nation*. Retrieved from: http://www.thenation.com/article/176036/inside-coursera-hype-machine# Accessed: May 17, 2015.

White, T. (May 8, 2014). *Open letter to the students, faculty, staff, and friends of San Jose State University*. California State University—Office of the Chancellor. Retrieved from: http://www.docstoc.com/docs/169779759/sjsu_administrative_review.pdf Accessed: May 23, 2015.

Wiebe, E., Thompson, I., & Behrend, T. (May, 2015). MOOCs from the viewpoint of the learner: A response to Perna et al. (2014). *Educational Researcher, 44*(4), 252–254.

Wildavsky, B. (May-June 2014). *Evolving toward significance or MOOC ado about nothing?* Forum of International Educator. Retrieved from: http://www.nafsa.org/_/File/_/ie_mayjun14_forum.pdf Accessed: May 23, 2015.

8

THE FOURTH WAVE

The Reconciliation of Blended and MOOC Technologies (2014–2020)

Martin Ford, in his 2015 best-seller, *Rise of the Robots: Technology and the Threat of a Jobless Future*, describes a model in which technology evolves according to a series of starts, stops, and accelerations in an S-shaped pattern rather than a consistent diagonal linear development curve. He uses the airplane as an example of a technology that followed the S-curve model of downswings and upswings. In the early 1900s, basic aircraft technology was slow to develop until improvements were made to propellers in the 1920s. The second major aircraft technology development came with the introduction of jet engines, which were widely accepted in the 1950s. However, the supersonic Concorde, which could have ushered in a new era of airplane travel in the 1970s, proved economically unfeasible and was decommissioned in 2003. This diffusion of innovation theory has been adopted by a number of economists and others to explain technology evolution. Everett Rogers (2003), in his seminal book, *Diffusion of Innovation*, traces the theory to the French sociologist Gabriel Tarde, who plotted the original S-shaped diffusion curves in 1903. More recently, Clayton Christensen (1997, 2013) warned corporations and organizations of disruption and used the S-curve model to emphasize the acceleration step of technology adoption.

The S-curve diffusion of innovation model can be applied to online education (see Figure 8.1) as well. Indeed, the waves that are the organizational framework for this book can be viewed as a series of S-curve starts and stops beginning in the early 1990s. So far we have examined the three waves that spanned the 1990s to 2013. In this chapter, we examine the present and the near future. This Fourth Wave of online education commenced approximately in 2014 and will likely continue until about 2020. It extends and combines the development of the Second Wave (blended learning) with the Third Wave (well-designed MOOC content) and incorporates a variety of new pedagogies using multiple approaches and

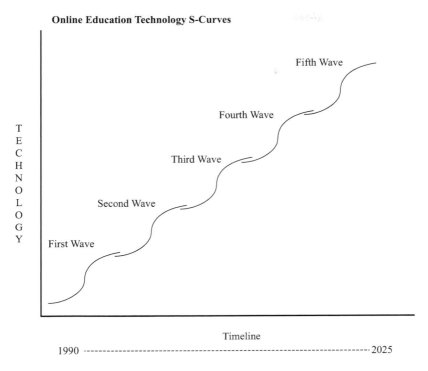

Online Education Technology S-Curves

FIGURE 8.1 S-Curves of Online Education (1990–2025) Depicting Five Waves

instructional tools. In a sense, it is the reconciliation of the pedagogical benefits of blended learning and the access/cost benefits of MOOC models. The Fourth Wave is also ushering in a number of new facilities and approaches that were in their nascent stages in previous waves. These include:

1. Learning analytics
2. Adaptive or differentiated learning
3. Expansion of competency-based instruction
4. Open educational resources (OER)
5. Interactive media (simulations, multiuser virtual environments, and games)
6. Mobile technology

All of these, as well as traditional lectures, class discussions, laboratory work, and internships that are typical in face-to-face classes, will be at the disposal of faculty and instructional designers. The Fourth Wave is one in which pedagogy drives technology in a comprehensive and sophisticated blended learning environment relying on a variety of face-to-face and digital resources developed by individual faculty, by well-financed MOOC companies, and by other education service providers.

Blended/MOOC Models

As the Fourth Wave began, MOOC courses were growing at a significant rate. The total number of MOOCs grew 201 percent in 2014, and over the period 2013–2018, MOOCs are forecasted to grow at a compound annual growth rate of 56.61 percent (MOOCs Directory, 2015). According to the European Commission's Open Education Europa initiative, there were over 3,842 MOOC courses available worldwide as of January 2015. However, the vast majority of these courses were not taken for college credit. Blended courses for credit, on the other hand, were becoming commonplace in many colleges and universities. The future of both of these instructional technologies are bright but will be even brighter as they merge together. As mentioned in the previous chapter, Daphne Koller gave the keynote address at the 19th Annual Sloan Consortium Conference on Online Learning in November 2013. She commented on the current state of teaching and learning in higher education and provided insights into the direction that her company, Coursera, was taking to achieve profitability. She predicted a bright future for MOOCs but perhaps not strictly as providers of entire courses but rather as the providers of pedagogically sophisticated instructional materials that could be used in blended online formats. Her thought was that Coursera and other MOOC providers might rebrand themselves as producers of high-quality content giving faculty options in using the materials. Coming on the heels of Sebastian Thurn's comment in October 2013, that he was throwing in the towel and that "we [Udacity] have a lousy product," Koller's comments essentially ushered in the Fourth Wave of online education (Chafkin, 2013).

The online education technologies of the Fourth Wave have a good deal of appeal to administrators, faculty, and instructional designers because they allow educators to make decisions as to how best to use these technologies for their academic programs. Pat James, executive director of the multimillion dollar California Community College Online Education Initiative, in discussing the future of online education and MOOC technology, commented:

> The opportunity we have now is one that can put everything that we know works into one solution. This project will have all of the pieces funded— a great common course management system, instructional design support, 24/7 help desk support, orientation for students, professional development for faculty, standards for design, and standards for qualifications, mentors, coaches and student services. Everything we have fought for, piece by piece, can happen here in one grand plan. . . . My recent foray into the MOOCs showed me what our university colleagues don't know. I think our work will help them, too. All of the students of California stand to gain. It's always been about access and now it can be about success, too.
>
> (James, 2014)

While many colleges, especially those in the for-profit sector, will continue to provide fully online courses and programs, most colleges are looking to add or blend online and rich-MOOC type content into a variety of new formats at the program and/or course level. Many different models are evolving, depending upon the level of instruction, the discipline, the preferences of faculty and instructional designers, and the nature of the student body. The emphasis, particularly in the United States, is on pedagogical value rather than on cost benefits. In other countries, especially those where there are not enough colleges and universities to serve growing populations, costs efficiencies as provided by the pure MOOC model are and will continue to be significant drivers of academic and course development. As a result of this next step in online education, MOOC providers are seeing competition grow more intense as new MOOC companies come on the scene and as some colleges use their own resources to develop MOOC materials. It is estimated that there are more than forty MOOC providers worldwide, with the number growing (Class Central, 2015).

One Size Does Not Fit All

The American higher education system comprises a multitude of institutions: from community colleges that have done an incredible job of providing access to research universities and medical schools that are the envy of every country in the world. We have for-profits, not-for-profits, private, public, and religious-affiliated schools. The students who attend these institutions are different and as diverse as the schools themselves. The student who is eighteen years old, attends an Ivy League school, lives in a dormitory, scores in the 90 percentile on the SATs, and aspires to go to law school is not the same student who is thirty-five years old, attends a community college, has a full-time job and family, needs to take remedial courses in basic skills, and hopes to be a health care worker. The faculty who teach laboratory chemistry courses are not the same as those who teach political philosophy, or those who teach basic accounting, or those who teach clinical nursing practice. One size does not fit all. How these varied institutions, students, and faculty approach instruction is different. Blended learning models, however, allow for all of these to integrate technology into teaching and learning. Add well-developed content and software platforms such as those that are being provided with MOOC technology, and the possibilities are endless. In this section, an examination will be made of the ways blended learning and MOOC technology are being used, in some cases, to provide academic programs and courses in the Fourth Wave of online education.

Required Courses in Large-Section Classes

At the undergraduate and graduate levels, large-section courses that enroll hundreds of students and generally take place in auditorium-like classrooms are prime candidates for blended/MOOC technology. Large-section courses have become mainstays at most large public and private, nonprofit universities. These classes typically are offered for foundation, general survey, and required general education courses. Large-section courses generally are seen as a cost-beneficial way of providing instruction rather than a pedagogically valuable one. These courses have also been the targets of various types of instructional technology including flipped classrooms, clicker devices, and online recitation sessions. Since the late 1990s, the National Center for Academic Transformation (2005), led by Carol Twigg, has provided leadership in using information technology to redesign learning environments and has provided a number of models directed specifically at improving large-section courses. They are prime candidates for blended and MOOC technology.

The traditional, face-to-face, large-section model is a three-hour course that consists of a large lecture session and a smaller recitation session. During the lecture session, faculty provide content in the form of a lecture and/or media presentation, but because of the large number of students, the ability to ask questions and interact is limited. The recitation sessions are much smaller, and students are able to ask questions and interact with each other as well as with a faculty member, who frequently is a graduate assistant. A large section course for 800 students might meet for two hours with a "star" lecturer or presenter in an auditorium and then meet for recitations with a graduate assistant for one hour. Each recitation might be as small as twenty students, thereby generating as many as forty sections. The ability of students to interact and ask questions is facilitated in the smaller recitation session. The National Center for Academic Transformation maintains a website containing case studies of colleges that have transformed basic courses, including large sections, using technology. Many of these are using blended learning environments. In one common transformation, the large lecture in maintained as a face-to-face experience and the recitation is moved into an online activity. A major pedagogical benefit of moving the recitation into an online activity is that students can begin asking questions immediately and do not have to wait for the recitation meeting at its appointed time and place. To put this another way, if a large, face-to-face lecture takes place on a Monday, a student need not wait until Tuesday, Wednesday, or perhaps later to ask a question.

MOOC technology can also add a new dimension to these models. For example, the University of Arizona, which has had a number of major blended learning initiatives, announced in 2015 that it was joining with edX to offer an online freshman year that will be available worldwide with no admissions process and full university credit. The focus of this model is to blend MOOC content into many of the first-year large-section courses of the mainstream baccalaureate programs. In what it calls the Global Freshman Academy, each credit will cost $200, but students will not have to pay until they pass the courses, which will be offered on the edX platform. The courses will be designed by University of Arizona faculty and will integrate content and materials available from edX (Lewin, 2015). Many other colleges are examining similar approaches.

Professional Graduate Programs

For decades, professional graduate programs in business administration, teacher education, health, and the technical fields have been very popular. These programs generally are not expensive to offer, can accommodate large numbers of students, and frequently are taught by adjunct faculty who have experience in these fields. Furthermore, these programs generally provide important credentials and certifications required by employers, governing boards, or professional organizations. As a result, there are substantial numbers of students employed in these fields who need to enroll or are interested in enrolling in these programs. Because many of these students are employed full-time, the related graduate programs are prime opportunities for online education that allow students to fit their studies into their otherwise busy lives. A number of excellent online and blended programs have been developed over the past decade in these professional academic areas, many of which are offered by the top schools in the country.

Babson College in Wellesley, Massachusetts, offers a blended learning MBA program in entrepreneurship that combines online classes, face-to-face sessions at its San Francisco or Wellesley campuses, and virtual collaboration activities "to make the most of your time, your learning, your network, and your investment" (Babson College, 2014). This approach allows a student to finish an MBA in 21 months. As described at the college's website:

> Face-to-face sessions occur approximately every seven weeks, Friday-Saturday. Online learning averages 20 hours per week, and reflects readings, case preparation, contributing to asynchronous and real-time discussions, and active participation in team-based exercises and projects. The Web-based elements are delivered via state-of-the-art distance learning tools.
>
> *(Babson College, 2014)*

Babson College's MBA program is consistently ranked by *U.S. News and World Report* as the number one graduate program in the country in entrepreneurship, ahead of universities such as Stanford, Harvard, and Yale (U.S. News and World Report, 2015).

In 2014, the Georgia Institute of Technology, in partnership with Udacity and AT&T, launched a new master's degree in computer science using a MOOC platform. The total tuition cost for the degree will be $6,600, far less than the $45,000 on-campus price. The program is underwritten by a $2 million grant from AT&T, which plans to use the program for its own professional training and for recruiting prospective employees. By design, courses in the program enroll hundreds of students, not thousands, as is typical of many MOOC courses. At the time of this writing, the program was enrolling 400-plus students per semester. The average age of the students in the online program is 34, while the average residential student is 23. An initial evaluation of student academic performance in the new program indicated that grade point averages were basically the same as the campus-based program (Straumshein, 2014).

In 2013, The Wharton School of Business at the University of Pennsylvania announced The Wharton Foundation Series, consisting of four core courses offered in its MBA program. These include Introduction to Financial Accounting, Operations Management, Marketing, and Corporate Finance. They will be free and offered as MOOCS in partnership with Coursera. The four courses in the series are six to ten weeks long. Each consists of a combination of prerecorded lectures and interactive features such as discussion boards that allow students to ask questions and get answers from the professor or an assistant. Don Huesman, director of the Innovation Group at Wharton, commented that:

> These MOOC courses are not watered-down versions of Wharton's on-campus classes. In fact, some professors at the school are using the MOOC content in their own classes, asking students to watch the lessons beforehand so that class time can be used for discussion—a practice typically known as the flipped classroom.
>
> *(Lavelle, 2013)*

Approximately 700,000 students in 173 countries enrolled in these courses in the first year they were offered. Huesman also was quoted as saying that:

> Wharton has no plans to accept the [MOOC] certificates for course credit should students subsequently enroll at Wharton, adding that "there's a very different experience that happens in a two-year immersion in a community of scholars that culminates in a degree." But he says that what students learn in the online classes can be used to "test out" of the required courses just as those with prior knowledge of the subject matter can do now.
>
> *(Lavelle, 2013)*

The Wharton model has been adopted by other colleges, where free MOOC courses are used to attract students to their programs but by themselves do not culminate in a degree. J.A. Byrne, writing for *Poets and Quants*, in an article titled "The future of the MBA: An unbundled, blended degree," sees the Wharton program as the future for most MBA programs (Byrne, September 17, 2014).

The Wharton blended/MOOC model is representative of how many university master's programs are evolving, Most of these programs either limit the number of MOOCs a student can take, do not offer the MOOC courses for credit, limit enrollments, or use the MOOCs as an adjunct to the regular MBA program. One might ask why these programs don't go the full online MOOC route. Fully online master's programs have been available for a number of years, but the massive and free approach of MOOCs is still being evaluated and in some cases rejected by college faculty and administrators. A 2014 case involving Harvard University's

School of Business (HSB) received a lot of attention on this very issue (Byrne, June 3, 2014; Useem, 2014). The HSB administration and faculty decided to opt out of edX, Harvard and MIT's funded MOOC provider, and instead offered a new pre-MBA program (HBX) with online courses not in a MOOC format. It is clear that the HBX program/courses are not substitutes for the Harvard MBA program; they are intended to give liberal arts students fluency in what it calls "the language of business" (Useem, 2014). As reported in the *New York Times*:

> Its HSB dean, Nitin Nohria, faced the school's biggest strategic decision since 1924—Should Harvard Business School enter the business of online education, and, if so, how? . . .
>
> Universities across the country are wrestling with the same question—call it the educator's quandary—of whether to plunge into the rapidly growing realm of online teaching, at the risk of devaluing the on-campus education for which students pay tens of thousands of dollars, or to stand pat at the risk of being left behind.
>
> At Harvard Business School, the pros and cons of the argument were personified by two of its most famous faculty members. For Michael Porter, widely considered the father of modern business strategy, the answer is yes—create online courses, but not in a way that undermines the school's existing strategy. "A company must stay the course," Professor Porter has written, "even in times of upheaval, while constantly improving and extending its distinctive positioning."
>
> For Clayton Christensen, on the other hand, whose 1997 book, "The Innovator's Dilemma," propelled him to academic stardom, the only way that market leaders like Harvard Business School survive "disruptive innovation" is by disrupting their existing businesses themselves.
>
> *(Useem, 2014)*

J.A. Byrne, former editor of *Business Week* and *Fast Company*, analyzed the school's decision as follows:

> Essentially, Harvard Business School is relying on the strength of its core business and changing incrementally, rather than casting away what it does best and trying to start something truly new and disruptive. . . .
>
> "I think the big risk in any new technology is to believe the technology is the strategy," Porter commented: "Just because 200,000 people sign up, doesn't mean it's a good idea."
>
> Especially, it should be added, if there is no revenue from the 200,000 people who sign up for a MOOC (Massive Open Online Courses). It's not that MOOCs directly hurt a school's existing business. But to the extent that they cost money and siphon off the time and energy of a school's best professors, taking them away from paying customers, they're hardly a winning strategy.

. . . Yet, many other business schools and universities have rushed into the MOOC market on the basis that it is giving them valuable brand exposure the world over.

Who's right? Porter, for sure.

(Byrne, June 3, 2014)

This debate is playing itself out in colleges and universities throughout the country as educators try to integrate new technology into their programs. It will continue for the remainder of the Fourth Wave. In a bit of irony, the first online course developed by HBX was *Disruptive Strategy*, taught by Clayton Christensen.

Undergraduate Liberal Arts Programs at Private, Nonprofit Colleges

The higher education sector that has been the slowest to enter into online education is the small, residential liberal arts colleges. This is not surprising, since a fundamental aspect of these schools is the social environment they provide their students: small class sizes, emphasis on sound pedagogy, comfortable dormitories, and a plethora of social activities designed to build community and lifelong friendships. However, administrators and faculty have begun to see the possible pedagogical benefits of providing online learning experiences for their students. First, it enables these schools to expand their course offerings. Second, the immediacy, interactivity, and group reflection of online learning can have significant pedagogical value. Third, it also allows students to have experiences in collaborative activities using media and digital technology, which many see as beneficial for career purposes.

The Harvard Business School (HBX) courses described in the prior section are offered specifically to other organizations and colleges. Individual students register for these courses only through an HBX partner organization. In its short history, HBX has found a number of willing partners, especially among small, private liberal arts colleges. For example, HBX announced in May 2015:

It has entered into agreements to work with several U.S. liberal arts colleges to provide additional benefits for their students taking the Credential of Readiness (CORe) program. CORe is an online program, consisting of approximately 150 hours of learning, for students and early career professionals to learn the fundamentals of business on a highly engaging and interactive platform designed by Harvard Business School faculty.

The newly-announced colleges are Carleton College of Northfield, MN; Grinnell College of Grinnell, IA; Hamilton College of Clinton, NY; Wellesley College of Wellesley, MA; and Williams College of Williamstown, MA. The agreements with these colleges increase student access to CORe by enabling HBX to offer increased levels of need-based financial aid for the program and guaranteeing space in CORe for students of the participating colleges. HBX announced a similar partnership with Amherst College on April 27, 2015. These agreements are based on a similar arrangement that has been in place for Harvard College students since summer 2014. . . . "The HBX CORe program has been designed to teach the fundamentals of business to college students and prepare them for the workplace," said Harvard Business School professor Bharat Anand, faculty chair of HBX.

(Harvard Business School Website, 2015)

These partnerships appear to be a win-win. They allow the liberal arts colleges to expand their curricula and provide their students with access to business courses. They also provide revenue for the Harvard Business School and can serve as feeders to its MBA programs. Harvard may be tapping into a trend wherein small, private colleges are becoming more interested in online learning experiences for their students.

The Teagle Foundation, which was established to support and strengthen liberal arts education, established a grant program titled *Hybrid Learning and the Residential Liberal Arts Experience, in 2014*. The aims of this program are to:

- Identify and support models that integrate online education into the residential liberal arts experience in ways that speak to both the quality of student learning and questions of institutional capacity.
- Encourage the formation of communities of practice from multiple institutions.
- Create a knowledge base of concepts and strategies related to hybrid learning in liberal arts institutions that can be shared with others.

(Teagle Foundation Website, 2015)

The grant program description also specifically mentions the centrality of the faculty in developing online course materials;

The Teagle Foundation approaches the challenges of improving teaching and learning with the conviction that the faculty must lead the way. In hybrid learning models, faculty expertise remains central to the work: they still design courses and curricula, lead discussions, provide feedback, and interact face-to-face with students. Inevitably, a robust hybrid learning initiative requires the support of senior leadership and others on campus, but faculty members, in collaboration with instructional technologists, ensure that the model is thoughtfully designed and well delivered. Faculty members also monitor the impact of the content and pedagogy of this approach on student learning.

(Teagle Foundation Website, 2015)

In 2014–15, the Teagle Foundation awarded fourteen grants to consortia whose main purpose was to share in the design of hybrid or blended courses. More than sixty small, residential liberal arts colleges are involved in these consortia. The blended model makes a great deal of sense for these colleges since it allows them to maintain their brands as having small, pedagogically sound academic programs while integrating the beneficial elements of online learning technology.

For-Profit, Selective Undergraduate Liberal Arts Colleges

The Minerva Project, based in San Francisco, was established in 2012 "to provide an extraordinary liberal arts and sciences education to the brightest, most motivated students in the world" and admitted its first class in fall 2014 (Minerva, 2015a). Minerva, perhaps the first of its kind, was founded by entrepreneur Ben Nelson, whose aim was to provide an alternative to the traditional liberal arts college. Its teaching model is based largely on principles developed by Stephen M. Kosslyn, a former Harvard dean and psychologist. It has a highly selective admissions process that includes assessments, interviews, and writing samples. Minerva is a for-profit entity and has received private funding to build its programs and will forgo any form of federal government financial aid or assistance. Minerva raised an initial $25 million from investors such as the venture capital firm Benchmark. Tuition, housing, and student fees total approximately $22,000 per year (Minerva, 2015b).

Minerva uses a blended learning model utilizing a combination of face-to-face and online activities. It uses a proprietary Active Learning Forum platform, designed especially for Minerva, which has a number of customized, built-in pedagogical features. Professors conduct sessions via live video and use interactive learning features such as collaborative breakout clusters, debates, quizzes, polls, dynamic document creation, and real-time simulations. It uses freely available content from such entities such as Khan Academy. All courses are taught as intimate seminars, with classes maximized at nineteen students.

An important feature of the Minerva model is that there are no academic departments, and its curriculum focuses on interdisciplinary study and global cultural experiences. For the first two semesters, students meet as a group and take courses at its main campus in San Francisco. Each of the succeeding six semesters is held in campuses at different cities such as Hong Kong, New York, Berlin, and Buenos Aires. At the time of this writing, it was too early to evaluate the experiences of its first cohort of students, but it appears to be a well-thought-out alternative to a traditional liberal arts education. Online technology is the integral facilitator of its pedagogical approaches, its curriculum, and its global context.

Enhancing Online Education

The Fourth Wave is also characterized by greater interest in a number of approaches that enhance online education. In this section, several of these will be presented:

- Big data and learning analytics
- Adaptive or differentiated learning

- Expansion of competency-based instruction
- Open educational resources (OER)
- Interactive media (simulations, multiuser virtual environments, and games)
- Mobile technology

All of these technologies have been evolving for a number of years. In the following sections, each will be examined in terms of its contributions to the enhancement of online education.

Big Data and Learning Analytics

Big data and learning analytics comprise the next generation of the decision-making applications and software that have been evolving for the past thirty or more years as part of database management systems. The decision-support software of the 1980s and the concept of data-driven decision making popularized in the 1990s have evolved into big data systems that rely on software approaches referred to as analytics. Big data is a generic term that assumes that the information or database system(s) used as the main storage facility is capable of storing large quantities of data longitudinally and down to very specific transactions. For example, college student record-keeping systems have always maintained outcomes information on students such as grades in each course. This information was used by institutional researchers to study patterns of student performance over time, usually from one semester to another or one year to another. In a big data scenario, data would be collected for each student transaction in a course, especially if the course is delivered electronically online. Every student entry on a course assessment, discussion board entry, blog entry, or wiki activity could be recorded, generating thousands of transactions per student per course. Furthermore, this data would be collected in real or near real time, as it is transacted, and then analyzed to suggest courses of action. Analytics software is the class of software applications that assists in this analysis.

The generic definition of analytics is similar to data-driven decision making. Essentially it is the science of examining data to draw conclusions and, when used in decision making, to present paths or courses of action. In recent years, however, the definition of analytics has expanded to incorporate elements of operations research such as decision trees and strategy maps to establish predictive models and to determine probabilities for certain courses of action. It uses data-mining software to establish decision processes that convert data into actionable insight, uncover patterns, alert and respond to issues and concerns, and plan for the future. This might seem to be an overly complicated definition, but the term "analytics" has been used in many different ways in recent years and has become part of the buzzword jargon that sometimes emanates from new technology applications and products. Alias (2011) defined four different types of analytics that could apply to instruction, including web analytics, learning analytics, academic analytics, and action analytics. The trade journal *Infoworld* referred to analytics as:

> One of the buzzwords around business intelligence software [that] . . . has been through the linguistic grinder, with vendors and customers using it to describe very different functions.
>
> The term can cause confusion for enterprises, especially as they consider products from vendors who use analytics to mean different things.
>
> *(Kirk, 2006)*

Goldstein and Katz (2005), in a study of academic analytics, admitted that they struggled with coming up with a name and definition that was appropriate for their work. They stated that they adopted the term "academic analytics" for their study but that it was an "imperfect label." What is critical to the definition of analytics is the use of data to determine courses of action and potentially to substitute for human judgment and experience, especially in applications with a high volume of transactions (Ford, 2015). Common examples of analytics applications are ecommerce companies such as Amazon.com or Netflix examining website traffic, purchases, or navigation patterns to determine which customers are more or less likely to buy particular products (i.e., books, movies). Using these patterns, companies send notifications to customers of new products as they become available.

In higher education, analytics are beginning to be used for a number of applications that address student performance, outcomes, and persistence including:

1. Monitoring individual student performance
2. Disaggregating student performance by selected characteristics such as major, year of study, ethnicity, etc.
3. Preventing attrition from a course or program
4. Analyzing the effectiveness of standard assessment techniques and instruments such as quizzes and exams

Several early adopters of learning analytics systems have received a lot of favorable attention. Rio Salado Community College, for instance, implemented the Progress and Course Engagement (PACE) system for automated tracking of student progress. To develop PACE, Michael Cottam, associate dean for instructional design at Rio Salado, indicated that:

> As we crunched data from tens of thousands of students, we found that there are three main predictors of success: the frequency of a student logging into a course; site engagement—whether they read or engage with the course materials online and do practice exercises and so forth; and how many points they are getting on their assignments. All that may *sound* simple, but the statistics we encounter are anything but simple. And we've found that, overwhelmingly, these three factors do act as predictors of success. . . .
>
> The reports we generate show green, yellow, and red flags—like a traffic light—so that instructors can easily see who is at risk. We can predict, after

the first week of a course, with 70 percent accuracy, whether any given student will complete the course successfully (with a grade of "C" or better). That's our "eighth day" at risk model. A second model includes weekly updates using similar predictive factors.

(Crush, 2011)

Rio Salado instructors can review student engagement at any time throughout the course, and data in PACE is maintained on a real-time basis. Several other colleges such as Northern Arizona University and Purdue University have developed similar applications. Northern Arizona University's early warning alert and retention system is called *Grade Performance System (GPS)*. Purdue University has a *Course Signals System* designed to increase student success in the classroom. Both *GPS* and *Course Signals* detect early warning signs and provide interventions that might help students do better in their courses.

There are a number of concerns with the development of big data/learning analytics applications for education. First, in order for big data and learning analytics applications to function well, data need to be accurate and timely. As a result, their benefits are maximized in fully online courses more so than blended or traditional, face-to-face courses.

Second, there are not enough individuals trained to use big data and analytics appropriately, so colleges and universities seeking to develop big data/learning analytics applications have found it difficult to attract experienced personnel. Because of the dearth of expertise, there is a tendency to use instructional templates that are integrated into course/learning management systems. These, although convenient, may be overly simplistic.

Third, and perhaps the most serious concern, is that since learning analytics requires massive amounts of data collected on students and integrated with other databases, colleges need to be careful about privacy, data profiling, and the rights of students in terms of recording their individual behaviors. While college classes have always involved evaluating student performance and academic behavior, learning analytics takes the recording of behavior to another level and scope. As well-intentioned as learning analytics might be in terms of helping students succeed, this "big data" approach may also be seen as "big brother is watching" and as an invasion of privacy that some students would rather not have imposed upon them. Precautions need to be taken to ensure that the extensive data collections of student instructional transactions are not abused in ways that potentially hurt individuals.

Adaptive Learning

The work of Patrick Suppes and Richard Atkinson during the 1960s and 1970s at the Institute for Mathematical Studies in the Social Sciences at Stanford University was introduced in Chapter Four of this book. Their work in developing computer-assisted instruction (CAI) was a major breakthrough in the way computers could be used in education. Computer software programs were developed that could teach and maintain records of student progress. Although this early programmed instruction was developed in the drill and practice style, Suppes and Atkinson set the stage for the future of computerized instructional systems. By the 1990s, the programs they developed mostly for the K–12 were being referred to as intelligent learning systems (ILS), which were far more sophisticated than the earlier CAI models. ILS took advantage of digital hardware advances that made greater use of graphics and media to provide more stimulating instruction activities. They also operated within database software systems that facilitated the maintenance of more detailed student performance indicators. ILS continued to evolve into what are now termed adaptive, differentiated, or personalized learning. These systems take advantage of learning analytics and artificial intelligence software to monitor student progress and performance very closely and are able to provide timely adjustments to the presentation of instructional material. Adaptive learning systems have the ability to be customized to the personal needs of each individual student. As described by one adaptive learning software provider:

> [Adaptive learning] monitors how the student interacts with the system and learns, leveraging the enormous quantities of data generated by a student's online interactions with ordinary (textbook-like) and extraordinary (game- and social-media-like) content, with teachers and peers, and with the system itself. It assesses not only what a student knows now but also determines what activities and interactions, developed by which providers, delivered in what sequence and medium, most greatly increase the possibility of that student's academic success.
>
> *(Kuntz, 2010)*

Many adaptive learning systems continue to be developed for K–12 education. They are particularly popular in "credit-recovery" programs, where high school students can make up courses that they failed to complete and need for graduation. In more recent years, adaptive learning systems have been developed for higher education. These systems can be used as stand-alone applications, with a teacher minimally involved, or in a blended learning environment where students spend some time in a traditional class and some time on an online adaptive learning system. They are also being integrated into textbook materials and course and learning management systems such as Blackboard and Desire2Learn. MOOC providers have begun to utilize adaptive learning as part of their course materials as well. Adaptive learning approaches are enjoying a degree of success in subject areas such as mathematics that require a good deal of scaffolding or building upon previous skills and knowledge in order to advance to a next level of understanding and mastery.

A number of colleges, universities, textbook publishers, and large education software companies such as Pearson, McGraw-Hill, and Blackboard have agreements with adaptive learning providers. CCKF, Inc. (Dublin, Ireland) has contracts for its Realize[it] adaptive software with colleges and universities in the United States including the University of Central Florida, the University of Texas, and Indiana University. Its largest contract is with the for-profit Career Education Corporation, where Realize[it] is being used in 300 sections of courses in English, mathematics, and business management (Riddell, 2013).

Knowillage Systems (Vancouver), the creator of the adaptive learning engine LeaP, was acquired by the CMS/LMS provider Desire2Learn. LeaP enables teachers to personalize learning paths and specializes in using natural language processing techniques and analytics to assist students struggling with course material.

The publishing company Macmillan entered into a partnership with the adaptive learning companies Knewton and PrepU. The latter focuses on college-level biology, nursing, chemistry, and psychology courses.

John Wiley & Sons, Inc., and Snapwiz, a Fremont, California-based company that specializes in adaptive and personalized learning solutions, announced the launch of *WileyPLUS with ORION*, the initial offering to come out of a partnership aimed at giving students highly personalized experiences that improve learning outcomes. Their solution goes further in creating adaptive, collaborative, and interactive learning spaces than anything currently on the market. *WileyPLUS with ORION* will be included at no extra cost to students using *WileyPLUS* across some of Wiley's leading titles in subjects such as Introduction to Business, Introduction to Psychology, Financial Accounting, and Anatomy and Physiology.

Adaptive learning has definitely found a niche as an enhancement to existing course modalities (fully online, face-to-face, blended), although its greatest popularity at the time of this writing is probably in blended learning environments. In all likelihood, its popularity will continue in various modes for the remainder of the Fourth Wave.

Competency-Based Online Education

Competency-based online education and the Western Governors University were presented in Chapter Five of this book. Competency-based education requires students to demonstrate competency(ies) in a subject area to receive credit for a course rather than simply attending or participating in formal class (online or face-to-face) activities. Competencies can be demonstrated by performing successfully on pre-established assessments that include testing, essay writing, and other activities. The Western Governors University (WGU) was conceived in 1995, chartered in 1996 as a private nonprofit university in 1997, and began accepting students in 1999. It has evolved into a national university, serving more than 55,000 online students from all fifty states. In addition, a number of other states, including Indiana, Texas, Missouri, Tennessee, and Washington, have created state-affiliated WGUs that offer the same programs and curricula. The most interesting copy of WGU is probably Southern New Hampshire University (SNHU). In 2009, SNHU was a small New England university with 2,000 residential students. A new president initiated a competency-based online program and enrollments grew to almost 40,000 in five years (Kahn, 2014). While WGU and SNHU have received much of the attention, other colleges and universities such as the University of Wisconsin, Northern Arizona University, the University of Texas, and Capella have also launched competency-based programs. Whether competency-based online education is an important model that will flourish in the years to come or is a modest alternative that will have a limited student market is the question.

While schools have been delivering competency-based education offline for decades, the online model developed by WGU provides a convenience that has a lot of appeal to adult learners (Wiese, 2014). Many of these adult learners work full-time, and their goals for a higher education are primarily career-oriented. Others are college dropouts who already have some college credits and who see a competency-based online program as a way to finish a degree. International students who live in countries with limited access to higher education are attracted to competency-based online programs as well, especially if they are offered by an accredited American institution.

On the other hand, competency-based programs have been criticized for giving credit for what students already know (Neem, 2011). In addition, low graduation rates (O'Shaughnessy, 2012) and very high student to faculty ratios (Career Index, 2015) at schools like WGU are reasons for concern. However, the impressive enrollment growths at WGU and SNHU cannot be ignored. Whether such programs will expand extensively throughout higher education in the foreseeable future is questionable. It is quite possible that a number of competency-based providers will partner with corporate, public, and private entities to develop customized programs that align competencies with industry needs. In all likelihood, competency-based online programs will grow for a limited market of working adults and international students.

Open Educational Resources

The open source movement is one of the most interesting aspects of the Internet. As more and more people use the Internet, software and applications are being made available and shared freely among online communities. The Internet is so ubiquitous, convenient, and social that many people are willing to give freely of much of what they produce on it, although there have always been technical people willing to share their work and ideas. In the early days of computer programming (the 1950s and early 1960s), a culture of sharing existed among coders and other technicians. One of the early programming languages, FORTRAN, was built on the idea of storing and using subroutines that could be utilized in many programs. FORTRAN programmers typically made a copy of a subroutine and gave it to others with similar applications. Grace Hopper was mentioned earlier in Chapter Four as popularizing the use and sharing of subroutines. While many of these subroutines were small helpful applications perhaps to improve the speed of sorting a file or to connect more efficiently one computing device to another, there was also some large-scale "freeware" available. The Statistical Package for the Social Sciences (also discussed in Chapter Four) developed in the 1960s is a prime example. The Internet has spurred a plethora of open source software such as Linux, Adobe Reader, Google products, Moodle, and iPad apps. It was only natural that the same would happen for some software designed for online instruction.

Open educational resources (OER) are electronic resources that are available for free or for very reduced costs for use in teaching and learning. OER includes a wide array of materials including textbooks, reading material (e.g. case studies), simulations, games, tests, quizzes, assessment tools, presentations (e.g. PowerPoint), and multimedia. OER materials are provided by faculty, instructional designers, and some commercial entities that are willing to share their work and intellectual property with others. Organizations such as Merlot, MIT's OpenCourseWare Project, and the Creative Commons have established large repositories of materials that faculty and others can access freely. While most textbook authors still work with traditional publishing companies and receive royalties, there are a growing number who make their books available as free resources on the Internet. Many faculty put their lectures on YouTube for free access by other faculty and students. For example, a YouTube.com search for "analysis of variance" or ANOVA will result in hundreds of videos by faculty and others explaining the intricacies of this statistical procedure. With the recent advent of flipped classrooms, the posting of lectures and class presentations has become commonplace using YouTube, podcasting, and other free media websites. Course developers such as Khan Academy and some MOOC providers are also making much of their content available online for free. Faculty and instructional designers no longer need to develop all aspects of a course but can instead search for free and appropriate course content and integrate it as needed. This trend will continue to accelerate as more faculty integrate freely available content into their courses, and it will spur further the development of online education, especially blended learning.

How do the traditional textbook publishers adjust or compete with the OER movement? In many cases, they are trying to integrate their content with some limited OER. Publishing companies are still profitable and authors still receive royalties, but traditional printed books are giving way to ebooks that can be purchased or rented at much less expense. The purchase of an ebook can include access and direction to other free web-based materials and media. These "accompanying" websites enhance the textbook so that it resembles an online course, with each book chapter the equivalent of a weekly class session or module. PowerPoint presentations, video lectures, and assessments are now routinely found on the websites of major college textbooks. This will suffice for the near future, but further down the road, textbook publishers will have to rethink their traditional book model.

Interactive Media: Simulations, Multiuser Virtual Environments, and Educational Games

Interactive media refer to any media-based learning activity that allows students to engage with material (i.e., manipulate, make decisions, alter outcomes) as opposed to passive media such as video or film, which only allow viewers to watch and listen. In this section, the term *interactive media* will refer to the trio of simulations, multiuser virtual environments (MUVE), and games, all of which hold great promise for online education. Before continuing, it is appropriate to define these three terms.

Simulations attempt to copy real-life processes, environments, or procedures in a virtual form that allows students to manipulate them and see the results of their actions. Scientific experiments, ecological systems, and historical or current events can be duplicated by using computer simulation models to represent the real-life situations. For instance, a simulation at McGill University called *The Open Orchestra* gives music students the feel of playing with a full orchestra in order to familiarize them with the sound of different musical instruments. In chemistry classes, reactions can be simulated so that students can immediately and safely see the result of adding a chemical or changing its amount or potency. In fact, a good deal of science research today in areas such as astronomy depends extensively upon simulated processes and environments. As a result, the move to simulations in science courses is generally accepted and even encouraged.

Multiuser virtual environments, or MUVEs, provide virtual environments in which students can participate in a variety of activities with other students and participants. A generic MUVE such as *Second Life* provides the user with tools for developing and manipulating avatars in virtual environments. It leaves the nature of the interactions and activities to the imaginations of the participants. A teacher, for example, could assign a group project activity utilizing a *Second Life* experience. Project themes related to identity, gender, and race can take on interesting meanings in a MUVE. Proponents argue that the freedom to develop and manipulate avatars in a virtual environment unleashes a plethora of creativity on the part of the users that can be beneficial within a wide range of educational activities.

Educational games use the challenge of a competitive digital environment to teach content and/or skills. Games, as entertainment for the general populace, have become incredibly popular. According to the Entertainment Software Association (2015), 155 million people in the United States or 51 percent of households own a dedicated video game console, and the average age of a video game player is 35. It is only natural that game technology found its way into instruction. Educational games are particularly useful in presenting problem-solving scenarios that focus on critical thinking, where students use cognitive, analytical, and reflective process skills. The material is presented in game format so that students compete with one another or with the computer. A classic example of an educational game popular in economics and business programs for many years is to have students compete with one another as traders in the stock market over some period of months to see who can maximize an initial investment of "play money." In the immediacy of the online environment, this game takes on whole new dimensions, as stocks can be monitored on an hourly basis and across time zones. Similar games representing real-life situations or case studies are also becoming popular in a number of other professional programs such as health (e.g., dealing with an emergency situation) and education (e.g., developing a school district budget with competing constituents).

James Gee (2007), a theoretical linguist, is an often-quoted proponent of gaming. In an interview, he summed up his views of the benefits of interactive media such as games:

> Video games are like an external version of the mind. When we understand things and plan actions we run game-like role-playing simulations in our heads. In a sense, our mind is a game engine. We can combine elements from disparate experiences and create fantasies and think through complex problems.
>
> System thinking involves being able to think in terms of complex interacting variables that make a system more than the sum of its parts. We most certainly want to see much of the social and natural world in these terms. . . .
>
> Video games are complex systems composed of rules that interact. Gamers must think like a designer and form hypotheses about how the rules interact so they can accomplish goals and even bring about emergent results. Thinking like a designer in order to understand systems is a core 21st Century skill. . . .
>
> Understanding oral and written language involves essentially running video-game like simulations in our heads. We run problem-based simulations where we try out various actions in our heads (as ourselves or someone else) and gauge their possible consequences.
>
> *(Shapiro, 2014)*

Gee is not alone in his views about the benefits of interactive media. Joichi Ito, the director of the MIT Media Lab, supports much of what Gee says and adds:

> I don't think education is about centralized instruction anymore; rather, it is the process establishing oneself as a node in a broad network of distributed creativity. . . .
>
> Neoteny, one of my favorite words, means the retention of childlike attributes in adulthood: idealism, experimentation and wonder.
>
> *(Ito, 2011)*

Jane McGonigal (2011), the former director of games research and development at the Institute for the Future, sees games as transforming real life and as able to be used to increase student's resilience and well-being. Bryan Alexander (2014), senior fellow, National Institute for Technology in Liberal Education, sees interactive media, especially their role-playing features, as "the future of higher education." With so many respected thinkers supporting interactive media and gaming in particular, it is likely that their future in education and especially online education is secure, but there are still issues that need to be considered.

First, it takes time and skill to develop interactive media applications, and the skills necessary are typically beyond the technological knowledge of most faculty and instructional designers. Second, it is possible to purchase an existing instructional game (or access to it through a website) if it has all the content, skill development, and features that a faculty member or instructional designer is interested in. The organization Online Colleges maintains a website (see: http:// www.onlinecolleges.net/about/) containing dozens of education games, many of which can be tested for little or no fee. However, many pedagogues prefer to customize instructional materials and do not like to feel that they do not have control of a critical part of their class. In addition, some media are available at the proprietor's website, which charges fees on a per-user basis; this can become expensive. Third, instructional media can require a good deal of class time, forcing the instructor to choose either a game, simulation, or MUVE over some other course activity(ies).

Despite these issues, interactive media have a future in online education, especially simulations, which already are catching on rapidly in science courses. Gaming and MUVEs will progress more slowly but will nonetheless continue to appear in online education.

Mobile Technology

Mobile technology is another important element of the Fourth Wave of online education. Like other technologies, it did not suddenly appear on the scene but evolved from the microcomputers of the 1980s, to the laptops of the late 1990s and early 2000s, and to the tablets and smartphones of the present day. As each of these devices appeared, instructional technology changed. Today, laptops or tablets are the primary devices of choice among students for their studies even though they may also have smartphones that can access much of the course material. While phones keep students connected to course material and allow them to respond and contribute to specific questions, for deep reading and careful analysis, it appears that laptops, tablets, or e-readers are preferred. An EDUCAUSE Center for Analysis and Research (2014) study of undergraduates found that of all students saying they used the following devices for class-related purposes:

- 70 percent used laptops
- 59 percent used smartphones
- 35 percent used tablets

Among students who owned their own devices:

- 74 percent used laptops
- 66 percent used smartphones
- 62 percent used tablets

(Dahlstrom & Bichsel, 2014, p. 14)

In this same study, of the 99 percent of the students who owned mobile devices: 8 percent owned just one device; 92 percent owned at least two devices; and 59 percent owned three or more devices.

The work of the EDUCAUSE Center for Analysis and Research is well-respected, and these data support the notion that students are using their mobile devices extensively, but they are picking and choosing which devices to use depending upon the nature of their interactions. It is likely that short, concise messages are fine on smartphones but reading substantive articles and other text might be best accomplished on a laptop or tablet. While this report did not study the use of books and other paper-based text, it can be assumed that a good deal of reading is done using these "mobile devices" also.

The Pew Research Center–Internet, Science, and Technology (2014) conducted a survey of American reading habits. The findings indicated that:

As of January 2014, some 76% of American adults ages 18 and older said that they read at least one book in the past year. Almost seven in ten adults (69%) read a book in print in the past 12 months, while 28% read an e-book, and 14% listened to an audiobook.

(Zickuhr & Rainie, 2014)

For printed book lovers, this might be positive news, but the breakdown by the age of the survey population shows significant differences. For example, in examining the percentage of different age populations that used an ebook for their reading in 2014:

Age Group	18–29	30–49	50–64	Older than 65
Percentage	47%	42%	35%	17%

(Zickuhr & Rainie, 2014)

Furthermore, the trend for younger people is definitely on the upswing; comparing the results for three years 2012, 2013, and 2014, the percentage of 18- to 29-year-olds using ebooks increases from 25 percent to 35 percent to 47 percent, respectively.

For faculty and instructional designers of online education, these data provide important information on mobile technology use among the population, and especially students. The implications are that students are likely to use a mix of devices to access course material, that formatting of course material should be friendly to mobile technologies, and that students can be expected to keep up to date with online discussion activities. Also, while it is especially convenient to upload much reading material to a course website so that students can easily download it onto their devices, faculty should not compromise their standards and should feel free to assign a substantive book(s) that is not available in electronic form. The use of mobile technology also has implications related to cloud computing, popular social media websites (i.e., Facebook, Twitter, and LinkedIn), and data security, all of which take on new dimensions in a hand-held world. With the proliferation and widespread use of mobile devices, online education becomes more integrated into the daily lives of students and is no longer something apart.

Policy Issues in the Fourth Wave

A number of policy initiatives arose during the Fourth Wave that have significant ramifications for online education.

Free College

One of the more provocative policy considerations of the Fourth Wave at the state and federal levels was the consideration of free college. Free college tuition may not seem to directly impact online education, but in fact it does, because if such a policy were to be enacted across the country, it would swell college enrollments beyond the capacity of the brick and mortar institutions. Tennessee started the discussion of free college when it launched "Tennessee Promise," a scholarship and mentoring program focused on increasing the number of students that attend college in the state. It provides students a last-dollar scholarship, meaning the scholarship will cover tuition and fees not covered by the Pell grant, the HOPE scholarship, or other state student assistance funds. Students may use the scholarship at any of the state's thirteen community colleges, twenty-seven colleges of applied technology, or other eligible institutions offering the associate's degree program.

While removing the financial burden is key, a critical component of the Tennessee Promise is the individual guidance each participant will receive from a mentor, who will assist the student to navigate the college admissions process. This is accomplished through mandatory meetings that students must attend in order to remain eligible for the program. In addition, Tennessee Promise participants must complete eight hours of community service per term enrolled as well as maintain satisfactory academic progress (2.0 GPA). The program admitted its first students in fall 2015; however, several colleges asked for a delay for one year so that they could staff and gear up for the number of new students they anticipated (Bennett, 2015).

The Tennessee Promise has spurred interest in the idea of free tuition in other states and at the federal level. In July 2015, Oregon announced it would be establishing a free community college program. Mississippi was also considering a free tuition plan for community college students. President Barack Obama in his 2015 State of the Union Address, citing the Tennessee Promise, proposed support for free community college tuition across the country. His proposal called for the federal government to fund 75 percent of the program and for the states to fund the remaining 25 percent. Since it came so late in his presidency, President Obama's proposal was largely symbolic, with little chance of passing in the U.S. Congress during the remainder of his tenure. Several other Democrats, including former Secretary of State Hillary Clinton, Senator Bernie Sanders, and Senator Elizabeth Warren, have gone a step further and have made proposals for debt-free college for all students enrolled in state-funded two-year and four-year institutions. It is likely that discussion of free college tuition will become more rigorously debated over the next several years, and if the Tennessee Promise is successful, other states will enact similar programs.

California Decides to Expand Access to Community Colleges via Online Education

As part of an overall $197 million increased funding package in 2014, Governor Jerry Brown, the California State Legislature, and the California Community Colleges agreed to establish the California Community College Online Education Initiative (OEI). This initiative was established in part because for the five-year period between 2008 and 2013, enrollment in the California Community Colleges had declined by 485,000 students. To re-establish California's tradition of universal access to a higher education, the OEI was conceived. The goals of OEI were:

- Increase the number of college associate degree graduates and transfers to four-year colleges
- Improve retention and success of students enrolled in Online Course Exchange courses
- Increase California Community Colleges education for the underserved and underrepresented including individuals with disabilities and those with basic skills needs
- Increase ease of use and convenience of the online experience
- Decrease the cost of student education
- Significantly increase demand for online course delivery
  (California Community College Online Education Initiative Website, 2014)

Pilot courses were offered in spring 2015, and the full launch of OEI followed in fall 2015. It is projected that within three years (2015–2018) more than 600,000 students will take advantage of courses offered through OEI.

While a number of states have had similar initiatives, the OEI is mentioned for several reasons. First, the scale and scope of the project makes it the largest such online education undertaking in public higher education. Second, the goals of the initiative are very clear in terms of increasing access to higher education. Third, the nature of OEI courses is that they will be faculty-led and designed to improve retention and success of students.

Gainful Employment—U.S. Department of Education

One of the more heated policy discussions relating to financial aid and online education centered on the U.S. Department of Education (U.S.DOE) proposal of new regulations calling for demonstration of the gainful employment of students. In 2011, the U.S.DOE issued a draft of new policies requiring colleges with career-oriented programs to comply with a new gainful employment rule. Those that did not would stand to lose access to federal student-aid programs. To meet the "gainful employment" standards, a program would have to show that the estimated annual loan payment of a typical graduate did not exceed 20 percent of his or her discretionary income or 8 percent of total earnings. In response to judicial challenges, the U.S.DOE revised its proposal in 2014. The U.S.DOE estimated that the new policy could affect about 1,400 programs serving 840,000 students. Ninety-nine percent of these programs are offered by for-profit schools, and a large percentage of these are online programs. The proposal generated heated debate among policymakers and college representatives. As reported by the Associated Press:

> Education Secretary Arne Duncan says the department wants to make sure that programs that prey on students don't continue abusive practices. However, Steve Gunderson, president and CEO of the Association of Private Sector Colleges and Universities, calls the effort "nothing more than a bad-faith attempt to cut off access to education for millions of students who have been historically underserved by higher education." On Capitol Hill, Sen. Tom Harkin, D-Iowa, chairman of the Senate Health, Education, Labor and Pensions Committee, that has aggressively investigated the industry, commends the new rule. He also said that the rule does little to stop colleges that offer poor quality programs where most of the students drop out.
> *(Hefling, 2014)*

A major lawsuit seeking to stop the U.S.DOE from enacting the new rule was brought by the Association of Private Sector Colleges and Universities. In July 2015, a judge ruled in favor of the U.S.DOE. As reported in *The Chronicle of Higher Education:*

> The department originally introduced the rule in 2011. The effort was dealt a major setback a year later, when a section of the rule was thrown out as

a result of an earlier court challenge by the association, the main lobbying group for for-profit colleges. The group's second challenge, to a revised rule, used many of the same arguments, asserting that the department had exceeded its authority in issuing the rule and that the rule was capricious and arbitrary.

In his ruling on Tuesday, Judge John D. Bates of the U.S. District Court for the District of Columbia dismissed those claims, saying the association "throws a host of arbitrary-or-capricious arguments against the wall in hope of a different outcome. None of them stick."

(Thomason, 2015)

At the time of this writing, the new gainful employment rule was expected to take effect in the latter part of 2015.

Another major case related to gainful employment and U.S.DOE involved Corinthian colleges. The saga of the for-profit but now-defunct Corinthian colleges made headlines in 2015 when the U.S. Department of Education announced that it was implementing a plan that would forgive the debt of students who were victimized by Corinthian. Corinthian at one time was one of the largest for-profit college operations in the country, but in 2014, it became a symbol of fraudulent practices in securing student loans. According to investigators, Corinthian schools charged exorbitant fees, lied about job prospects for its graduates, and in some cases, encouraged students to lie about their circumstances to get more federal aid. In a plan orchestrated by the U.S.DOE, some of the Corinthian schools were closed while others were sold before the chain filed for bankruptcy in 2015 (Flaherty, 2015). In an unprecedented action, the U.S.DOE discharged much of the student debt. At Heald College alone, one of several Corinthian schools, over 40,000 student borrowers took on more than $540 million in loans.

The [U.S.DOE] department's action is notable for several reasons. For one, it has agreed to provide loan discharges to thousands of students at Corinthian's Heald College based on its own finding that the college systematically misled students about its job-placement rates. It has also put into motion the steps for a discharge process for other students who believe they have been defrauded by their college. And for the first time in history, the department plans to appoint a special master to review claims by students who contend they deserve loan discharges because they were defrauded by Corinthian or other colleges.

"It's a significant change," says Robyn Smith, a lawyer at the National Consumer Law Center who calls the creation of the process a welcome sign "that the department recognizes there are large numbers of students who have been harmed."

(Blumenstyk, 2015)

This action on the part of the U.S.DOE put state agencies, accreditors, and others on notice that they need to do more to protect students from fraudulent practices.

> Senator Elizabeth Warren, who has proposed moving the student-loan complaint system out of the Education Department and into the Consumer Financial Protection Bureau, says the department ought to be able to balance the two priorities when it comes to loan discharges for fraud. The department "has power to cut off aid to fraudulent schools long before students are hurt and taxpayer dollars are wasted," she said in a written statement to *The Chronicle*. "If they don't want taxpayers to pay for discharges when students get cheated, [department officials] should invest the time and resources early to make sure predatory schools never cheat those students in the first place."
>
> *(Blumenstyk, 2015)*

It will be interesting to see how this plays out in other situations where students believe they were misled by college recruiters.

Summary

The focus of this chapter is the Fourth Wave of online education, specifically during the years 2014 to 2020. The primary Fourth Wave model integrated the best features of the Second Wave (pedagogical/blended learning) models and the Third Wave (MOOC student access/content) models. In a sense, it is a reconciliation of the pedagogical benefits of blended learning and the access/cost benefits of MOOC models. A number of new models were presented that included online, blended, and MOOC features. The Fourth Wave is also ushering in a number of new facilities and approaches that were in their nascent stages in previous waves. The Fourth Wave is categorized primarily as one where pedagogy drives technology in a comprehensive and sophisticated blended learning environment relying on a variety of face-to-face and digital resources developed by individual faculty, by well-financed MOOC companies, and by other education service providers. A number of policy issues including the free tuition movement, the California Community College Online Education Initiative, new federal proposals for gainful employment qualifications, and the discharging of student loans were discussed.

References

Alexander, B. (2014). Gaming the future of higher education. Blog posting: *The Academic Commons for a Liberal Education*. Retrieved from: http://www.academiccommons. org/2014/07/24/gaming-the-future-of-higher-education/ Accessed: June 17, 2015.

Alias, T. (2011). Learning analytics: Definitions, processes, and potential. Unpublished paper. Retrieved from: http://learninganalytics.net/LearningAnalyticsDefinitions ProcessesPotential.pdf Accessed: June 8, 2015.

Babson College (2014). Blended learning MBA program. Retrieved from: http://www.babson.edu/admission/graduate/Pages/blended-learning-program.aspx Accessed: June 5, 2015.

Bennett, J. (June 14, 2015). Tennessee Promise students lag behind on volunteer work. *The Daily Herald.* Retrieved from: http://columbiadailyherald.com/news/local-news/tennessee-promise-students-lag-behind-volunteer-work Accessed: June 20, 2015.

Blumenstyk, G. (June 18, 2015). How a for-profit's implosion could be a game-changer for college oversight. *The Chronicle of Higher Education.* Retrieved from: http://chronicle.com/article/How-a-For-Profit-s-Implosion/230979/ Accessed: June 20, 2015.

Byrne, J.A. (June 3, 2014). Why Clayton Christensen is wrong (& Michael Porter is right). Blog posting: *inFluencer.* Retrieved from: https://www.linkedin.com/pulse/20140603145153-17970806-why-clayton-christensen-is-wrong-michael-porter-is-right Accessed: June 6, 2015.

Byrne, J.A. (September 17, 2014). The future of the MBA: An unbundled, blended degree. *Poets & Quants.* Retrieved from: http://poetsandquants.com/2014/09/17/the-future-of-the-mba-an-unbundled-degree/ Accessed: June 5, 2015.

California Community College Online Education Initiative (2014). *Goals.* California Community Colleges Online Education Initiative Website. Retrieved from: http://ccconlineed.org/goals Accessed: June 20, 2015.

Career Index (2015). *Western Governors University.* Career Index Website. Retrieved from: http://www.educationnews.org/career-index/western-governors-university/ Accessed: April 18, 2015.

Chafkin, M. (December 2013). Udacity's Sebastian Thrun: Godfather of free online education, changes course. *Fast Company.* Retrieved from: http://www.fastcompany.com/3021473/udacity-sebastian-thrun-uphill-climb Accessed: May 12, 2015.

Christensen, C. (1997). *The innovator's dilemma: When new technologies cause great firms to fail.* Boston: Harvard Business Review Press.

Christensen, C. (2013 Reprint). *The innovator's dilemma: When new technologies cause great firms to fail.* Boston: Harvard Business Review Press.

Class Central (2015). Class Central 2011–2015. Retrieved from: https://www.class-central.com/providers Accessed: June 2, 2015.

Crush, M. (December 14, 2011). Monitoring the PACE of student learning: Analytics at Rio Salado Community College. *Campus Technology.* Retrieved from: http://campustechnology.com/Articles/2011/12/14/Monitoring-the-PACE-of-Student-Learning-Analytics-at-Rio-Salado-College.aspx?Page=1 Accessed: June 10, 2015.

Dahlstrom, E. & Bichsel, J. (2014). *ECAR study of undergraduate students and information technology, 2014.* Research Report. Louisville, CO: ECAR, October 2014. Retrieved from: https://net.educause.edu/ir/library/pdf/ss14/ERS1406.pdf Accessed: June 18, 2015.

Entertainment Software Association (2015). Essential facts about the computer and video game industry. Retrieved from: http://www.theesa.com/wp-content/uploads/2015/04/ESA-Essential-Facts-2015.pdf Accessed: June 18, 2105.

Flaherty, A. (June 8, 2015). Gov't to erase debt for students who attended now-defunct Corinthian schools. *Associated Press.* Retrieved from: http://www.huffingtonpost.com/2015/06/08/corinthian-loan-debt_n_7539122.html Accessed: June 20, 2015.

Ford, M. (2015). *Rise of the robots.* New York: Basic Books.

Gee, J.P. (2007). *What video games have to teach us about learning and literacy,* 2nd Edition. New York: Palgrave Macmillan Trade.

Goldstein, P.J. & Katz, R.N. (2005). *Academic analytics: The uses of management information and technology in higher education.* Boulder, CO: EDUCAUSE Center for Applied Research.

Harvard Business School Website (2015). *HBX, Harvard Business School's online education initiative, announces additional agreements with liberal arts colleges.* Boston: Harvard Business School. Retrieved from: http://www.hbs.edu/news/releases/Pages/hbx-liberal-arts-colleges.aspx Accessed: June 7, 2015.

Hefling, K. (October 30, 2014). Obama administration announces final gainful employment rule. *Associated Press.* Retrieved from: http://www.huffingtonpost.com/2014/10/30/obama-gainful-employment-rule-for-profit_n_6074652.html Accessed: June 20, 2015.

Ito, J. (December 5, 2011). In an open-source society, innovating by the seat of our pants. *New York Times.* Retrieved from: http://www.nytimes.com/2011/12/06/science/joichi-ito-innovating-by-the-seat-of-our-pants.html?_r=2 Accessed: June 17, 2015.

James, P. (May 13, 2014). The CCC Online Education Initiative vision: How did we get here? *TechEdge.* Retrieved from: http://ccctechedge.org/opinion/miscellaneous/428-the-ccc-Online-education-initiative-vision-how-did-we-get-here Accessed: June 14, 2015.

Kahn, G. (January 2, 2014). The Amazon of higher education. *Slate.* Retrieved: http://www.slate.com/articles/life/education/2014/01/southern_new_hampshire_university_how_paul_leblanc_s_tiny_school_has_become.html Accessed: April 18, 2015.

Kirk, J. (February 7, 2006). 'Analytics' buzzword needs careful definition. *Infoworld.* Retrieved from: http://www.infoworld.com/t/data-management/analytics-buzzword-needs-careful-definition-567 Accessed: June 7, 2015.

Koller, D. (November, 2013). *Online learning: Learning without limits.* Keynote presentation at the 19th Annual Sloan Consortium Conference on Online Learning. Orlando, FL. http://www.irrodl.org/index.php/irrodl/article/view/882/1823 Accessed: May 17, 2015.

Kuntz, D. (2010). *The Knewton Blog: What is adaptive learning?* Knewton Website. Retrieved from: http://www.knewton.com/blog/adaptive-learning/what-is-adaptive-learning/ Accessed: June 11, 2015.

Lavelle, L. (September 13, 2013). Wharton puts first-year MBA courses online for free. *Bloomberg Business.* Retrieved from: http://www.bloomberg.com/bw/articles/2013-09-13/wharton-puts-first-year-mba-courses-online-for-free Accessed: June 5, 2015.

Lewin, T. (April 25, 2015). Promising full college credit, Arizona State University offers online Freshman program. *New York Times.* Retrieved from: http://www.nytimes.com/2015/04/23/us/arizona-state-university-to-offer-online-freshman-academy.html Accessed: June 4, 2015.

McGonigal, J. (2011). *Reality is broken: Why games make us better and how they can change the world.* New York: Penguin Press.

Minerva (2015a). *Minerva: Achieving extraordinary.* Minerva Project Website. Retrieved from: https://www.minerva.kgi.edu/about/ Accessed: June 23, 2015.

Minerva (2015b). *Minerva: Admissions, tuition and fees.* Minerva Project Website. Retrieved from: https://www.minerva.kgi.edu/admissions/tuition_fees Accessed: June 23, 2015.

MOOCs Directory (2015). MOOCs Co. Retrieved from: http://www.moocs.co/ Accessed: June 3, 2015.

National Center for Academic Transformation (2005). *Who we are?* Saratoga Springs, NY: National Center for Academic Transformation Website. Retrieved from: http://www.thencat.org/whoweare.html Accessed: June 4, 2015.

Neem, J. (April 1, 2011). Online university doesn't offer 'real college education.' *Seattle Times.* Retrieved from: http://www.seattletimes.com/opinion/online-university-doesnt-offer-real-college-education/ Accessed: April 18, 2015.

O'Shaughnessy, L. (2012). Fifty colleges with the best and worst graduation rates. *CBS Money Watch Website*. Retrieved from: http://www.cbsnews.com/news/50-private-colleges-with-best-worst-grad-rates/ Accessed: April 18, 2015.

Riddell, R. (2013). Adaptive learning: The best approaches we've seen so far. *EducationDive*. Retrieved from: http://www.educationdive.com/news/adaptive-learning-the-best-approaches-weve-seen-so-far/187875/ Accessed: June 12, 2015.

Rogers, E.M. (2003). *Diffusion of innovations*, 5th Edition. New York: The Free Press.

Shapiro, J. (2014). Games can advance education: A conversation with James Paul Gee. *Mindshift*. Retrieved from: http://ww2.kqed.org/mindshift/2014/07/03/games-can-advance-education-a-conversation-with-james-paul-gee/ Accessed: June 17, 2015.

Straumshein, C. (June 6, 2014). One down, many to go. *Inside Higher Education*. Retrieved from: https://www.insidehighered.com/news/2014/06/06/one-semester-students-satisfied- unfinished-georgia-tech-online-degree-program Accessed: June 6, 2015.

Teagle Foundation Website (2015). *Request for proposals: Hybrid learning and the residential liberal arts experience*. New York: The Teagle Foundation. Retrieved from: http://www.teaglefoundation.org/teagle/media/library/documents/rfps/Hybrid-Learning-RFP-Fall-2014_1.pdf?ext=.pdf Accessed: June 7, 2015.

Thomason, A. (June 23, 2015). Gainful-employment rule survives for-profit group's court challenge. *The Chronicle of Higher Education*. Retrieved from: http://chronicle.com/blogs/ticker/gainful-employment-rule-survives-for-profit-groups-court-challenge/101079?cid=at&utm_source=at&utm_medium=en Accessed: June 23, 2015.

Useem, J. (May 13, 2014). Business school disrupted. *New York Times*. Retrieved from: http://www.nytimes.com/2014/06/01/business/business-school-disrupted.html?_r=0 Accessed: June 6, 2015.

U.S. News and World Report (2015). Best graduate schools: Entrepreneurship. Retrieved from: http://grad-schools.usnews.rankingsandreviews.com/best-graduate-schools/top-business-schools/entrepreneurship-rankings Accessed: June 5, 2015.

Wiese, M. (October 17, 2014). The real revolution in online education isn't MOOCs. *Harvard Business Review*. Retrieved from: https://hbr.org/2014/10/the-real-revolution-in-online-education-isnt-moocs/ Accessed: June 13, 2015.

Zickuhr, K. & Rainie, L. (2014). *A snapshot of reading in America in 2013*. Pew Center for Research—Internet, Science, & Technology. Retrieved from: http://www.pewinternet.org/2014/01/16/a-snapshot-of-reading-in-america-in-2013/ Accessed: June 18, 2015.

9

THE FIFTH WAVE

Maturation (2021–2029)

Drew Faust, the president of Harvard University, in a message to the World Economic Forum in 2015, described three major forces that will shape the future of higher education:

1. The influence of technology
2. The changing shape of knowledge
3. The attempt to define the value of education

She went on to extol the facilities that digital technology and communications will provide for teaching, learning, and research. She sees great benefits in technology's ability to reach masses of students around the globe and to easily quantify large databases for scaling up and assessment purposes. On the other hand, she made it clear that "residential education cannot be replicated online" and stressed the importance of physical-being interaction and shared experiences.

On the nature of knowledge, she stated that the common organization of universities by academic departments may disappear because "the most significant and consequential challenges humanity faces" require investigations and solutions that are flexible and not necessarily discipline specific. Doctors, chemists, social scientists, and engineers will work together to solve humankind's problems.

On defining value, she accepts that quantitative metrics are now evolving that can assess the importance of meaningful employment and lifelong fulfillment in a career. But she also believes that higher education provides something very valuable, that it gives people "a perspective on the meaning and purpose of their lives," and that it was not possible to quantify this type of student outcome. She concluded that:

> So much of what humanity has achieved has been sparked and sustained by the research and teaching that take place every day at colleges and universi-

ties, sites of curiosity and creativity that nurture some of the finest aspirations of individuals and, in turn, improve their lives—and their livelihoods. As the landscape continues to change, we must be careful to protect the ideals at the heart of higher education, ideals that serve us all well as we work together to improve the world.

(Faust, 2015)

While Faust presented three key elements in higher education's future, it is the interplay of these elements that will become most crucial in predicting its future. Will technology drive the shape of knowledge and the definition of value, or will it be the other way around? Techno-centrists see technology as the driver, while others who look at higher education holistically see technology as a tool serving the needs of the other elements.

During its Fifth Wave (2021–2029), online education will mature. Internet technology will be integrated into the vast majority of all college instruction. A wide variety of delivery designs, some fully online and some blended, will be the rule throughout higher education. Students will come to expect every course to have online components that provide access to content and tools for interacting with faculty and fellow students. Colleges and universities that carefully plan, develop, and integrate online education will do well in this new environment. Those that do not will struggle. This chapter provides an examination of the maturation of online education as it will occur in the 2020s and will also speculate on possible future scenarios for higher education. Chapter Ten will go further into the 2030s and beyond.

Predicting the Future

Any attempt at predicting the future is based on calculated speculation. "What" is difficult enough, but the "when" is even more difficult. Niels Bohr, the Danish physicist, was fond of saying that "prediction is very difficult, especially if it's about the future." While he did not originate this quote, he fervently believed it. Levitt and Dubner (2014), the authors of the best-seller *Freakonomics,* tell the following story of Nobel laureate Thomas Sargent during an interview:

Moderator: "Tonight, our guest: Thomas Sargent, Nobel laureate in economics and one of the most-cited economists in the world. Professor Sargent, can you tell us what CD rates will be in two years?"

Sargent: "No."

(Levitt & Dubner, 2014, p. 27)

Levitt & Dubner go on to reference Paul Krugman, another Nobel laureate in economics, who said that too many economists' predictions fail because they overestimate the impact of future technologies. They also point out that Krugman made erroneous predictions about the growth of the Internet. Levitt & Dubner's comments illustrate the difficulty of prediction and are pertinent to our discussion of online technology and the future of higher education as well. Every attempt will be made not to overestimate the impact of technology and to take a measured and informed view of its potential in effecting higher education's future. To start, let's take a look at what others have said about the future of higher education.

Reviewing the Literature on Technology and Higher Education's Future

As mentioned in Chapter Eight, Clayton Christensen, in his 1997 book, *The Innovator's Dilemma*, laid out his theory of "disruptive innovation," which posits that corporations need to quickly and abruptly adjust to new technologies in order to survive. Christensen has applied the same theory to other organizations including colleges and universities. Christensen and Horn (2013) provide a most sobering prediction that, in the 2020s, it is possible that the "bottom 25% in every tier" of higher education will close or merge if they do not adapt to online education. This is a view widely popular among many leaders in private and public enterprises, but it is one to be taken with some caution, as Paul Krugman indicated. The most critical question is whether technology will be the driving force for change. Another is whether technology must be disruptive or integrated gracefully and in stages into an organization's plans and future directions. There have been a number of books and articles that posit higher education needs "disruptive" change in light of online technology. A good example of this thinking appeared in an editorial in *The Economist* (June 28, 2014) titled "Creative destruction: A cost crisis, changing labor markets and new technology will turn an old institution on its head." The editorial states that "the Internet, which has turned businesses from newspapers through music to book retailing upside down, will upend higher education." The editorial continues on to promote MOOC technology, the establishment of common standards, and national testing for all of higher education. An alternate view of MOOC technology recognizes its place in higher education as well as its need for significant maturation and modification before being widely adopted. As for a common set of standards and assessments, this idea has been tried extensively in K–12 education with the adoption of the federal government's No Child Left Behind (NCLB) education policy in 2001. NCLB has been less than successful, since most states sought and were granted waivers from its testing and assessment requirements. The latest reauthorization by the U.S. Congress of NCLB, in December 2015, significantly reduced standardized assessments/testing and Common Core requirements for K–12 education.

Since it would be too extensive an undertaking to review all of the pertinent literature, five authors of recent books on technology and the future of higher education have been selected to represent different perspectives based on their professional experience. They include a Washington, D.C.-based policy analyst, a director of a higher education investment fund, college administrators representing for-profit and nonprofit sectors of higher education, and an editor from *The Chronicle of Higher Education*.

The End of College . . .

Possibly the most strident call for a techno-centric change in higher education was published by Kevin Carey (2015) in *The End of College: Creating the Future of Learning and The University of Everywhere*. Carey directs the Education Policy Program at the New America Foundation in Washington, D.C. Carey's major criticisms in this book were leveled at what he calls the "hybrid" university, which integrates multiple missions of research, practical training, and the liberal arts. (As an aside, Carey's use of the term "hybrid" has no relationship to the concept of "blended learning" as used to describe a major form of online education.) He finds fault with the traditional teaching and learning in these institutions and concludes that they do not do enough to prepare students for lifelong careers. He is completely enmeshed in the possibilities of MOOC technology and joins a number of other individuals who see MOOCs as the silver bullets that will disrupt and revolutionize American higher education. His book, published in 2015 and probably written a little earlier, did not foresee the backlash to MOOCs. His subtitle, *The University of Everywhere*, is based on the concept that higher education will be available anyplace and at any time and that students will mix and match learning activities from multiple sources to build their own unique credential or degree. As a result of online education and specifically MOOC models, he calls on colleges to look beyond "the crumbling, ivy-choked confines of the hybrid university to find a world of possibility"(Carey, 2015, p. 255). He also sees the Minerva Project, described in Chapter Eight of this book, as one of the harbingers of The University of Everywhere.

Carey makes important references to historical figures such as Herbert Simon (artificial intelligence) and Patrick Suppes (computer-assisted instruction) but ignores much of the development of online education in the 1990s and early 2000s and the millions of college students enrolled in online education in community colleges, public universities, and for-profit schools during this period. He has two references to blended learning attributed to Daphne Koller, the president of the MOOC provider Coursera, and does not discuss the literature that goes back to the early 2000s. He mentions the United States Department of Education (2010) landmark meta-analysis study once and does not distinguish the key findings of online versus blended learning. Watters and Goldrick-Rab (2015), in a review of Carey's book, commented that:

> this narrative about higher education is an inch deep in shallow waters. It zooms past debates of history with barely a note of documentation for

its claims (indeed a total of 21 endnotes are provided for 5 entire chapters of text).

(Watters & Goldrick-Rab, 2015)

Carey's University of Everywhere is typical of the techno-centric view that technology is the driving force for the future of higher education. There is no doubt that colleges and universities will be doing a good deal more online education, but Carey should have dug deeper into the complex issues associated with his predictions, as Watters and Goldrick-Rab suggested.

College Disrupted . . .

In *College Disrupted: The Great Unbundling of Higher Education,* Ryan Craig (2015) raises many of the same issues as Kevin Carey but is far more moderate in his predictions. Craig is the Managing Director of University Ventures, an investment firm focused exclusively on higher education. He is concerned about the future of higher education but also cautions against unbridled reliance on technology and states:

> If colleges and universities are to avoid being replaced by some creation of Silicon Valley, they're going to have to answer the question of what students are actually learning and demonstrate how their programs benefit their students.
>
> *(Craig, 2015, p. 12)*

Craig's comment about the benefit of higher education is well taken. It is similar to what Harvard's President Drew Faust said, quoted earlier in this chapter. In essence, technology's impact will relate to other issues, such as the perceived value of a college credential. Craig also sees a combination of competency-based learning, adaptive learning, and gamification as forming the perfect blend of approaches to reform higher education. He suggests that whether this blend of approaches will be acceptable and successful or not will be determined in the next five years. If successful, he predicts that it will take at least twenty years to move much of higher education to this approach.

The Idea of the Digital University . . .

Frank McCluskey and Melanie Lynn Winter (2012), in *The Idea of the Digital University: Ancient Traditions, Disruptive Technologies and the Battle for the Soul of Higher Education,* make the case that nonprofit and for-profit higher education can learn a great deal from each other. McCluskey is a retired provost of the American Public University System (APUS), and Winter was the registrar at Walden

University, both for-profit, private universities with extensive online education programs. McCluskey and Winter make the important point that higher education's response to online technology depends extensively on individual colleges' understanding of their constituents and markets. They reference the work of Bob Zemsky (2005), who proposed that colleges and universities needed to be market smart and mission driven. McCluskey and Winter caution against "creeping Harvardism," or the tendency of colleges to try to be like Harvard or something that they are not. In essence, a tribal college is not a community college is not a research university is not a private residential liberal arts college. McCluskey and Winter also make the case that colleges and universities, in order to meet the needs of students, compete in the global marketplace, and address rising costs, must make greater use of data-driven decision making. Specifically, they espouse the possible benefits of predictive analytics for teaching and learning and completely negate any proposals for a common curriculum or evaluation system in higher education:

> The richness of our higher education landscape would be horribly damaged by any attempt to have a single curriculum or criteria [for evaluation] applied.
>
> *(McCluskey & Winter, 2012, p. 221)*

College UnBound . . .

Jeffrey Selingo is a writer and editor for *The Chronicle of Higher Education*. In 2013, he published *College (Un)bound: The Future of Higher Education and What It Means for Students*. His major thesis is that although higher education will be disrupted in the future, technology will not be the sole cause:

> The decade ahead for colleges and universities will be much different . . . and at the center of this disruption is a perfect storm of financial, political, demographic, and technological forces.
>
> *(Selingo, 2013, p. 58)*

Indeed, in higher education's future, technology will not be the only driver, and it may not be the main driver. Financial issues related to rising student tuition and reductions in state funding for public higher education will have significant effects on some sectors of higher education. The tuition-driven nonprofit and for-profit private sectors will compete rigorously for students and funding sources. At the same time, there have been calls from President Obama and several state governors to adopt free tuition policies in the community colleges. There have even been calls for debt-free public higher education in general. It is not unthinkable that some form of these policy proposals will be enacted over the next ten or more years. If so, financial pressures on the public sector will ease, but these colleges will have to rely heavily on technology to accommodate increasing numbers of students. Selingo did an excellent analysis of the rising costs of college as a force for adopting and integrating more technology. Using ten-year data (2000–2010) from the Delta Project, he observed that during this decade, instructional costs had been largely contained but that administration and facilities costs had increased significantly. In fact, at many large campuses, the number of administrators was now exceeding the number of full-time instructors. It is likely that as colleges implement more technology in instruction, budget decisions will have to be made about allocating or reallocating more funds to technical support services.

Selingo also focused on student demographics as a driver for some colleges. He observes, for instance, that the number of high school graduates in the Northeast will continue to decline at least thorough 2022. This demographic will have an impact on colleges and universities that draw heavily from this area of the country. These colleges will have to tap into new student populations from other parts of the country or the world in order to maintain enrollments. Furthermore, not all of these institutions will be able to enroll these students on their physical campuses but will rely on some form of online education. Selingo does not "see mass consolidations, downsizing, and closures in the coming years" (Selingo, 2013, p. 72). Instead, he sees colleges offering a combination of traditional courses, MOOC-type courses, and blended courses to meet the needs of students and to contain costs. Adaptive learning, competency-based programs, and fluid transfer credit policies will also become more common over the next decade. He concludes by citing a number of colleges and universities that have programs and approaches in sync with his future vision, including Arizona State University (online education), the University of Southern New Hampshire (competency-based education), and the University of Central Florida (blended learning).

Designing the New American University

Michael Crow is the president of Arizona State University (ASU). Prior to his appointment at ASU, he was a professor and administrator at Columbia University, where he was involved with the Fathom online education program. William Dabars is a Senior Research Fellow and Director of Research for the New American University in the Office of the President at ASU. He is also an associate research professor in ASU's School of Historical, Philosophical, and Religious Studies. Their book, *Designing the New American University*, published in 2015, provides readers with a model based on the practices, approaches, and policies that have moved ASU to over 76,000 students (2015 enrollment figure) and into the largest research university in the country. Many think that the ASU model portends the future of the American research university. Since their model focuses entirely on their role and position as a research university, they readily admit that it is not appropriate for all of higher education and perhaps not even for other research universities:

There is no single codified model for the American research university, . . . and there would appear to be a number of variants . . . [that] includes public and private universities that range considerably in scale. . . . The model for the New American University that we delineate is intended to complement the set of highly successful major research universities and is only one among many possible models.

(Crow & Dabars, 2015, p. 7)

Crow and Dabars also comment that each institution must implement the model according to its own unique situation, determined by:

its mission and setting; the characteristics of its academic community; the scope of its constituent colleges, schools and departments; and the extent of its willingness to undertake commitment to public service and community engagement.

(Crow & Dabars, 2015, p. 8)

In describing their model, emphasis is placed on how the constituents of ASU re-examined their mission and goals and redefined them as follows:

The university's four major objectives are to demonstrate leadership in academic excellence and accessibility; to establish national standing in academic quality; to establish ASU as a global center for interdisciplinary research, discovery, and development 2020; and to enhance local impact and social embeddedness.

(Crow & Dabars, 2015, p. 61)

Crow and Dabars go on to comment extensively on how online education and other technologies are enabling them to achieve their goals and objectives. Since adopting their model, ASU has embarked on a number of initiatives that use online education including blended learning, learning analytics, adaptive learning practices, and freshman year courses developed in partnership with edX. They state:

Through a combination of traditional classroom instruction and online technologies that deliver interactive content, monitor individual progress, and accommodate multiple learning styles, universities can deliver coursework customized to students that accelerates learning while lowering costs.

(Crow & Dabars, 2015, p. 274)

With regard to the administrative uses of technology, Crow and Dabars recommend a commitment to data-driven decision making in all aspects of its management and operations. The book concludes with a number of metrics that illustrate ASU's progress as the New American University. While some point to

ASU as the model for the future, others see problems with the large section sizes in some of the traditional courses and the growing numbers of untenured faculty (Warner, 2015). In Crow and Dabars' approach, technology is not the driver of change but the enabler. While they use a good deal of technology, theirs is not a techno-centric view of the future of higher education but a holistic one. Nor does it provide a quick fix. They state that it takes time to plan and as much as "a decade to operationalize" (Crow & Dabars, 2015, p. 17). In sum, they advise that colleges and universities must first understand what they are, what their missions are, and who their faculty and students are and then use the appropriate technology to meet these needs.

Maturation—The Digital University

Who among these authors is right about the future of higher education? They are all right. There are also overlaps among their predictions. Each of the authors predicts a future, at least through the decade of the 2020s, in which colleges take greater advantage of online education and evolve into digital universities. Carey's *University of Everywhere* is the 2020s evolution of the Alfred P. Sloan Foundation's *Anytime, Anywhere Online Education* grant program of the 1990s. Craig's *College Disrupted* espouses the benefits of combining competency-based learning, adaptive learning, and gamification to form the perfect blend of approaches for the future of higher education. McCluskey and Winter foresee a future digital model where colleges integrate a combination of fully online, blended, and face-to-face courses into their academic programs. Crow and Dabars caution that there is not any single model for the future of higher education. They recommend careful planning and blended approaches to develop what they term the *New American University*. Selingo focuses on the forces (financial, political, demographic, and technological) that will require higher education to respond to the diverse needs of students. Like Craig and McCluskey and Winter, he sees colleges offering a combination of traditional courses, MOOC-type courses, adaptive learning, competency-based programs, and blended learning. And like Carey, he also sees the need for more fluid transfer credit policies. In sum, all institutions through the 2020s will be using some aspect of online education to serve their students. That these approaches resemble a well-organized symphony of technology rather than a cacophony or a lot of noise with little coordination is most important to their success. This can be accomplished by careful planning and focusing on the goals and objectives of the institution to meet the needs of students rather than on the latest technology.

There is very little to indicate that there will be a mass disruption of colleges. The vast majority of the institutions that exist today will exist through the 2020s. The demand is great, and higher education will continue to attract students who see the value of a college education. Large public and private universities will offer a wide variety of academic programs geared increasingly to careers and employment. Students will have options for fully online programs, face-to-face programs, and especially blended programs. Every program and course will likely have an online component. New institutional models comparable to Western Governors University and the Minerva Project will evolve, but they will add to the mix of already existing institutions, not replace them. Of course, if there is a major national or international development such as an economic depression, a natural or manmade catastrophe, or a major technological breakthrough, higher education will be affected, as will all other elements of the world order.

Technological Breakthroughs

While we all hope or pray that there will not be any major world calamity such as a climate catastrophe, a great economic depression, or a global war, it is likely that there will be new technological developments that can have significant ramifications. The technologies selected to be discussed in this section are in evidence at the time of this writing but have not had a major impact on higher education. It is likely that their impact will be felt in the 2020s.

Nanotechnology

The simplest definition of nanotechnology is technology that functions at the atomic level. "Nano" refers to a billionth of a meter or the width of five carbon atoms. Governments around the world have been investing billions of dollars to develop applications using nanotechnology. These applications for the most part have focused on areas such as medicine, energy, materials fabrication, and consumer products. However, companies such as Intel and IBM have been developing nanochip technology, which has the potential to radically change the scope of all computing and communications equipment. IBM, for instance, announced in July 2015 a prototype chip with transistors that are just 7 nanometers wide, or about 1/10,000th the width of a human hair (Neuman, 2015). If this nanochip technology develops into commercial production, the whole concept of a digital computer may give way to a quantum computer that operates entirely on a scale the size of atoms and maybe smaller. As of this writing, quantum computers are in their infancy, but prototypes are exceeding the speed of conventional computers by 3,600 times or at the speed of today's supercomputers (Dodson, 2013). Another decade of research and development on quantum computers may find their speed thousands of times faster than the speed of today's supercomputers. The storage capacity of such equipment will replace the gigabyte (10^9) and terabyte (10^{12}) world of today with zettabyte (10^{21}) and yottabyte (10^{24}) devices. Large-scale digitization of all the world's data will occur, with access available on mobile devices. And all of this technology and computing power will be less expensive than it is now and will be available to everyone. Nanotechnology will provide the underlying base for the development of a host of new applications including those used in higher education.

Such a development will have as much of if not a greater impact on humankind than the Internet and World Wide Web.

Cloud Computing and Education Resources

In 1994, this author described a place called Futuretown in the year 2025, where people would be served by an all-inclusive Communications and Computer Services Utility (CCSU) (Picciano, 1994). This digital utility would provide all services related to computer, television, email, and financial transactions, and it would be a one-stop utility for all information and entertainment services. Government, corporate America, hospitals, schools, and colleges would all use this utility for their operations. In 1994, the Internet and World Wide Web were in their nascent stages of development. There were few applications available other than file transfer (ftp), email, and electronic messaging. Home access was nonexistent in most parts of the country, and where it was available, users relied on slow-speed dial-up modems. While there were some limited facilities for uploading and downloading images, video was impossible due to these slow-speed connections. This began to change as higher-speed connectivity became available via cable modems, fiber optics, and digital subscriber lines (DSL) in the early 2000s. With the improvement in the speed and quality of connectivity, cloud computing or simply "the cloud" evolved, wherein users no longer relied on their personal computers for storing files and running programs. Cloud computing services became available through major companies such as Google, Amazon, and Microsoft. Best-selling author Nicholas Carr describes cloud providers as having turned data processing into a utility operation that "allow vast amounts of information to be collected and processed at centralized plants" and fed into applications running on smartphones and tablets (Carr, 2014, p. 194). Essentially, cloud services can take responsibility for all file handling and storage as well as applications such as email, text messaging, and social networking.

On the education front, cloud computing has not been a major technology in most colleges and universities. While there has been some movement to low-cloud applications such as personal email and middle-cloud applications such as course and learning management systems, mission-critical applications such as student or financial database systems are not yet in the picture (Green, 2015). A survey of senior information technology officers in 2015 found:

> 12 percent of the survey participants report that their campus has moved or is converting to cloud computing for ERP (administrative) services. . . . And less than a fifth of institutions expect to be running mission-critical finance and student information systems on the cloud by Fall 2020.
>
> *(Green, 2015)*

By the mid-2020s, however, it is likely that the cloud will be providing a good deal of digital services including instructional applications. By then, there will be little need for colleges and universities to maintain their own course or learning management systems, and the implications of cloud computing for colleges are significant. First, instructors will be able to access large numbers of courses and course materials developed by other faculty or commercial developers. We are beginning to see some of this now with the open education resources (OER) movement, but an efficient and all-inclusive file-sharing system does not exist. While some websites and services assist with this, the vast majority of all course materials still reside on campus-based computer systems with restricted access. Furthermore, since many faculty presently customize their materials to their own courses, they are not thinking about the convenience sharing with others would provide. Second, the MOOC movement encourages high investment in course development. A single course might cost $1 million or more to develop and make available to a customer base. Some of the materials, especially media files, are well done and are attracting faculty who use them for their own non-MOOC courses. These courses also integrate state-of-the-art features such as learning analytics, adaptive/personalized learning, and micro assessments. At most colleges, this type of funding and the investment in course development required is a rarity but is beginning to catch on, usually in partnership with other colleges or corporate partners. Third, MOOC materials are setting a standard for high quality course content development and may in fact be leading to course standardization. This is especially true for the introductory courses that almost all colleges teach. If all of this course development is moved away from MOOC and other private developers and onto computer facilities in the cloud, the ease with which faculty and students can access course material will increase tremendously and be most attractive. It is not unfathomable to think that there will be great pressure both inside and outside higher education to make use of these course materials as well as entire courses. Policy makers who seek standards and promote common assessments will have readily accessible material available to them in the cloud. Perhaps most importantly, students also will have access to these courses and materials and will be able to develop their own programs of study with the guidance of faculty mentors and advisers.

Artificial Intelligence and Learning Analytics Software

As noted in Chapter Eight of this book, learning analytics is still in its developmental stages but is gaining traction as an important facility for teaching and learning. Learning analytics depends upon artificial intelligence (AI) techniques that use sophisticated algorithms to understand instructional processes. They also rely on large amounts of "big" data to build a series of decision processes. Significant increases in the speed and storage capabilities of computing devices that will be possible through nanotechnology will also increase the capabilities and accuracy of AI-driven learning analytics software. What is presently known as big data will be small in comparison to the "superbig" data that will be available with nano-based computer systems.

AI allows learning analytics to expand in real time to support adaptive and personalized learning applications. For these applications to be successful, data must be collected for each instructional transaction that occurs in an online learning environment. Every question asked, every student response, every answer to every question on a test or other assessment is recorded and analyzed and stored for future reference. A complete evaluation of students as individuals as well as entire classes is becoming more common. Alerts and recommendations can be made as the instructional process proceeds within a lesson, from lesson to lesson, and throughout a course. Students can receive prompts to assist in their learning and faculty can receive prompts to assist in their teaching. The more data available, the more accurate will be the prompts. By significantly increasing the speed and amount of data to be analyzed through nanotechnology, the accuracy and speed of adaptive or personalized programs will be improved. Faculty will make inquiries about individual students to understand particular strengths and needs. They will be able to use an "electronic teaching assistant" to determine how instruction is proceeding for individual students and the class as a whole. They will be able to receive suggestions about improving instructional activities. But the real change will come when adaptive and personalized programs actually do most of the teaching. While presently in their beginning stages, they will become more prevalent in the 2020s.

Low Cost/High Quality Media

Every year, the quality of digital media improves. Much of this improvement has occurred because of the increased speed and storage capacity of computer equipment. Digitally developed animation has come a long way since the early days of games like *Pacman*, *Pong*, and *Space Invaders*. Major motion picture companies now produce feature-length films with special effects that blur the distinction between real-life action and animation. Eventually digital animations will be indistinguishable from real-life filming. The film *Avatar* set the standard for an entire new level of sophistication in digital animation. At a cost of $500 million, *Avatar* dazzled audiences with its special effects in the fictional world of Pandora. This technology is finding its way into education applications with games, simulations, and multiuser virtual environments. The first educational applications in augmented reality, using special interfaces to see, hear, and interact with virtual environments, are also becoming available. In the 2020s, these applications will be far more sophisticated and will grow in popularity, especially for courses that already use gaming and simulations. The popular lectures delivered by the talking head star professor will be incredibly enhanced for students, who will use devices that allow their senses to feel subject matter in virtual learning environments. Furthermore, these educational applications will be relatively inexpensive to produce as the cost of computing in general continues to decline.

Policy Issues of the Fifth Wave

It is difficult to imagine what the policy issues will be in the 2020s during the Fifth Wave. Some of the unresolved issues discussed earlier in this book will continue to be discussed for many years to come. For example, providing free higher education is inevitable in the future, but exactly when is difficult to say. Accreditation specifically related to new forms of online education programs will continue to be discussed. These discussions in turn will require colleges to consider carefully their transfer credit policies. It is also likely that as more instruction moves to online formats, local college policy issues related to faculty workload and conditions of employment will arise. Contingent faculty (adjuncts, contract employees, nontenure-bearing titles) will continue to increase, with more of them being represented by collective bargaining. In sum, the 2020s will be a dynamic period for higher education policy at all levels, spurred by increased student enrollments and online technology.

Summary

This chapter speculated on the future of online education in the 2020s during its Fifth Wave. During this period, online education will have matured and Internet technology will have been integrated into the vast majority of all college instruction through a wide variety of delivery designs. Online education will be viewed as routine, and students will have come to expect that every course will have online components. Five books that were reviewed that examined the future of higher education specifically considered whether technology was the driving force or whether technology was a tool used to respond to larger issues facing higher education. The conclusion drawn from this review was that no single model will dominate higher education in the 2020s and that colleges will adjust and modify programs and courses in a number of ways using online education techniques. The chapter also considered the effects of a new technological breakthrough such as widespread use of nanotechnology in the design of computer chips and the implications for cloud computing, artificial intelligence, and media production. The chapter concluded with a brief consideration of policy issues that might exist in the 2020s.

References

Carey, K. (2015). *The end of college: Creating the future of learning and the University of Everywhere.* New York: Riverhead Books.

Carr, N. (2014). *The glass cage: Automation and us.* New York: W.W. Norton and Company.

Christensen, C.M. (1997). *The innovator's dilemma: When new technologies cause great firms to fail.* Boston: Harvard Business Review Press.

Christensen, C.M. & Horn, M.B. (November 1, 2013). Innovation imperative: Change everything. Online education as an agent of transformation. *New York Times.* Retrieved from: http://www.nytimes.com/2013/11/03/education/edlife/online-education-as-an-agent-of-transformation.html Accessed: July 23, 2015.

Craig, R. (2015). *College disrupted: The great unbundling of higher education.* New York: Palgrave/Macmillan.

Crow, M.M. & Dabars, W.B. (2015). *Designing the New American University.* Baltimore: Johns Hopkins Press.

Dodson, B. (May 13, 2013). D-Wave quantum computer matches the tenth ranked supercomputer for speed. *Gizmag.* Retrieved from: http://www.gizmag.com/d-wave-quantum-computer-supercomputer-ranking/27476/ Accessed: July 18, 2015.

The Economist (June 28, 2014). Editorial. Creative destruction: A cost crisis, changing labour markets and new technology will turn an old institution on its head. Retrieved from: http://www.economist.com/news/leaders/21605906-cost-crisis-changing-labour-markets-and-new-technology-will-turn-old-institution-its Accessed: July 10, 2015.

Faust, D. (2015). Three forces shaping the university of the future. *World Economic Forum.* Retrieved from: https://agenda.weforum.org/2015/01/three-forces-shaping-the-university-of-the-future/ Accessed: July 9, 2015.

Green, K. (2015). *The 2015 campus computing survey.* Encino, CA: The Campus Computing Project. Retrieved from: http://www.campuscomputing.net/item/2015-campus-computing-survey-0 Accessed: November 23, 2015.

Levitt, S.D. & Dubner, S.J. (2014). *Think like a freak: The authors of Freakonomics offer to retrain your brain.* New York: William Morrow/HarperCollins Publishers.

McCluskey, F.B. & Winter, M.L. (2012). *The idea of the digital university: Ancient traditions, disruptive technologies and the battle for the soul of higher education.* Washington, DC: Westphalia Press.

Neuman, S. (July 9, 2015). IBM announces breakthrough in chip technology. *The Two-way: Breaking News from NPR.* Retrieved from: http://www.npr.org/sections/thetwo-way/2015/07/09/421477061/ibm-announces-breakthrough-in-chip-technology Accessed: July 17, 2015.

Picciano, A.G. (1994). *Computers in the schools: A guide to planning and administration.* New York: Merril/Macmillan.

Selingo, J. (2013). *College (un)bound: The future of higher education and what it means for students.* Boston: New Harvest/Houghton Mifflin Harcourt.

U.S. Department of Education (U.S. DOE), Office of Planning, Evaluation, and Policy Development (2010). Evaluation of evidence-based practices in online learning: A meta-analysis and review of online learning studies, Washington, DC. Retrieved from: http://www2.ed.gov/rschstat/eval/tech/evidence-based-practices/finalreport.pdf

Warner, J. (January 25, 2015). ASU is the "New American University"—It's terrifying. Blog Posting: *Inside Higher Education.* Retrieved from: https://www.insidehighered.com/blogs/just-visiting/asu-new-american-university-its-terrifying Accessed: July 13, 2105.

Watters, A. & Goldrick-Rab, S. (March 26, 2015). Techno fantasies. *Inside Higher Education.* Retrieved from: https://www.insidehighered.com/views/2015/03/26/essay-challenging-kevin-careys-new-book-higher-education Accessed: July 10, 2015.

Zemsky, R. (2005). *Remaking the American university: Market smart and mission centered.* New Brunswick, NJ: Rutgers University Press.

10

2030 AND BEYOND

In January 1956, Herbert Simon, Nobel laureate for economics (1978), told his students that over the Christmas break, he and his colleague Al Newell had developed a computer program that could do simple logic problems on what he termed "a thinking machine" (Brynjolfsson & McAffee, 2014). He spent the next several years developing computer programs that could solve more sophisticated problems and play games. In 1958, he predicted that a digital computer would be the world chess champion by 1968 (Crevier, 1993). Simon was right about the computer chess champion, but off by about thirty years. In 1997, an IBM computer named Deep Blue beat the world chess champion, Gary Kasparov. Ten years later, chess programs comparable to the one on Deep Blue were running on ordinary personal computers and laptops.

The Herbert Simon vignette illustrates the difficulty of predicting the future. Even a great mind like Simon might foresee what will happen but has great difficulty in predicting when it will happen. This is especially true in the highly dynamic and fluid world of digital technology. The purpose of this chapter is to speculate on possible new technologies that will have major impacts (as opposed to incremental changes) on higher education. The possibilities discussed will likely occur sometime after 2030. They may occur ten, twenty, thirty, or more years later. While the focus of this chapter is higher education, these technologies will impact other human endeavors as well, much like the Internet did in the 20th century.

In Chapter One, Stephen Johnson was referenced as saying that technological innovations "have set in motion a much wider array of changes in society than you might reasonably expect" (Johnson, 2014, p. 2). For example, President Barack Obama and NASA have announced a project to send humans to the planet Mars by 2030. The next Mars Rover, designed to gather information, will be launched in 2020 and will include computing equipment using the large-scale miniaturized technology discussed in Chapter Nine (NASA Jet Propulsion Laboratory, 2015). Major federally funded programs such as NASA's 1960s space program fueled a number of major breakthroughs in digital technology in the following decades, especially with regard to micro-computing technology. At that time, computer memory and central processing unit components in particular changed radically from expensive metallic magnetic core storage to relatively cheap semiconductor silicon chips. It is quite possible that new NASA projects such as the Mars Rover and subsequent landing will also result in major advances in digital technology. It will be interesting to see how NASA will make greater use of nanotechnology and quantum systems in its probes, rovers, and other space exploration equipment.

At the same time as these changes continue to unfold in digital technology, neuroscience research is accelerating at a very rapid pace. Many well-established teams of individuals are focusing on mapping brain functions. Mapping involves developing an understanding on how certain thought functions occur and how the brain processes information from our senses. Experiments using digital technology are now duplicating certain brain functions. While this work is very rudimentary at the present, it will likely be possible to improve some brain functions using digital technology in a couple of decades. At some point, the combined digital and biological research and development will yield breakthroughs that will have ramifications for all humankind.

The Computer and the Mind

Ray Kurzweil, one on the world's best known futurists, has spent his lifetime studying man-machine interfaces. Trained as a computer scientist at MIT, in 2012, Kurzweil was appointed a director of engineering at Google, where he directs a team developing machine intelligence and natural language understanding. He has been described as "the restless genius" by *The Wall Street Journal* and "the ultimate thinking machine" and the "rightful heir to Thomas Edison" by *Forbes*. PBS selected Kurzweil as one of sixteen "revolutionaries who made America" over the past two centuries.

Kurzweil (1992, 2000, 2006, 2013) has published several best-sellers on manmachine interfaces. He predicts that sometime in the late 2030s or 2040s, a singularity will occur in which computers will be developed that can take over certain brain functions (Kurzweil, 2006). A central idea of his prediction rests on what he calls *the law of accelerating returns* or LOAR:

> an evolutionary process inherently accelerates and . . . its products grow exponentially in complexity and capability . . . it pertains to both biological and technological evolution.
>
> *(Kurzweil, 2013, p. 4)*

The key to Kurzweil's LOAR is exponential growth, especially when applied to the capacity, capability, and speed of computer chip technology and central processing units (CPUs). CPUs provide basic control/communication, memory, and arithmetic/logic functions on all digital computing devices, whether super-computers or the microchip in a microwave oven. As discussed in Chapter Nine, nanotechnology and quantum computing are evolving so that in another decade or so, quantum computers will have speeds thousands of times faster than today's supercomputers. In addition, the storage capacity of such equip-ment will dwarf the gigabyte (10^9) and terabyte (10^{12}) storage devices of today with zettabyte (10^{21}) and yottabyte (10^{24}) capabilities. Kurzweil envisions this technology developing computer-brain interfaces that will significantly expand the ability to think, to reason, and to create knowledge. Eventually, this technol-ogy will mature to the point where its capacity and speed will exceed that of the human brain. When this happens, the aforementioned singularity will occur that begins the transfer of the human mental capacities to mind or "thinking" machines. He posits that these machines will be capable of improving and rec-reating themselves while significantly expanding and improving their mental capacities. Kurzweil (2013) credits John von Neumann with first using the word "singularity" in 1958 in the context of human technological history. He also establishes that while he understands that a computer is not a brain, it can "become a brain if it is running brain software" based on algorithms that simulate brain activity (Kurzweil, 2013, p. 181). Kurzweil describes a host of possibilities that include integrating and enhancing the senses, especially seeing and hearing, with neural implants that are designed to expand mental and memory capacities in the neocortex, the part of the brain where the most complex human mental activities take place. He also predicts that intelligent self-generating nanobots will be infused into our bloodstreams to keep our bodies healthy at the cellular and molecular levels.

> They [nanobots] will go into our brains noninvasively through the cap-
> illaries and interact with our biological neurons, directly extending our
> intelligence.
>
> *(Kurzweil, 2013, p. 279)*

Kurzweil goes on to mention that while intelligent nanobots might seem overly futuristic and may not be available for three decades, cell-sized devices have already been developed that detect and destroy cancer cells in the bloodstream.

Kurzweil is a computer scientist and has great faith in the benefits and the potential of technology. However, his predictions are not without critics. In fact, a number of prominent computer scientists, neuroscientists, and biopsycholo-gists such as Daniel Dennett, Rodney Brooks, David Gelernter, and Paul Allen question Kurzweil, especially regarding the algorithmic comparisons of com-puters and the brain. New York University psychology professor Gary Marcus wrote a highly critical review in *The New Yorker* of Kurzweil's *How To Create A Mind*, stating that:

> Kurzweil's pointers to neuroanatomy serve more as razzle-dazzle than real evidence for his Theory . . . what I find is that it's a very bizarre mixture of ideas that are solid and good with ideas that are crazy.
>
> *(Marcus, 2012)*

Miguel Nicolelis, a research neuroscientist at Duke University, dismissed Kurzweil's coming singularity as "a bunch of hot air," and went on further to declare that:

> the brain is not computable and no engineering can reproduce it. You could have all the computer chips ever in the world and you won't create a consciousness.
>
> *(Murray, 2013)*

However, Nicolelis does not dismiss the idea that human intelligence will be augmented by digital technology in the 2030s or beyond. He himself has developed and conducted experiments on monkeys using what he terms *neuroprosthesis* devices. While rudimentary at present, neuro- prostheses are not that far afield from Kurzweil's neural implants.

Just as provocative as neural implants are brain-machine interfaces that allow multiple physical brains to work together (i.e., teacher and student brains) in a common digital environment. Miguel Nicolelis and colleagues at Duke University astonished neuroscientists in 2015 by reporting on what is generally believed the first experiment using brain networks or brainets in monkeys to collaboratively solve a problem. The results of their experiment were reported in *Nature* as follows:

> Traditionally, brain-machine interfaces (BMIs) extract motor commands from a single brain to control the movements of artificial devices. Here, we introduce a Brainet that utilizes very-large-scale brain activity (VLSBA) from two (B2) or three (B3) nonhuman primates to engage in a common motor behaviour. A B2 generated 2D movements of an avatar arm where each monkey contributed equally to X and Y coordinates; or one monkey fully controlled the X-coordinate and the other controlled the Y-coordinate. A B3 produced arm movements in 3D space, while each monkey generated movements in 2D subspaces (X-Y, Y-Z, or X-Z). With long-term training we observed increased coordination of behavior, increased correlations in neuronal activity between different brains, and modifications to neuronal representation of the motor plan. Overall, performance of the Brainet improved owing to collective monkey behavior. These results suggest that primate brains can be integrated into a Brainet, which self-adapts to achieve a common motor goal.
>
> *(Ramakrishnan et al., 2015, p. 1)*

As one editorial noted:

> The idea of interconnected brains sounds a bit terrifying, especially since the Duke University team behind this study argues that it's also possible with people and even plans to try and create human brain-to-brain networks.
>
> . . . There are a lot of perks to going the extra mile and creating human brain-to-brain networks. For instance, brainets could help with the rehabilitation of individuals with limited mobility and sensitivity by allowing them to tap into and mimic the neuronal activity of healthy volunteers.
>
> . . . Experiments like the ones carried out by scientist Miguel Nicolelis and his colleagues are bound to pave the way for the development of so-called organic computers, i.e. brains linked together and able to synchronize to solve more or less complex problems.
>
> *(Softpedia Editorial, 2015)*

Neural implants, nanobots, and brainets may seem like science fiction, and doubts rightfully exist regarding their realization in the next several decades. At the same time, well-respected scientists who themselves express concerns and misgivings are devoting time, energy, and resources to developing man-machine interfaces that minimally augment brain function if not radically change the way humans use their brains and intelligences. In 2016, the Defense Advanced Research Projects Agency (DARPA), a branch of the U.S. Department of Defense, announced a new initiative to implant neural devices into brains of soldiers to facilitate digital interfacing. DARPA is the same agency that initiated the development of the Internet in 1960s. As stated on its website:

> A new DARPA program aims to develop an implantable neural interface able to provide unprecedented signal resolution and data-transfer bandwidth between the human brain and the digital world. The interface would serve as a translator, converting between the electrochemical language used by neurons in the brain and the ones and zeros that constitute the language of information technology.
>
> *(Defense Advanced Research Projects Agency, 2016)*

In 2015, a team of scientists at The Ohio State University announced that they had "grown" the first human brain in a laboratory. The brain, engineered from adult human skin cells and grown in a dish for fifteen weeks, is about the size of a pencil eraser, according to the university. It has the maturity of a five-week-old fetal brain, and contains 99 percent of the genes in a fully developed human fetal brain (Caldwell, 2015). The implications of all of this brain function research for intelligence and knowledge development are extensive, including the potential to significantly alter how education and instruction are delivered. If brain functions can be augmented by any of the technologies mentioned, the nature of our instructional paradigms will need to change dramatically.

The New Supercloud!

Discussions of digital technology in the future frequently lead to speculation about robotics. Most of these discussions focus on manufacturing, assembly lines, and other tasks that can be most easily subjected to specific algorithmic sequences or programs. Martin Ford (2015) reviews various possibilities in *The Rise of the Robots: Technology and the Threat of a Jobless Future* and makes several predictions. He does not see a world controlled by *Terminator* or *Star Wars* androids but allows that digital technology will surely lead to more robotic applications in certain industries. These applications will be enhanced by artificial intelligence software that will be far more advanced than the present-day versions. Artificial intelligence software will be expanded with man-machine interfaces to take advantage of breakthroughs in neuroscience. For the next ten years or so, Ford sees current online learning, augmented by artificial intelligence software, evolving into more seamless and more widely accepted adaptive or personalized instructional applications similar to those discussed in Chapter Nine. But what about beyond the 2020s? What can educators expect? Adaptive or personalized learning applications will grow and become more sophisticated over the next decade but will not evolve into full acceptance until the 2030s or beyond. The true teaching machine will become common in the post-2030 period. Instruction will be delivered on a personal, laptop, or mobile digital device that will access a "supercloud" network computer for instruction.

The term supercloud is used to distinguish it from existing cloud computing, already generally available from Google, Microsoft, Amazon and others. Current cloud facilities and their evolution over the next decade will essentially consist of digital utility systems that provide access to generic applications in communications, entertainment, and information retrieval. They will become as routine as electric, cable TV, and telephone utilities are today. Several prototypes exist at MIT and in Europe and China of "supercloud" networks that essentially provide access to a host of applications similar to the cloud services that exist today, albeit with far more capacity and capability. In the 2030s, however, a new type of supercloud computer service will evolve that will go beyond utility functions. It will be more personalized and more integrated into people's daily lives. In Stanley Kubrick's *2001: A Space Odyssey*, HAL, the computer that controlled all the functions of the spacecraft, is an illustration of a supercloud computer that will provide services geared to our everyday existence. It will wake us up, make our breakfast, set the day's schedule, start the car (giving us the option of driving ourselves or using a self-drive feature), handle many of our work activities, and entertain us in the evening with movies, culture, games, and sports. This supercloud computer will also provide a host of important services such as medical diagnoses, legal consultations, advice on financial investments, and education. It will have access to the world's knowledge including books, reports, digital copies of art and architecture, video archives of speeches, music and dance productions, medical databases, legal databases, and secondary and postsecondary education courses. It will also have a friendly interface so that requests will be handled via spoken natural language. Doctors will be required by their HMOs to do all of their diagnoses using this HAL-type supercloud computer. Scientists will see much of their laboratory work conducted through simulations on a supercloud computer. Judicial systems will rely extensively on the supercloud to arrive at judgments.

All education will be integrated within the supercloud. It is likely that many colleges will merge and/or consolidate during the 2030s or beyond. Large public university systems will likely utilize one central administration center that provides the full extent of support services presently provided by individual colleges. Faculty will be knowledge managers and tutors who produce, disseminate, and help students to acquire and gain understanding of humankind's nature, existence, and future. Faculty will also be required to use a supercloud computer to prepare programs of instruction personalized to each of their students and to assess progress according to national standards. Many class or student group activities will be optional and will occur synchronously or asynchronously on the supercloud computer network. This supercloud network computer will be a game-changer for education and for every other profession and occupation. "Big Brother" will have arrived.

Artificial Intelligence and the End of Humanity

Will artificial intelligence be the end of humanity? The future described here generates mixed reactions among people. On one hand, there are many great benefits to be derived from intelligent man-machine systems. They provide valuable assistance in endeavors such as health, medicine, and education, as well as the overall advancement of human society. On the other hand, there are concerns about the dangers of the loss of control of our lives, our existence, and our future. These issues go well beyond education, colleges, and universities. Critical to the development and advancement of intelligent machines is artificial intelligence software. Stephen Hawking, one of the preeminent physicists of the 20th and 21st centuries, created headlines when he stated in a 2014 interview that:

> I think the development of full artificial intelligence could spell the end of the human race. Once humans develop artificial intelligence, it will take off on its own and design itself at an ever-increasing rate.
>
> *(Holley, 2014)*

Hawking, because of amyotrophic lateral sclerosis (ALS), has been confined to a wheelchair for most of his life and is dependent on a number of digital technologies for his mobility and communication with others. His speech is only possible because of artificial intelligence technology that assists him in forming words and sentences that reflect his thoughts. This technology uses an infrared switch to detect the motions in his left cheek muscle, which he uses to select individual characters and build sentences. A cursor scrolls across the keyboard on Hawking's wheelchair-mounted tablet. When the cursor reaches the letter Hawking wants, he moves his cheek and an infrared switch picks up the motion. In this way he can build words and sentences which are sent to his voice synthesizer (Hawking, 2015). Even though Hawking has benefitted extensively from current artificial intelligence technology, he nevertheless issued his grave warning that, unchecked, it threatens humankind's very existence.

Hawking is not alone in his concerns. In 2014, Stanford University invited leading thinkers from several institutions to begin a 100-year effort to study and anticipate how artificial intelligence will affect every aspect of people's lives. This project, called the *One Hundred Year Study on Artificial Intelligence* or *AI100*, was the idea of computer scientist and Stanford alumnus Eric Horvitz, a Distinguished Scientist and Director of Microsoft Research's Main Laboratory in Redmond, Washington. He is also a former president of the Association for the Advancement of Artificial Intelligence (AAAI). It was in his capacity as president of AAAI that Horvitz convened a conference in 2009 at which top researchers considered advances in artificial intelligence and its influences on people and society, a discussion that illuminated the need for continuing study of AI's long-term implications. Horvitz and Russ Altman, a professor of bioengineering and computer science at Stanford, have formed a committee that will select a panel to begin a series of periodic studies on AI's effect on automation, national security, psychology, ethics, law, privacy, democracy, and other issues. In a statement issued at a conference convened by Horvitz and Altman, Stanford President John Hennessy stated:

> Artificial intelligence is one of the most profound undertakings in science, and one that will affect every aspect of human life. . . . Given Stanford's pioneering role in AI and our interdisciplinary mindset, we feel obliged and qualified to host a conversation about how artificial intelligence will affect our children and our children's children.
>
> *(Cesare, 2014)*

In a white paper describing the need and purpose of the *AI100*, Horvitz outlined several areas for the study. While praising the possibilities of artificial intelligence and the rich opportunity for "better understanding the impressive capabilities of the brain via computational models, methods, metaphors, and results," he speculated whether the field also faces:

> potential challenges to privacy that might come to the fore with advances in AI research and development, including efforts in machine learning, pattern recognition, inference, and prediction? What are the implications for privacy of systems that can make inferences about the goals, intentions, identity,

location, health, beliefs, preferences, habits, weaknesses, and future actions and activities of people? What are the preferences and levels of comfort of people about machines performing such inferences? How might people be protected from unwanted inferences or uses of such inferences? Are there opportunities for innovation with new forms of insightful (yet lightweight?) regulatory guidance, policies, or laws?

(Horvitz, 2014)

The challenges are formidable, and while Horvitz convenes the world's most accomplished researchers and scientists in the field to study artificial intelligence, there are few if any restrictions on unscrupulous individuals and entrepreneurs regarding weapons development, breaching of national security systems, and profiteering from advanced artificial intelligence technology.

The Future of Life Institute (2015) initiated an open letter titled *Research priorities for robust and beneficial artificial intelligence* expressing the same concerns about artificial intelligence development as described in the white paper issued by Horvitz. The open letter is signed by Stephen Hawking, Elon Musk (founder of SpaceX and Tesla Motors), Steve Wozniak, (co-founder of Apple), and many of the world's top computer scientists. Their concerns reflect the concerns of humanity over our ability to control the advancements of artificial intelligence in what Ray Kurzweil called the coming *singularity*.

Summary

This chapter examined new digital technologies that will have major impacts on most human endeavors including higher education in the year 2030 and beyond. Predicting what will happen in the future is difficult; the timing of predictions in particular is very speculative. In this chapter, the work of futurist Ray Kurzweil was featured, especially with regard to the singularity, when man-machine technology will begin to outperform human brain functions and will begin to repair and replicate itself. It is likely that technology to augment the human brain such as neural implants, intelligent, self-generating nanobots, and brainets are likely to evolve in the post 2030 timeframe. Many of these technologies will communicate with and rely on supercloud computer networks that will be far more advanced than the cloud computing of the present day. Artificial intelligence will dominate much of the man-machine interface technologies, and concerns are arising about the loss of control over humanity's future to technology. Major thinkers, including Stephen Hawking, have issued warnings to this effect.

References

Brynjolfsson, E. & McAffee, A. (2014). *The second machine age: Work, progress and prosperity in a time of brilliant technologies.* New York: W. W. Norton and Company.

Caldwell, E. (2015). *Scientist: Most complete human brain model to date is a 'brain changer.'* Posting on The Ohio State University. Retrieved from: https://news.osu.edu/news/2015/08/18/human-brain-model/ Accessed: August 19, 2015.

Cesare, C. (2014). Stanford to host 100-year study on artificial intelligence. *Stanford News*. Retrieved from: http://news.stanford.edu/news/2014/december/ai-century-study-121614.html Accessed: August 17, 2015.

Crevier, D. (1993). *AI: The tumultuous history of the search for artificial intelligence*. New York: Basic Books.

Defense Advanced Research Projects Agency (2016). Bridging the bio-electronic divide: New effort aims for fully implantable devices able to connect with up to one million neurons. Retrieved from: http://www.darpa.mil/news-events/2015–01–19 Accessed: January 25, 2016.

Ford, M. (2015). *The rise of the robots: Technology and the threat of a jobless future*. New York: Basic Books.

Future of Life Institute (2015). Research priorities for robust and beneficial artificial intelligence: An open letter. Retrieved from: http://futureoflife.org/AI/open_letter Accessed: August 17, 2015.

Hawking, S. (2015). *The computer*. Posting on Stephen Hawking website. Retrieved from: http://www.hawking.org.uk/the-computer.html Accessed: August 19, 2015.

Holley, P. (December 2, 2014). Stephen Hawking just got an artificial intelligence upgrade, but still thinks AI could bring an end to mankind. *The Washington Post*. Retrieved from: http://www.washingtonpost.com/news/speaking-of-science/wp/2014/12/02/stephen-hawking-just-got-an-artificial-intelligence-upgrade-but-still-thinks-it-could-bring-an-end-to-mankind/ Accessed: August 17, 2015.

Horvitz, E. (2014). One-hundred year study of artificial intelligence: Reflections and framing. Unpublished white paper. Stanford University. Retrieved from: https://stanford.app.box.com/s/266hrhww2l3gjoy9euar Accessed: August 17, 2015.

Johnson, S. (2014). *How we got to now: Six innovations that made the modern world*. New York: Riverhead Books.

Kurzweil, R. (1992). *The age of intelligent machines*. Boston: MIT Press.

Kurzweil, R. (2000). *The age of spiritual machines: When computers exceed human intelligence*. New York: Penguin Books.

Kurzweil, R. (2006). *The singularity is near: When humans transcend biology*. New York: Penguin Books.

Kurzweil, R. (2013). *How to create a mind: The secret of human thought revealed*. New York: Penguin Books.

Marcus, G. (November 15, 2012). Ray Kurzweil's dubious new theory of mind. *The New Yorker*. Retrieved from: http://www.newyorker.com/books/page-turner/ray-kurzweils-dubious-new-theory-of-mind Accessed: August 12, 2015.

Murray, P. (2013). Leading neuroscientist says Kurzweil singularity prediction a "bunch of hot air." *SingularityHub*. Retrieved from: http://singularityhub.com/2013/03/10/leading-neuroscientist-says-kurzweil-singularity-prediction-a-bunch-of-hot-air/ Accessed: August 12, 2015.

NASA Jet Propulsion Laboratory (2015). *Mars future rover plans: Launch 2020*. NASA Website. Retrieved from: http://mars.nasa.gov/mars2020/mission/rover/ Accessed: July 30, 2015.

Ramakrishnan, A., Ifft, P.J., Pais-Veira, M., Byun, Y.W., Zhuang, K.Z., Lebedey, M.A., & Nicolelis, M.A. (2015). Computing arm movements with a monkey brainet. *Nature*

Scientific Reports, *5*, Article number: 10767; doi:10.1038/srep10767. Retrieved from: http://www.nature.com/srep/2015/150622/srep10767/full/srep10767.html Accessed: August 14, 2015.

Softpedia Editorial (2015). *Brainets: A higher form of communication or downright terrifying?* Softpedia Website. Retrieved from: http://news.softpedia.com/news/brainets-a-higher-form-of-communication-or-downright-terrifying-486662.shtml Accessed: August 14, 2015.

EPILOGUE

In *A Christmas Carol* by Charles Dickens, the miserly Ebenezer Scrooge is visited on Christmas Eve by the ghost of his former business partner Jacob Marley as well as the Ghosts of Christmases Past, Present, and Future. The novel takes place in London during the 1840s. The Ghosts take a reluctant Scrooge on a time-travel voyage to see the people, places, and things that have and will matter to him. The past reflects memories of childhood, love, and career. The present has some joys but also illuminates the stark realities of London's poor, its orphans, its prisons, and its workhouses. The future is dark and haunting. Scrooge sees the empty chair where Bob Cratchit's lame son, Tiny Tim, would normally sit. The visit to the future ends as Scrooge faces his own mortality in the form of a tombstone inscribed with his name. He asks the Ghost:

> "Before I draw nearer to that stone to which you point, answer me one question. Are these the shadows of the things that Will be, or are they shadows of things that May be . . . ?"

The Ghost continued to point downward to the grave by which it stood.

> "Men's courses will foreshadow certain ends, to which, if persevered in, they must lead," said Scrooge. "But if the courses be departed from, the ends will change. Say it is thus with what you show me!"
>
> *(Dickens, 1843)*

I opened this book by commenting about an exchange I had with a young associate professor who approached me after I gave a talk about online education in New York in November 2014. Our discussion centered on the future of higher education, and she specifically asked if I thought that in ten years she would be out of a job. My answer to her was that she would not be displaced anytime soon but that the way she teaches would change and evolve. I stand by this comment. In the foreseeable future, the role of the faculty will remain strong in most institutions, but they must be alert to technologies and adjust accordingly to those that may be of benefit to their students. American higher education as an institution will change also. In fact, it has been evolving and will continue to do so in response to digital technologies. Administrators, faculty and support staffs have ushered in many changes to the way our colleges operate, including how faculty teach and how students learn. These changes are best implemented in planned, carefully developed projects, programs, and initiatives rather than by disruptive sudden upheavals. What is critical is that colleges and universities be open to changing and adapting. Use technologies that are beneficial, question those that are not, but most important, do not ignore them. Let the academy control the technologies and do not let the technologies control the academy.

Reference

Dickens, C. (1843). *Project Gutenberg E-Book version of A Christmas Carol.* Project Gutenberg. Retrieved from: http://www.gutenberg.org/files/46/46-h/46-h.htm Accessed: September 7, 2015.

ABOUT THE AUTHOR

Anthony G. Picciano is Professor and Executive Officer of the PhD Program in Urban Education at the City University of New York (CUNY) Graduate Center. He is also a member of the faculty in the graduate program in Education Leadership at Hunter College, the doctoral certificate program in Interactive Pedagogy and Technology at the CUNY Graduate Center, and the CUNY Online BA Program in Communication and Culture. He has held several administrative appointments at the City University and State University of New York.

Dr. Picciano started his career working with computer systems in the late 1960s. He taught his first college-level course in computer programming and systems analysis in 1971. In the 1970s and 1980s, he was involved with developing computer facilities, computer-assisted instruction (CAI) laboratories, and data networks at the City University of New York. He started teaching online in 1996.

In 1998, Dr. Picciano co-founded CUNY Online, a multimillion dollar initiative funded by the Alfred P. Sloan Foundation that provided support to faculty using the Internet for course development. He was a founding member and continues to serve on the Board of Directors of the Online Learning Consortium (formerly the Sloan Consortium).

Dr. Picciano's research interests are education leadership, education policy, Internet-based teaching and learning, and multimedia instructional models. With Jeff Seaman, Dr. Picciano has conducted major national studies on the extent and nature of online and blended learning in American K–12 school districts. He has authored numerous articles and frequently speaks and presents at conferences on education and technology. He has authored thirteen books including:

Conducting Research in Online and Blended Learning Environments: New Pedagogical Frontiers (2016, Routledge/Taylor & Francis).

Blended Learning: Research Perspectives, Volume 2 (2014, Routledge/Taylor & Francis)

The Great Education-Industrial Complex: Ideology, Technology, and Profit (2013, Routledge/Taylor & Francis),

Educational Leadership and Planning for Technology, 5th Edition (2010, Pearson)

Blended Learning: Research Perspectives, Volume 1 (2007, The Sloan Consortium)

Data-Driven Decision Making for Effective School Leadership (2006, Pearson)

Distance Learning: Making Connections across Virtual Space and Time (2001, Pearson)

Educational Research Primer (2004, Continuum)

Dr. Picciano was elected to the Inaugural Class of the Sloan Consortium's Fellows in recognition of "outstanding publications that have advanced the field of online learning." Dr. Picciano was the 2010 recipient of the Sloan Consortium's *National Award for Outstanding Achievement in Online Education by an Individual.*

Visit Dr. Picciano's website at http://anthonypicciano.com.

INDEX